Exchange Rate Regimes

Exchange Rate Regimes

Fixed, flexible or something in between?

Imad A. Moosa

First published 2005 by
PALGRAVE MACMILLAN
Houndmills, Basingstoke, Hampshire RG21 6XS and
175 Fifth Avenue, New York, N.Y. 10010
Companies and representatives throughout the world

PALGRAVE MACMILLAN is the global academic imprint of the Palgrave
Macmillan division of St. Martin's Press, LLC and of Palgrave Macmillan Ltd.
Macmillan® is a registered trademark in the United States, United Kingdom
and other countries. Palgrave is a registered trademark in the European
Union and other countries.

ISBN-13: 978–1–4039–3672–1
ISBN-10: 1–4039–3672–2

This book is printed on paper suitable for recycling and made from fully
managed and sustained forest sources.

A catalogue record for this book is available from the British Library.

Library of Congress Cataloging-in-Publication Data
Moosa, Imad A.
  Exchange rate regimes : fixed, flexible or something in between? /
Imad A. Moosa.
    p. cm.
  Includes bibliographical references and index.
  ISBN 1–4039–3672–2 (cloth)
  1. Foreign exchange. 2. Foreign exchange rates. I. Title.
  HG3851.M665 2005
  332.4′5—dc22
                                                        2004060799

10   9   8   7   6   5   4   3   2   1
14   13 12 11 10 09 08 07 06 05

Printed and bound in Great Britain by
Antony Rowe Ltd, Chippenham and Eastbourne

To Nisreen and Danny

Contents

List of Tables

List of Figures

Preface

I have always been interested in exchange rate regime choice as a result of my general interest in exchange rate economics. However, I became particularly interested in the choice and consequences of exchange rate regimes when I was appointed as an economic adviser to the US Treasury on matters related to monetary reform in Iraq following the collapse of Saddam Hussein's regime in April 2003. In May 2003, I travelled to Baghdad where I joined a group of economists and bankers from the US Treasury to examine the monetary aspects of the reconstruction of Iraq. In particular, we dealt with the issue of introducing a new currency and the associated exchange rate regime. Later on, we were joined by a group of IMF economists who visited for a short period of time to offer advice. As a result of the consultation process, we got involved in a heated debate that boiled down to a single question: should Iraq adopt a currency board or managed floating? For a large number of reasons pertaining to the special situation in Iraq, I firmly believed in and argued for the choice of an extreme regime like a currency board. Unfortunately for me (and for the people of Iraq), the managed-floating camp won the match by sheer numbers, certainly not on the basis of logical arguments that took into account the tragic situation in Iraq.

When I finished my mission in Baghdad in June 2003, I returned to Melbourne, determined to go through the extensive literature on exchange rate regime choice, motivated by the desire to remove any shadow of doubt in my mind on the soundness of my arguments (for a currency board and against managed floating). After studying the literature carefully and thoroughly, I became more convinced than I had been of the validity of my views. As a by-product, I gained sufficient knowledge of the literature on exchange rate regime choice to write a book on the subject. Hence, I took on a project that has produced this nine-chapter book.

The book presents what may be a comprehensive, but certainly an up-to-date, survey of the literature on exchange rate regime choice, dealing with three interrelated issues. The first issue is the conventional and never-ending debate on fixed versus flexible exchange rates. The second issue is that of the determinants of exchange rate regime choice. The book surveys the theory of and evidence on the factors that determine the regime chosen by a country with particular characteristics. The third issue is the effect of the exchange rate regime on the macroeconomy. In other words, it is the question of whether or not exchange rate regimes affect macroeconomic performance, putting special emphasis on growth and inflation. Unfortunately, no clear-cut answers emerge, except on the hazard of generalizing stylized facts. When it comes to exchange rate regime choice, the underlying issues should be considered on a case-by-case basis, pondering objectively while discarding ideology and avoiding dogma. Although I am not a fan of currency boards, I strongly believe that this would have been the best choice for Iraq. A case study that discusses this issue in detail is presented in Chapter 9.

This book would not have materialized without the help and encouragement I received from family, friends and colleagues. My utmost gratitude must go to my wife and children who had to bear the opportunity cost of writing this book and endure the agony caused by the trip to Baghdad, knowing that I might face hazards of all kinds. My wife, Afaf, not only bore most of the opportunity cost of writing the book but proved, as always, to be my best research assistant by producing the elegant diagrams shown in the book. I am grateful to my colleagues at the Department of Economics and Finance, La Trobe University, with whom I have shared many of the ideas expressed in this book. Out of my colleagues at La Trobe, I am particularly grateful to Buly Cardak, to whom I always resort when I hit a wall. Buly was instrumental in the endeavour to make sure that the extensive list of references found at the end of this book was complete, up to date, accurate and consistent with the text. I am also grateful to Xiangkang Yin, Robert Waschik, Harry Clarke, Greg Jamieson and the two Colleens: Colleen Stoate and Colleen Harte. Other La Trobe colleagues provided some insights in the stimulating atmosphere of the John Scott Meeting House. Hence, I should thank Greg O'Brien, Bill Horrigan, Bob Parsons and Rodney Adams.

The major part of this book was written in Kuwait during my tenure at the Gulf University for Science and Technology (GUST). I received extensive help from colleagues at GUST but in particular I would like to thank Razzaque Bhatti, Mark Olson and Hussain Al-Sharoufi who read the manuscript and came up with numerous suggestions (not to mention identifying some errors that escaped my attention). I would also like to thank some of my other colleagues at GUST, including Abdulla Al-Refaee, Nabil Al-Haj, Shaima Ashkanani, Masoud Al-Kandari, Nayef Al-Hajraf, Wajeeh Al-Hamed, Mustafa Al-Dabbos and Syed Saud.

Ahmed Al-Kawaz of the Arab Planning Institute deserves a special thank you, not only for encouraging me to write a piece on the monetary aspects of the reconstruction of Iraq (Moosa, 2004b), but also for providing the data used in this book. My previous and current students at La Trobe deserve to be mentioned here, and so I would like to thank Hussein Al-Muraikhi, Rashed Al-Enzi, Jamal Al-Turkait, Kelly Burns and Sean Patterson. I should not forget to mention the support I received from my friends Ron Ripple, Nabeel Al-Loughani, Talla Al-Deehani and Khalid Al-Saad. Last, but not least, I would like to thank Jacky Kippenberger and Katie Button of Palgrave for encouragement, support and positive feedback.

Naturally, I am the only one responsible for any errors and omissions in this book. It is dedicated to my beloved children, Nisreen and Danny.

Kuwait   IMAD A. MOOSA

List of Abbreviations

ADF   augmented Dickey–Fuller statistic
ARMA autoregressive moving average
BIS   Bank for International Settlements
CBI   Central Bank of Iraq
CBK   Central Bank of Kuwait
CPI   Consumer Price Index
DEM   German mark
DF   Dickey–Fuller statistic
DW   Durban–Watson statistic
ECU   European currency unit
EEC   European Economic Community
EMCF European Monetary Cooperation Fund
EMS   European Monetary System
EMU   European Monetary Union
ERM   exchange rate mechanism
EU   European Union
EUA   European Unit of Account
EUR   Euro
FDI   foreign direct investment
GBP   British pound
GCC   Gulf Cooperation Council
GDP   gross domestic product
GNP   gross national product
IMF   International Monetary Fund
JPY   Japanese yen
KWD   Kuwaiti dinar
OCA   optimum currency area
PPP   purchasing power parity
PSFM Price–specie flow mechanism
SDR   Special Drawing Right
UIP   uncovered interest parity
USD   US dollar
VAR   vector autoregressive representation

List of Abbreviations

1
Background and Overview

Introduction

Before the collapse of the Bretton Woods system of fixed but adjustable exchange rates in 1971, most countries had declared par (fixed) values for their currencies against the US dollar, with a margin of 1 per cent above and below the par values. They also had the obligation to maintain the par values unless they could demonstrate the presence of a 'fundamental disequilibrium' (as opposed to temporary or transitory disequilibrium) in the balance of payments, in which case the par values could be changed subject to the approval of the International Monetary Fund (IMF). The UK, for example, utilized this scheme twice by devaluing the pound in 1949 and 1967. The word 'most' is used here because a small number of countries did not maintain fixed par values. Some countries in Latin America experienced high inflation rates that made it necessary for them to pursue a policy of gradual depreciation (what has become to be known as a crawling peg), and both Lebanon and Canada had extensive experience with floating exchange rates (the Canadian experiment with floating lasted between 1950 and 1962).

The Bretton Woods agreement, therefore, defined the specifics of the exchange rate regime (fixed but adjustable rates) and the exchange rate policy of maintaining the exchange rate within a predefined range through intervention and otherwise (for example, by using interest rates as a policy tool). According to Salvatore *et al.* (2003) the exchange rate regime choice debate seemed to have come to an end in 1944 when most of the free-market economies signed up to the Bretton Woods system of fixed but adjustable exchange rates. However, that was not the case because the conventional wisdom of the time, which formed the foundation of the Bretton Woods system, was challenged in the early 1950s in a classic article by Friedman (1953). This article has become a landmark in the literature on the fixed versus flexible exchange rates debate and the literature on exchange rate regime choice at large.

The debate on exchange rate regime choice is certainly not new or recent. Many times during the past 150 years or so, decisions on exchange rate regime choice needed to be made, giving rise to heated arguments involving economists and politicians. Corden (2002) starts his book on exchange rate regime choice with the case of the Indian rupee in the 1870s when Britain was on the gold standard while India was on the silver standard. When the price of silver fell sharply, the Indian rupee depreciated against the pound and other currencies, which raised the rupee cost of pound-denominated 'home charges' that India had to make to Britain. As a result, the choice of exchange rate regime became a debatable issue. In the nineteenth century also an important exchange rate regime question was the choice among the gold standard, the bimetallic standard, the silver standard and free coinage (non-metallic standard). Events that took place in the interwar period and the decision to adopt the Bretton Woods system in 1944 are examples of exchange rate regime choice. In the interwar period, for example, a decision was initially taken to return to the gold standard and then to abandon it, going through free floating. And even as far back as 1797, the decision by Britain to suspend the gold standard was an exchange rate regime choice (Bordo and Schwartz, 1997). Thus, the question of exchange rate regime choice has been around for a long time. Corden (2002) distinguishes between exchange rate regime choice and exchange rate choice within a given regime. For example, the decision to return to the gold standard in the interwar period was a regime choice, but selecting the par value of the (fixed) exchange rate was an exchange rate choice.

Apart from the never-ending debate on the pros and cons of floating as opposed to fixed exchange rates, the issue of regime choice was not that crucial, but things changed following the transformation of the international monetary system in 1971. This transformation has provided countries with a far wider range of exchange rate regimes than was previously available. The post-Bretton Woods system allowed different types of exchange rate arrangements to emerge, and these were formally legalized as possible choices in the Second Amendment of the IMF's Articles of Agreement on 1 April 1978. Countries could opt to link to an external standard such as a single currency, to the Special Drawing Rights (SDR) or to a self-selected basket of currencies. Those countries wishing for greater flexibility could choose clean (or free) floating, managed floating with varying degrees of intervention, or a rule for officially controlling exchange rate movements according to objective indicators. Variants of these schemes have also appeared, such as pegging to an undisclosed basket of currencies, with the authorities reserving the right to make occasional shifts in the rate or to operate the scheme within fairly wide margins.

With the emergence of a more exotic menu of exchange rate regimes, increasing attention has been paid to the rationale for choosing one type of regime over another. Because major industrial countries have adopted floating (except European countries that are now in a currency union), the issue of exchange rate regime choice mostly pertains to developing countries. Immediately following the collapse of the Bretton Woods system, developing countries declared their preference for a 'system of stable exchange rates based on adjustable par values', a view that was expressed in a communiqué issued on 24 March 1973 following the third meeting of the ministers of the Intergovernmental Group of Twenty Four on International Monetary Affairs. This view was reiterated in another meeting of the Group, held in Paris in June 1975. The communiqué stated the following:

> On exchange rates, Ministers reaffirmed the stand that they had taken in the previous meeting against the legalization of floating other than in particular circumstances subject to conditions which should take account of the characteristics of countries and in a manner designed to prevent undue instability in the value of major trading currencies. Ministers expressed support for amendments envisaging a return at the appropriate time to a system of par values, containing provision for the establishment of central rates, and empowering the Fund to authorize individual countries to continue the float thereafter in particular circumstances.

Developing countries were unable to maintain their exchange rates against major currencies by pegging their currencies against one of them. The selection of an exchange rate regime by a developing country in a world of floating among major currencies is typically viewed as involving a sequence of choices or considerations, bearing in mind the objective of striking a balance between microeconomic efficiency and macroeconomic stability. To start with, there is the question of whether or not to adopt floating, leaving the exchange rate to be determined entirely by the forces of supply and demand in a free foreign exchange market. With the emphasis on the role of the market in exchange rate determination, the question then is whether the conditions exist (in developing countries) to allow floating. This question can also be based on the fixed versus flexible exchange rates debate in the light of characteristics such as susceptibility of the economy to internal and external disturbances, the openness of the economy and attitude towards inflation. If it is believed that floating is not an option, a decision should then be taken for the determination of the link between the domestic currency and some external standard: would it be better to choose a single currency peg or a basket peg? One approach is to choose a peg so as to reduce or offset as far as possible the effects on, or costs to, the economy of exchange rate variability. Another approach is to view the choice of a peg as involving broader policy considerations than those related to short-term exchange rate variability. These are core issues that this book deals with in some detail.

One has to bear in mind that exchange rate regime choice represents a dilemma for developing countries. A developing economy faces a trade-off between exchange rate stability (that is needed to promote trade, investment and growth) and the need for flexibility to maintain price competitiveness. For reasons that will be revealed later, it has been established that floating exchange rates are not suitable for developing countries. But fixed exchange rates are difficult to maintain under high capital mobility in this era of financial deregulation. Hence, the choice may fall on something in-between, but this is no good for the proponents of the bipolar view (also called the two-corner solution) who envisage the inevitability of going for either strictly fixed or completely flexible exchange rates. All of these considerations are also important for countries planning to issue a new currency, because the decision regarding the choice of exchange rate regime and the degree of currency convertibility needs to be made before issuing the new currency. The choice, according to Quirk and Short (1993), 'has a major impact on the degree to which the country controls its monetary and exchange rate policies, and thus the acceptability of the new currency'. The choice also determines which macroeconomic variables bear the burden of long-term adjustment (the exchange rate, international reserves, the price level or the interest rate). All of these considerations have to be taken care of in a constantly changing environment characterized by increased capital mobility, exposure to foreign exchange risk, greater internationalization of balance sheets, increased openness to international trade, shifts of exports towards manufacturers, trade diversification, greater interregional trade and declining inflation (Mussa *et al.*, 2000).

One point of terminology must be clarified here concerning the use of the words 'flexible' and 'floating'. Most economists use the two words interchangeably, but it is arguable that they may not mean the same thing. For example, Wickham (1985) maintains the view that flexibility does not necessarily imply that the exchange rate is determined by the interaction of market forces (that is, free or clean floating). On the other hand, Edwards and Levy-Yeyati (2003) make it explicit that they use the terms 'floating' and 'flexible' interchangeably. The same goes for Friedman (1953), who defines a 'system of flexible or floating exchange rates' as 'exchange rates freely determined by private dealings and, like other market prices, varying from day to day'. Although Wickham's argument makes a lot of sense, the discussion in this book is based on using the two words interchangeably. By and large, the word 'flexible' is typically used in a generic sense to mean the opposite of 'fixed' (the latter is also used to describe arrangements in which the exchange rate assumes various degrees of 'fixity'). What we should bear in mind, however, is that the precise meaning of the word 'floating' is 'perfectly flexible', which is what the word 'flexible' in the title of this book means. It must also be mentioned that the words 'regime' and 'arrangement' (and also 'system') are used interchangeably (no problem in this case).

Having clarified this point, it may be useful to go through some of the interesting controversies arising from the fixed versus flexible exchange rates debate. The first is the Joseph Stiglitz versus the IMF case, which pertains to the debate because intervention in the foreign exchange market is needed for any regime other than free floating. The extent of intervention may also determine or contribute to the degree of exchange rate flexibility. Stiglitz (2003) (justifiably) finds it strange that the IMF, an institution that strongly believes in the power of the market, should advocate a policy of market intervention as a necessary measure to keep a currency from depreciating (implying that the Fund is against floating). Stiglitz further argues that one of the central reasons for the failure of its policies throughout the Asian crisis of 1997–98 is that the IMF employed an outdated economic model, leading to the conclusion that it is important to prevent domestic currency depreciation. The IMF defends its position (which seems to be inconsistent with the philosophy of *laissez-faire*) on the grounds that market failure results in exchange rate overshooting. This stance is motivated by worries about the adverse inflationary effect of depreciation, but Stiglitz argues that rising oil prices also have inflationary effects (yet, the IMF does not advocate intervention in the oil market). He also argues that there is no concrete evidence supporting the proposition that inflation has adverse effects on economic growth as long as it remains moderate (see, for example, Moosa, 1997). It seems, he argues, that the adverse effects on growth of an overvalued currency are far greater than those of the inflation induced by depreciation. The IMF holds the view that depreciation may produce contagion, which leads to a disruption of global financial markets. However, neither theory nor evidence provides a convincing support for this proposition.

In another case, Mundell (2003) criticizes the haphazard nature of the shift to flexible exchange rates (in the early 1970s), arguing that it was by no means well-planned and that few events in international monetary history have been more poorly prepared. There was very little analysis of how a system of managed flexible exchange rates would work out. There was little, if any, recognition of what would be given up by abandoning the existing international system. Moreover, Obstfeld and Rogoff (1995) argue that when the postwar system of exchange rates collapsed in the early 1970s, few imagined just how volatile exchange rates would be in the ensuing floating-rate era. Fewer still anticipated how difficult it would be to establish any systematic connection between exchange rate movements and the underlying changes in economic fundamentals, even at fairly long horizons. Little wonder, then, that so many observers have called for policies to restore limits on exchange rate fluctuations. However, Obstfeld and Rogoff conclude that 'stuffing the genie of floating exchange rates back in its bottle is easier said than done'.

At this point it seems appropriate to introduce the concept of the classic macroeconomic trilemma: the idea that of the three policy objectives of fixed exchange rates, open capital markets (capital mobility) and autonomous monetary policy, only two can be mutually consistent. The intuitive explanation is rather simple: when a country credibly and permanently pegs its currency against another currency (let us call it the anchor currency), the domestic interest rate will be equal to the interest rate of the anchor country. Obstfeld *et al.* (2004a) use the concept of the trilemma to explain the interwar crises, which (they argued) arose out of the inability of governments to pursue consistent policies in a rapidly changing political and economic environment.

The concept of the exchange rate

One way of considering the choice between exchange rate regimes is to ask how various regimes affect the level and path of the real exchange rate relative to its appropriate value and trajectory. However, exchange rate regime choice primarily and practically pertains to the fixity or variability of the nominal (not the real) exchange rate. Both fixed and flexible nominal exchange rates are, in principle and in appropriate circumstances, capable of securing balance of payments adjustment by altering the real exchange rate. At this stage, we need to define the concept of nominal and real exchange rates.

The nominal exchange rate between two currencies, x and y, can be expressed as $E(x/y)$. This expression refers to the price of one unit of currency y in terms of currency x (the number of units of x per one unit of y). This exchange rate is nominal because it is not adjusted for changes in prices. It is bilateral because it is an expression of two currencies in terms of one another.

If $E(x/y)$ rises, then this would indicate appreciation of y and depreciation of x, and vice versa. This is because a higher value of E indicates that one unit of y after its appreciation is worth more than before in terms of the number of units of x. Thus, we refer to the rise and fall of exchange rates but the appreciation and depreciation of currencies. When $E(x/y)$ changes between two points in time (0 and 1) from $E_0(x/y)$ to $E_1(x/y)$, then the rate of appreciation or depreciation of currency y is given by

$$\dot{E}(x/y) = \frac{E_1(x/y)}{E_0(x/y)} - 1 \tag{1.1}$$

where $\dot{E}(x/y)$ is the percentage change in the exchange rate measured as the x price of a unit of y, and hence it is the percentage change in the value of currency y. Remember that E is the variable whose value changes between time 0 and time 1, but (x/y) is the unit (or units) of measurement. The expression (x/y) may be dropped for simplicity but we have to make sure that it is (x/y), not (y/x).

The corresponding change in the value of currency x can be calculated in two ways. The first is to calculate it as the percentage change of the reciprocal rate, $E(y/x)$. The reciprocal rate is expressed as

$$E(y/x) = \frac{1}{E(x/y)} \tag{1.2}$$

which says that the exchange rate measured as the price of one unit of x is the reciprocal of the exchange rate measured as the price of one unit of y. Then we calculate the appreciation (positive change) or depreciation (negative change) of x as the percentage change of $E(y/x)$. Hence

$$\dot{E}(y/x) = \frac{E_1(y/x)}{E_0(y/x)} - 1 \tag{1.3}$$

The other method that can be used for the same purpose is to calculate the percentage appreciation or depreciation of x directly from the percentage change in the value of currency y as

$$\dot{E}(y/x) = \frac{1}{1 + \dot{E}(x/y)} - 1 \tag{1.4}$$

This exchange rate notation can be used to illustrate the point made earlier about the ability of a country to maintain its exchange rate against major currencies by pegging its currency to one major currency under a system of fixed exchange rates. If x is the currency of a developing country and $y_i(y_j)$ is major currency $i(j)$, then

$$E(x/y_i) = \frac{E(x/y_j)}{E(y_i/y_j)} \tag{1.5}$$

Under fixed exchange rates, $E(y_i/y_j)$ is constant. If the developing country pegs to currency y_j ($i \neq j$), then the exchange rates of x against y_i will be constant, given that $E(x/y_j)$ is constant by definition.

The real bilateral exchange rate is the nominal rate adjusted for domestic and foreign prices. Hence

$$R(x/y) = E(x/y)\left[\frac{P_y}{P_x}\right] \tag{1.6}$$

where P_y and P_x are the price levels in the countries whose currencies are y and x respectively. It is obvious from equation (1.6) that real appreciation of currency y (a higher R) comes from nominal appreciation (higher E) or from a higher P_y relative to P_x (country y having a higher inflation rate than country x). Notice, however, that while the behaviour of the nominal exchange rate, $E(x/y)$, is determined in part by the exchange rate regime, it is the behaviour of the real exchange rate, $R(x/y)$, that is crucial for the economy. For example, under fixed exchange rates, E is constant, which means that the real exchange rate is determined entirely by the inflation differential. Under flexible exchange rates, and assuming that purchasing power parity (PPP) holds, any rise in E will be offset by a corresponding fall in the price ratio, which leaves R unchanged.

These principles on the relationship between the real and nominal exchange rates can be represented diagrammatically as in Figures 1.1–1.3. In Figure 1.1, if inflation is higher in country y than in country x, the price ratio line will rotate upwards to represent a rising price ratio. Under fixed exchange rates, E will not change but R will rise. Figure 1.2

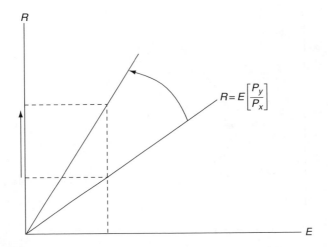

Figure 1.1 The effect of a rising price ratio under fixed exchange rates

represents the case of flexible exchange rates when purchasing power parity (PPP) does not hold. As E rises, R will also rise without any change in the price ratio. Finally, Figure 1.3 shows the case of flexible exchange rates when PPP holds precisely. As the price ratio falls (because of a lower

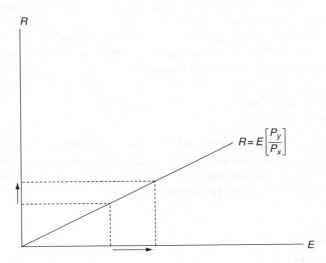

Figure 1.2 The effect of changes in the nominal exchange rate when PPP does not hold

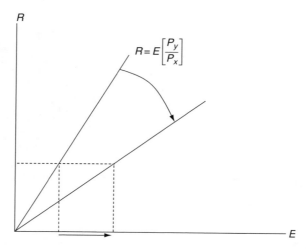

Figure 1.3   The effect of changes in the nominal exchange rate when PPP holds

inflation rate in y) the nominal exchange rate rises, but nothing happens to the real exchange rate. The constancy of the real exchange rate despite changes in the nominal rate is a crucial prediction of the PPP hypothesis.

The effective (or multilateral) exchange rate is an index of the value of a currency against several currencies. Let $E(x_1/y)$, $E(x_2/y)$, ..., $E(x_m/y)$ be the bilateral exchange rates of currency y against the currencies $x_1, x_2, \ldots, x_m$. If there is a base period, 0, then the effective exchange rate of currency y at time t is calculated as

$$e_t = \sum_{i=1}^{m} w_i \left[\frac{E(x_i/y)_t}{E(x_i/y)_0} \right] \tag{1.7}$$

where w_i is the weight assigned to currency x_i. When a currency is pegged to a basket, the objective is to stabilize the effective exchange rate, e_t. The weights can be export weights, import weights or bilateral trade weights, which are given respectively by

$$w_i = \frac{X_i}{\sum X_i} \tag{1.8}$$

$$w_i = \frac{M_i}{\sum M_i} \tag{1.9}$$

$$w_i = \frac{X_i + M_i}{\sum X_i + \sum M_i} \qquad (1.10)$$

where X_i is exports to country i, M_i is imports from country i and $X_i + M_i$ is the total bilateral trade with country i. The weights given by equations (1.8)–(1.10) result in the export-weighted, import-weighted and trade-weighted effective exchange rates (or exchange rate indices). These measures, however, are only approximations to the 'true' effective exchange rate, changes in which are intended to measure the hypothetical uniform change in the exchange rate of a currency against all other currencies that would be equivalent (in its effect on the balance of payments) to the pattern of exchange rate changes that actually occurred. No such comprehensive measure of the effective exchange rate exists.

The real effective exchange rate is calculated from the real bilateral exchange rates. Let P_i be the price level in the country whose currency is x_i. Then

$$r_t = \sum_{i=1}^{m} w_i \left[\frac{E(x_i/y)_t}{E(x_i/y)_0} \left(\frac{P_y}{P_i} \right)_t \right] \qquad (1.11)$$

where the price levels are measured as indices relative to the base period 0. Alternatively the real effective exchange rate can be calculated by adjusting the nominal effective exchange rate for the 'effective' price ratio, which gives

$$r_t = e_t \left[\frac{P_{y,t}}{\sum_{i=1}^{m} w_i P_{i,t}} \right] \qquad (1.12)$$

Under a basket peg, e does not change, in which case r will change according to the inflation differential, as in Figure 1.1.

Exchange rate volatility and misalignment

It is often claimed that one of the products of the current system of 'floating' exchange rates, which has been in operation since the early 1970s, is exchange rate volatility and misalignment. Exchange rate volatility refers to short-run fluctuations of the exchange rate around its mean value. The shift to floating exchange rates has indeed produced significant nominal exchange rate volatility. It is often argued that one reason for the emergence of financial risk management as a study discipline and a thriving professional activity is the shift by the Federal Reserve System to money supply targeting in 1979 and the general shift to floating following the collapse of the Bretton Woods system in 1971 (these two events produced interest rate volatility and exchange rate volatility, respectively).

Figure 1.4 shows the nominal bilateral exchange rates against the dollar (measured as the price of one dollar) of the yen, pound and Canadian dollar since December 1959. The change in volatility following the shift to floating is conspicuous. We can see that the yen/dollar exchange rate was rather stable prior to the shift to floating, but it was not completely fixed. This is because the exchange rates were allowed, under the Bretton Woods system, to move within a narrow range around their par values. The behaviour of the pound/dollar exchange rate tells the same story, except for the big jump in the exchange rate in November 1967 when the pound was devalued by 15 per cent. That was the second devaluation of the pound under the Bretton Woods system following the earlier devaluation of 1949 (one has to remember that the pound had been grossly overvalued). There is a slightly different story with the Canadian dollar, which had a floating exchange rate until 1962, and this is why we observe some volatility in the Canadian dollar/US dollar exchange rate prior to the collapse of the Bretton Woods system (during the earlier part of the sample period). Afterwards, volatility declined sharply because the Canadian dollar returned to the Bretton Woods system of fixed exchange rates. When the Bretton Woods system collapsed and the Canadian dollar was refloated, volatility reappeared. The same stories about the three exchange rates can be gleaned from Figure 1.5, which shows the month-to-month percentage changes in the three exchange rates.

While these graphs show that nominal exchange rates are more volatile under flexible exchange rate regimes, it has been argued that this issue is neither so simple nor so obvious (for example, Bartolini, 1996). Ghosh *et al.* (2002) cast doubt on this proposition, suggesting that nominal exchange rate volatility depends on the time horizon. They identify two features of exchange rate data: (i) nominal exchange rate volatility is greater under floating regimes at all horizons, and (ii) there is a tendency for volatility to decrease with the length of the time horizon. Finally, Jeanne and Rose (1999) cast doubt on the ability of purely macroeconomic models to explain regime-varying exchange rate volatility, suggesting instead models in which the structure of the foreign exchange market changes with the exchange rate regime. In this model, exchange rate volatility has two components: macroeconomic fundamentals and noise, which is uncorrelated with the fundamentals. The size of the noise component is endogenously determined, as it

(a) Japanese yen/US dollar

(b) British pound/US dollar

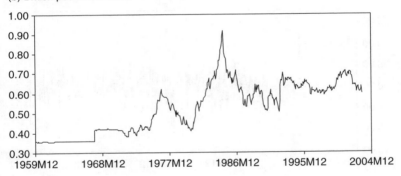

(c) Canadian dollar/US dollar

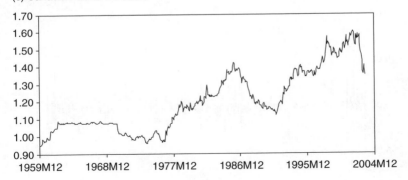

Figure 1.4 Nominal bilateral exchange rates

14

(a) Japanese yen/US dollar

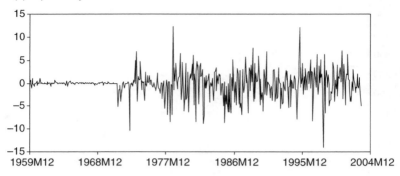

(b) British pound/US dollar

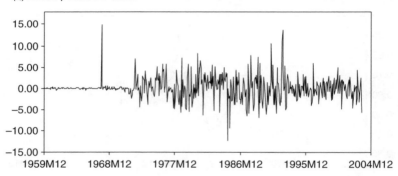

(c) Canadian dollar/US dollar

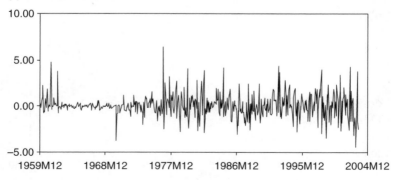

Figure 1.5 Percentage change in the nominal bilateral exchange rates

depends on the decision of noise traders with respect to entering the foreign exchange market.

Exchange rate misalignment refers to the deviation of the real exchange rate from its long-run equilibrium value. The problem here is how to calculate the long-run equilibrium value of the real exchange rate. There are indeed many sophisticated methods and models to calculate the long-run equilibrium value but the simplest and most intuitively appealing method is based on purchasing power parity. According to the PPP hypothesis changes in prices should be exactly matched by offsetting changes in the nominal exchange rate, so that the real exchange rate is unchanged. This necessarily means that the real exchange rate should be independent of the nominal exchange rate. Is this what the record actually shows? Not really.

Consider Figure 1.6, which shows consumer prices in the USA, Japan, the UK and Canada since December 1974. During the period covered by the graph, the UK had the highest inflation rate as prices went up by a factor of 5.2, whereas Japan had the lowest inflation rate with a factor of 0.9. Prices in the USA and Canada increased by factors of 2.6 and 2.7 respectively. Qualitatively, PPP held over the sample period in the sense that countries with higher inflation rates had depreciating currencies, and vice versa. Thus, the US dollar appreciated against the Canadian dollar and the pound but it depreciated against the yen, as shown in Figure 1.7. However, PPP does not seem to hold quantitatively, as changes in prices are not matched by (exactly or approximately)

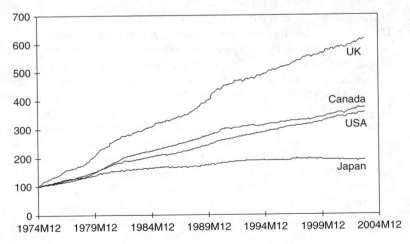

Figure 1.6   Consumer price indices (December 1974 = 100)

offsetting changes in nominal exchange rates. During the same period, the three nominal exchange rates changed by −63.1, 40.3 and 36.2 per cent, respectively. This is why the real exchange rates graphed in Figure 1.7 are not constant, exhibiting high correlation with the nominal exchange rates. If the base period of December 1974 was truly a period of equilibrium, then we may consider the initial level of the real exchange rate to be the long-run equilibrium level, which means that any subsequent deviation from this level is a measure of exchange rate mis-alignment. At the end of the period covered by Figure 1.7, the three real exchange rates were misaligned by −30, −19 and 30 per cent respectively.

Another way to look at misalignment is to measure the deviation of the actual nominal exchange rate from the PPP rate, which is the rate that would prevail if PPP held precisely. If the actual nominal rate is above (below) the PPP rate, this means that the US dollar is overvalued (undervalued). Thus, Figure 1.8 shows that the yen and the pound have been predominantly overvalued in terms against the US dollar but that the Canadian dollar has been predominantly undervalued. What is important for the discussion here is that all of these exchange rates appear to be misaligned.

The preceding discussion suggests the following characterization about the behaviour of floating exchange rates:

- Nominal exchange rates are highly correlated with the corresponding real rates. The nominal–real correlation coefficients are 0.96, 0.88 and 0.65 for the exchange rates of the Canadian dollar, Japanese yen and British pound respectively.
- The switch to floating rates has produced much more variability that cannot be explained by the variability of the fundamental determinants (Flood and Rose, 1999). The standard deviation of the percentage change in the exchange rate of the Canadian dollar against the US dollar increased from 0.69 during the period 1957–72 to 1.40 during the period 1972–2003. For the yen/dollar rate, the standard deviation increased from 0.58 to 3.31, and for the pound/dollar rate, it increased from 1.27 to 3.04. The relatively high standard deviation of the pound/dollar rate in the earlier period is due to the 1967 devaluation of the pound.
- Fundamentals cannot explain the behaviour of exchange rates over a short/medium-term horizon. This, however, does not mean that fundamental factors do not matter. For some forceful arguments for the importance and relevance of fundamentals, see Moosa (2002).
- Exchange rates tend to exhibit long-lived swings, with no apparent changes in fundamentals that are significant enough to justify the swings.

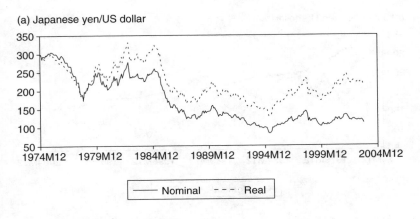

(a) Japanese yen/US dollar

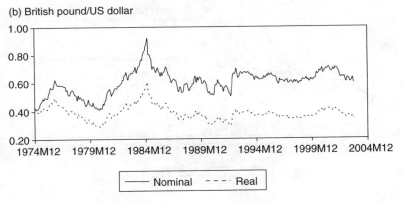

(b) British pound/US dollar

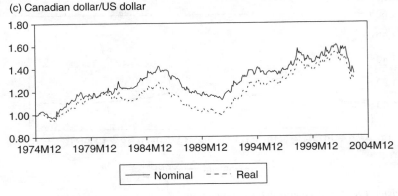

(c) Canadian dollar/US dollar

Figure 1.7 Nominal and real bilateral exchange rates

18

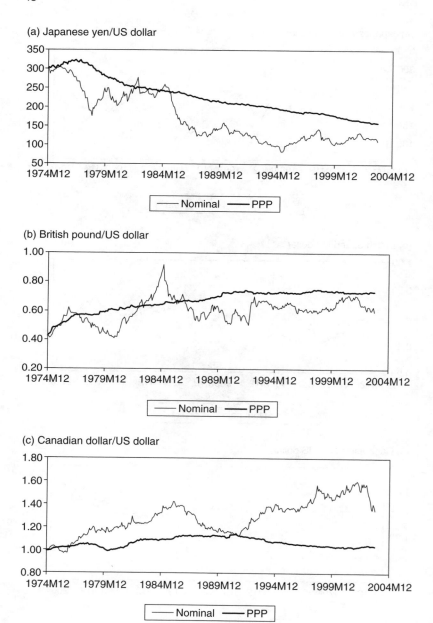

Figure 1.8   Nominal and PPP exchange rates

All of these observations, which are verified by Figures 1.6–1.8, have important implications. First, exchange rate volatility creates uncertainty that is harmful to international business and a depressing factor for international trade. Second, exchange rate misalignment distorts the pattern of comparative advantages, with adverse consequences for international trade. Finally, high correlation between the nominal and real rates means that changes in the former are translated into changes in the latter, implying that a nominal shock would be translated into a real shock. We have to remember that production and trading decisions, as well as competitiveness, depend on the real (not the nominal) exchange rate.

The observations that nominal and real exchange rates are highly correlated and that nominal rates are more volatile under flexible exchange rate regimes (as in Figures 1.6–1.8) seem to suggest that the volatility of the real exchange rate is dependent on the underlying exchange rate regime. Mussa (1986) believes that this is the case, arguing that 'the observed empirical regularities provide strong evidence against theoretical models that embody the property of nominal exchange rate regime neutrality'. However, the evidence obtained by Grilli and Kaminsky (1991) casts doubt on this claim. This evidence is based on an examination of the behaviour of real and nominal exchange rates over a period going back to 1885. They found that large differences in the volatility of real exchange rates between fixed and flexible exchange rate regimes are present only in the post-Second World War period. They concluded that what is crucial for real exchange rate behaviour is the particular historical period rather than the nominal exchange rate arrangement.

In a more recent study, Mendoza (2000) applied variance decomposition to the Mexican peso/dollar real exchange rate over the period 1969–2000. He concluded that a finding attributing most of the variation in the real exchange rate to fluctuations in the prices of traded goods and nominal exchange rates holds only in periods in which Mexico 'was not under a regime of exchange rate management'. During periods when Mexico had a managed exchange rate regime, the variability of the prices of non-traded goods relative to traded goods accounts for up to 70 per cent of the variability of the real exchange rate. Ghosh *et al.* (1997) found support for the proposition that real exchange rates are more volatile under fixed exchange rates.

Let us look at what has been happening since 1885. Figure 1.9 displays the behaviour of the nominal and real dollar/pound exchange rate since 1885 (annual observations). In Figure 1.9(a) the nominal and real exchange rates are plotted together, showing different degrees of correlation between the two rates across historical episodes. Figure 1.9(b) displays the volatility of the nominal and real exchange rates measured by the year-to-year percentage change. Table 1.1 reports measures of volatility and correlation over three historical episodes (1885–1913, 1949–72 and 1973–present). We can readily observe that, apart from

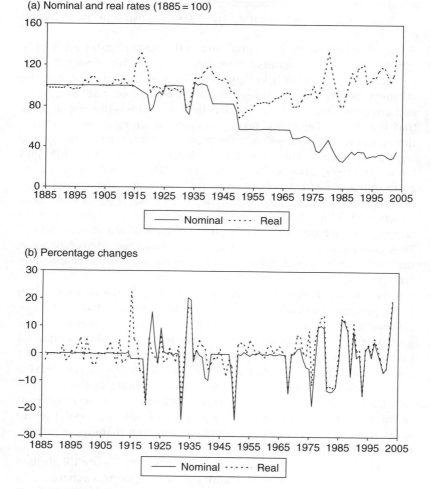

Figure 1.9   The dollar/pound exchange rate

Table 1.1 Volatility and correlation of the dollar/pound exchange rate

	1885–1913	1949–72	1973–2003	1885–2003
Standard deviation (nominal)	0.14	5.83	8.78	6.80
Standard deviation (real)	2.68	6.36	8.68	6.90
Correlation	0.21	0.13	0.24	0.09

the gold standard period, the volatilities of the real and nominal exchange rates are very close, indicating indeed that the nominal exchange rate regime is non-neutral as suggested by Mussa (1986). However, the results also support the findings of Grilli and Kaminsky (1991), who argued that the closeness of the volatilities of the nominal and real exchange rates is a post-Second World War phenomenon.

Patterns of exchange rate regime choice

During the period since 1870, four main exchange rate regime switches have taken place: (i) the adoption of the gold standard from 1870 to the outbreak of the First World War in 1914, (ii) the switch to flexible exchange rates in the interwar period, (iii) the adoption of the Bretton Woods system of fixed but adjustable exchange rates from 1944 to 1972, and (iv) the switch to the present system. On the other hand, Grilli and Kaminsky (1991) present the evolution of exchange rate regimes according to the following chronology: the gold standard (January 1879 to June 1914); the transition to wartime markets (July 1914 to November 1914); controlled floating (December 1914 to March 1919); the gold exchange standard (May 1925 to August 1931); the second interwar floating (September 1931 to August 1939); fixed exchange rates under the Bretton Woods system (October 1949 to May 1972); and the present system (March 1973 to the present time).

Figure 1.10 displays exchange rate regime choice using the most recent available data (obtained from the IMF's *Annual Report on Exchange Arrangements and Exchange Restrictions*, 2003). It shows that 48 per cent of the countries have fixed exchange rates; 54 per cent of these countries have hard pegs (no separate legal tender and currency boards), whereas the rest have conventional pegs (pegging to a single currency or a basket of currencies). Countries with flexible exchange rates comprise 44 per cent, of which 56 per cent adopt managed floating and 44 per cent have independent floating. Countries with intermediate regimes (defined

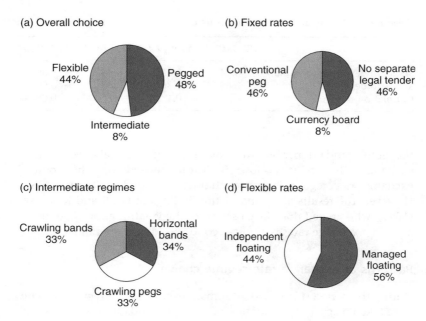

Figure 1.10   Exchange rate regime choice (2003)

here to include pegged currencies with horizontal bands, crawling pegs and crawling bands) comprise a minority of 8 per cent.

Changes in the pattern of exchange rate regime choice indicate a move towards flexible exchange rates and away from intermediate regimes. We have to be careful, however, that this classification is based on what countries report to the IMF, which may not be what they actually do. In Chapter 5, a distinction will be made between the IMF's (*de jure*) classification and the *de facto* classification of exchange rate regimes, which shows that a larger number of countries have intermediate regimes than is shown here. While the numbers represented by Figure 1.10 seem to support the 'hollowing out hypothesis', which postulates that countries have been shying away from intermediate regimes, the *de facto* classification supports the hypothesis of 'fear of floating', which postulates that (developing) countries claiming to have floating rates have rather rigid rates. These are issues that will be dealt with in detail in Chapter 5. We will also discuss the exit problem of why countries find it difficult to move from fixed exchange rates to more flexible ones.

But then there is the question of what we mean by 'intermediate' regimes. Some economists (for example, Bubula and Otker-Robe, 2003) define intermediate regimes to include conventional (soft) pegs as well as managed floating. The two extremes of fixed and floating exchange rates are in this case represented by hard pegs and independent floating. Bubula and Otker-Robe (2002) make it explicit that intermediate regimes include conventional pegs as well as crawling pegs, horizontal bands, crawling bands and tightly managed floating. If this is the case, then the distribution of exchange rate regimes looks completely different, as in Figure 1.11. It must be pointed out, however, that in any discussion of the hollowing out hypothesis, conventional pegs are regarded as intermediate regimes.

We will now consider some of the preliminary arguments involved in exchange rate regime choice. The traditional case for fixed exchange rates rests on two grounds. The first is the optimum currency areas argument: when there are close trade ties and similarity of production structures, a fixed exchange rate will encourage beneficial trade and capital flows. Mundell (1961) and Tower and Willett (1976) emphasized the advantages of forming a currency area such that there is a fixed exchange rate among the countries within the area but flexible rates with the rest of the world. The second is that a fixed exchange rate regime can be viewed as an anchor for monetary policy. The traditional argument in favour of a flexible exchange rate regime is that it allows countries to pursue independent monetary policy, which can be

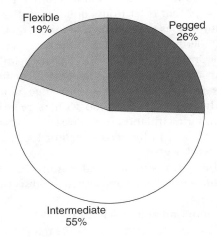

Figure 1.11   Exchange rate regime choice (soft pegs are classified as intermediate)

directed to the needs of the domestic economy. The exchange rate could then be a buffer to soften the impact of external shocks, such as changes in the terms of trade.

On the surface it seems that there is a tendency towards greater exchange rate flexibility, which is explainable in terms of the vastly expanded volume of international capital flows that have made the maintenance of fixed exchange rates rather difficult. Increased capital mobility has heightened susceptibility to financial disturbances, such as changes in interest rates, while enhancing the ability of flexible exchange rates to act as a buffer against shocks. But then there is a widespread belief that a system of floating exchange rates would not work in developing countries, because a successful operation of this system requires highly sophisticated financial structures involving forward and futures markets. There has also been the concern that floating rates could lead to a steep fall in the currency value as a result of balance of payments difficulties, which in turn could adversely affect price stability and output in the short run.

Quirk and Cortes-Douglas (1993) list the following explanations for why developing countries may opt for flexible rates:

- Without sufficient reserves to defend it, a fixed exchange rate is not credible.
- It is difficult for any country to determine a sustainable equilibrium exchange rate level under fixed rates, and the task becomes even more difficult if macroeconomic and structural reforms are under way. If the rate is set at a level that is far from equilibrium, the resulting effects may lead the authorities to reset the rate to rectify such errors, which in turn could undermine confidence in the currency.
- Macroeconomic instability (in the form of high inflation rates) has been evident in most of the countries opting for flexible exchange rates. In these circumstances, fixed exchange rates could not be adjusted quickly enough to keep up with price realignments. The desire to stop imported inflation from Russia led Latvia and Lithuania to float their currencies in the second half of 1992 (but subsequently they moved to hard pegs).
- The authorities may think for political reasons that if the market did the job, the influence of lobbies and vested interests would be reduced.

On the other hand, Garber and Svensson (1995) suggest four explanations for the desire to choose fixed exchange rates. These explanations include the following: (i) a fixed exchange rate system may minimize instability in real economic activity; (ii) it helps a central bank that otherwise lacks credibility to gain some credibility; (iii) the system 'muffles extraneous disturbances and insulates the economy from them'; and (iv) the system would provide 'a synthetic money market with the liquidity of the markets of the country that provides the vehicle currency'. They go on to demonstrate how a fixed exchange rate system operates and how it comes to an end. More recently, the theory of fear of floating has come to the surface, postulating the preference of developing countries for less flexible exchange rates (Calvo and Reinhart, 2002).

Aghevli and Montiel (1991) summarize the major findings and point out a common feature of the exchange rate regime literature. They argue that most of the studies have been developed for industrial countries engaged in short-run stabilization of output. The analysis is therefore focused on a narrow criterion of macroeconomic stability in the face of random transitory disturbances. Thus, it is likely that choosing to stabilize any single macroeconomic variable could perturb another variable that may also seem relevant to general welfare, in which case exchange rate regime choice is not unambiguously determined. Following Aghevli and Montiel (1991), the apparent solution to this problem is to specify a general welfare criterion that would consider these trade-offs. However, this may produce general results, depending directly on the predetermined weights given to each of the variables that the authorities wish to stabilize.

The choice of exchange rate regime is linked to some extent to the achievement of specific targets set by the authorities. It is more likely that these targets are related to internal and external imbalances. Therefore, correlation between exchange rate regime choice and real output, prices and balance of payments stabilization is expected. The following points can be made:

- When the objective is balance of payments stabilization, it is preferable to adopt flexible exchange rates to overturn disequilibrium. In this case, attention should be paid to the Marshall–Lerner condition, the degree of capital mobility and foreign reserves constraints.
- When the objective is to stabilize domestic prices, the financial discipline issue becomes paramount. In this case, a fixed exchange rate system imposes a degree of financial discipline by discouraging recourse to inflationary finance.
- When the objective is to stabilize real output, the exchange rate regime becomes mainly a shock absorber. The variability of real output is affected by different economic disturbances, in which case

the choice of the exchange rate regime is used to spread these effects. Therefore, the choice in this case depends on the nature of shocks and the structural characteristics of the economy (such as the degree of openness, capital mobility, wage indexation and development).

In view of these points, let us consider a country that faces high domestic inflation. If the exchange rate is already fixed, the authorities could opt for flexible exchange rates in order to avoid a balance of payments crisis. In this case, the target becomes avoiding an imminent external crisis rather than controlling inflation. If the country already has flexible rates, fixing the exchange rate amounts to imposing an anchor on the economy, which is conducive to controlling inflation. Therefore, the response to a high domestic inflation rate is not unique, depending on the target set by the policy-maker. Edwards (1996) presents a model assuming that the monetary authorities minimize a quadratic loss function that captures the trade-off between inflation and unemployment. The model is applied initially to the choice between fixed and flexible exchange rates, then it is extended to the choice between fixed but adjustable rates and flexible rates. Klyuev (2001) developed a model of exchange rate regime choice that is centred on the trade-off between internal price stability and external competitiveness while allowing for the institutional costs of altering the regime. The main implication of the model is the presence of a non-linear relationship between inflation and regime choice for the next period.

Sarno and Taylor (2002, p. 171) point out that the issue of choosing fixed as opposed to flexible exchange rates arose in the macroeconomic literature from an extension of the criteria to be considered in making the choice between a monetary policy of interest rate targeting and a monetary policy of money supply targeting within the IS–LM framework. These extensions are based on choosing monetary as well as exchange rate policy by minimizing a weighted sum of the variances of output and inflation. The conclusions of this strand of research is that if the variance of the LM (IS) shock is significantly larger than the variance of the IS (LM) shock, then a fixed (flexible) exchange rate regime is preferable. If there is no significant difference between the variances of the two shocks then managed floating is the optimal regime.

Perhaps it makes sense to close this discussion with Eichengreen's (1999a) argument that 'the economist is no more convincing than the shoe salesman when he insists that one size fits all'. Likewise, Frankel (1999) expresses the same idea through the title of his paper *No Single Currency Regime is Right for All Countries or at All Times*. It is, therefore, not possible (neither is it plausible) to argue that all countries should adopt floating rates. Hong Kong has good economic and political reasons to relinquish its monetary autonomy and commit to a currency board. In fact, Hong Kong has had a rather pleasant experience with its currency board. We will also argue that a country like Iraq, ravaged by war and hyperinflation, could benefit from a currency board (see a case study on Iraq in Chapter 9). France, Germany and other European countries have compelling reasons to go for a monetary union. But, Eichengreen argues, countries that are not prepared to delegate national monetary autonomy to a foreign central bank (as with a currency board) or to create a transnational entity, like the European Central Bank, will face pressures to move to a regime of greater exchange rate flexibility.

The verdict (in advance)

It is typically the case that the verdict is delivered at the very end, but on this occasion I have chosen to spell it out at the beginning. This book deals primarily with three controversial issues pertaining to exchange rate regime choice:

- The fixed versus flexible exchange rates debate.
- The factors that determine exchange rate regime choice.
- Macroeconomic performance under various exchange rate regimes.

On three counts, the analysis and the evidence presented in this book convey the message that there are no clear-cut conclusions. When we consider the debate on the choice between fixed and flexible exchange rates in their generic forms, no obvious favourite emerges, as both have their advantages and disadvantages. And when we consider the suitability of a specific regime within the wide spectrum between the two extremes, we do not reach the conclusion that 'one size fits all'. It all depends on the country in question, and any attempt to generalize the issue is bound to be ideologically driven. On the factors determining exchange rate regime choice, we will again find no clear correspondence between the determining factors and the selected regime. This would be the case whether the matching is done via casual empiricism or via rigorous empirical work. As far as macroeconomic performance is concerned, no strong and robust association can be found between exchange rate regimes and macroeconomic performance, and this is particularly the case for output growth (the relationship is less weak for inflation). Although incorporating the distinction between various classification schemes (of exchange rate regimes) and among countries according to the level of development produces less ambiguous results, the association is still not that convincing.

There is no doubt that the exchange rate regime is important, but we should not assign more importance to this factor than it actually deserves. If growth theory tells us that tens of variables can explain cross-country differences in growth, it sounds bizarre to say that country A has a better growth record than that of country B because country A chose exchange rate regime X whereas country B chose exchange rate regime Y. Of course it is not always like that in the literature, but ideologically driven views tend to be dogmatic in this sense. Likewise, one cannot say that fixed exchange rates are superior to flexible rates under all circumstances. And we cannot attribute the choice of a certain regime by a certain country to certain characteristics because of the likelihood of finding another country with similar attributes that has chosen a different regime. The verdict, therefore, is that the role of the exchange rate regime should not be exaggerated while the determinants and consequences cannot be generalized. Hopefully, the material presented in the following chapters will justify this verdict.

2
The Role of the Exchange Rate in the Economy

Macroeconomic linkages through exchange rates

The exchange rate provides a key macroeconomic linkage between the domestic economy and the rest of the world that takes place through the goods and asset markets. In the goods market, the exchange rate establishes linkages between domestic and foreign prices through the relationship

$$P = \alpha + \beta EP^* \tag{2.1}$$

where P is domestic prices, P^* is foreign prices and the exchange rate is expressed as the domestic currency price of one unit of the foreign currency. The parameters that reflect transaction costs and other market imperfections are α and β. This is a linear relationship between domestic prices and foreign prices expressed in domestic currency terms. It shows that the higher the exchange rate, other things being equal, the higher the price of foreign goods in the home country ($\partial P/\partial E > 0$). The same relationship can be seen in Figure 2.1, which depicts P as a function of P^*. As the exchange rate rises (the domestic currency depreciates) the line $P = \alpha + \beta EP^*$ rotates upwards, leading to higher P for the same level of P^*. This happens either directly (because the domestic price of imported goods rises) or indirectly (because domestic firms can afford to raise their prices when competitors' prices rise). Some of the effect is transmitted through the labour market, as workers may demand wage increases when higher import prices raise the cost of living. Governments that are aware of this connection would prefer to stop depreciation but if they do so in the face of domestic inflation they risk a loss in competitiveness. Naturally, the effect of domestic currency appreciation

29

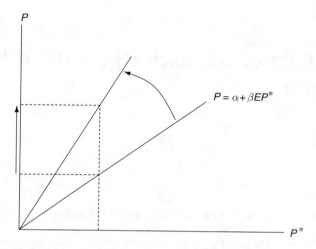

Figure 2.1 The effect of a rising exchange rate on domestic prices

on domestic prices can be augmented by a rise in foreign currency prices as shown in Figure 2.2. On the other hand, it can be seen in Figure 2.3 that domestic currency appreciation (falling exchange rate) can offset the effect of rising foreign prices.

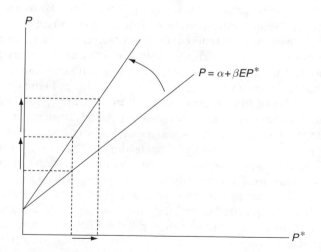

Figure 2.2 The effect of domestic currency depreciation and rising foreign prices on domestic prices

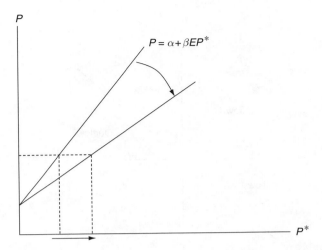

Figure 2.3 The effect of domestic currency appreciation and rising foreign prices on domestic prices

The asset markets also have exchange rate linkages. The choice among assets depends on the trade-off between risk and return, a linkage that can be expressed in terms of uncovered interest parity (UIP), which may be written as

$$i = i^* + \dot{E}^e \tag{2.2}$$

where i is the domestic interest rate, i^* is the foreign interest rate and $\dot{E}^e$ is the expected change in the exchange rate. If we relax the assumption of risk neutrality, the condition becomes

$$i = i^* + \dot{E}^e + \rho \tag{2.3}$$

where ρ is the risk premium. Equation (2.3) can be rewritten as

$$i - i^* = \dot{E}^e + \rho \tag{2.4}$$

Under fixed exchange rates, $\dot{E}^e = 0$ and if $\rho = 0$ then $i = i^*$, a condition that requires capital mobility. If this condition is not met and capital moves across borders in an unrestricted fashion, then (depending on the configuration of interest and exchange rates) the underlying country may experience capital inflow or outflow. This is shown in Figure 2.4.

Microeconomic linkages through the exchange rate involve resource allocation. When the real exchange rate makes the economy highly

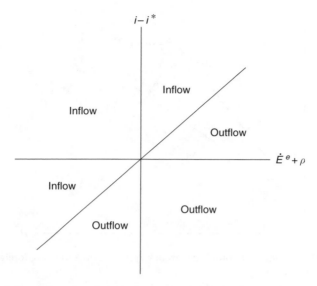

Figure 2.4   Interest and exchange rate configurations and capital flows

competitive, resources are drawn into the traded goods sector, which is mirrored in the factor market by a new allocation of resources. The economy becomes trade-oriented, with rising employment of capital and labour in the export- and import-competing sectors. The distribution of income is also affected. If the country has a traditional export sector (for example, agriculture or mining), then a very competitive exchange rate will make traditional exports profitable. There are also implications for the asset markets. When domestic returns are below foreign returns, capital flight will occur, leaving a smaller amount of resources available for domestic investment. Moreover, those who indulge in capital flight (for example, those who can fake trade invoices) often do so at the expense of those who do not (perhaps because they cannot).

Exchange rate policies/regimes affect the external balance and the internal balance through their effects on total spending (via the demand for money) and on the competitiveness of traded goods. According to Collier and Joshi (1989), the external balance should be interpreted as the achievement of a sustainable current account deficit (a deficit that is consistent with a realistic medium-run projection of foreign capital inflow). The internal balance is a more complex target as it has employment (or output) and inflation as its components. Policy-makers would like to have high employment and output and low inflation, but complications are introduced by the fact that there may be a trade-off between these sub-targets (as implied by the Phillips curve). Exchange rate regimes/policies affect the internal balance because the price of a currency has an important direct influence on the general price level (as we have seen), and an important indirect influence on the level of aggregate economic activity. Microeconomic efficiency, or the efficiency of resource allocation, is important for the objective of maximizing real income. Exchange rate regimes/policies affect efficiency in two ways: (i) by affecting the uncertainty surrounding the outcome of economic transactions (particularly foreign-trade transactions), and (ii) by making the imposition of trade restrictions more or less likely.

Exchange rate fluctuations as a source of risk and uncertainty

Some cynical commentators say that the shift from fixed to flexible exchange rates following the collapse of the Bretton Woods system in the early 1970s resulted in the promotion of telex operators to foreign exchange dealers. Beyond the humour in this statement, the effects of this shift have been more profound in terms of the (increased) uncertainty surrounding the outcome of financial and commercial cross-border transactions. The shift has led to the emergence of two thriving and interrelated industries: exchange rate forecasting and foreign exchange risk management. The problem is that forecasting exchange rates is much more difficult than predicting who will win a penalty shoot-out between England and another team in a World Cup or a European Cup quarter-final, or even the inflation rate to prevail next year. Given that exchange rate forecasting is used extensively in financial decision-making, the shift has created problems as well as opportunities for multinational businesses and, indeed, businesses with exposure to the outside world. In fact, even businesses that do not deal with the outside world are exposed to foreign exchange risk because exchange rate changes may induce foreign competitors to enter the domestic market.

International financial operations, such as capital budgeting, are much more complicated under flexible exchange rates because another dimension of risk (foreign exchange risk) is added. In the case of domestic currency financing, the cost of financing is equal to the interest rate on the domestic currency, which is known in advance. Financing in a foreign currency under fixed exchange rates means that the cost of financing is equal to the interest rate on the foreign currency, which is also known in advance. Thus, it is possible, under fixed exchange rates, to compare the two known costs and choose the cheaper financing mode (domestic currency or foreign currency financing). Under flexible exchange rates, the cost of financing in a foreign currency is equal to the interest rate on the foreign currency plus the percentage change in the exchange rate (the percentage change in the value of the foreign currency). This component is not known in advance, which means that an element of risk is introduced into foreign currency financing. The comparison of the costs of financing will not be straightforward (for more details, see Moosa, 2003, 2004c).

Under flexible exchange rates, the outcome of cross-border commercial transactions will not be known with certainty because of exchange rate fluctuations. Consider the case of an exporter who sells his products in foreign markets. This exporter faces exposure to foreign exchange risk, in the sense that his total revenue in domestic currency terms fluctuates as the exchange rate fluctuates. Consider the following equations for the derivation of domestic currency revenue:

$$R = PQ \tag{2.5}$$

$$Q = f(P^*) \tag{2.6}$$

$$P^* = \alpha + \beta \left(\frac{P}{E}\right) \tag{2.7}$$

where R is domestic currency revenue, P is the domestic price of the product, Q is the quantity sold, P^* is the foreign price of the product and E is the exchange rate measured as the price of one unit of the foreign currency. Equation (2.5) defines domestic currency revenue as the product of the domestic price and the quantity sold. Equation (2.6) is a demand function in which the quantity sold in the foreign market depends on the foreign currency price of the product. Equation (2.7) relates the foreign currency price to the domestic price, where α and β represent the effect of market imperfections and transaction costs. The exporter can choose to set the price in foreign currency terms (in which case P^* will be fixed) or in domestic currency terms (in which case P will be fixed). Alternatively, the price can be set in foreign currency terms but the domestic currency price is adjusted to offset partially any adverse exchange rate movement. We will now consider what happens to the domestic currency revenue as the exchange rate changes.

Figures 2.5–2.7 are diagrammatic representations of equations (2.5)–(2.7). Figure 2.5 represents the case when the exporter uses foreign currency pricing, which means that the foreign currency price does not

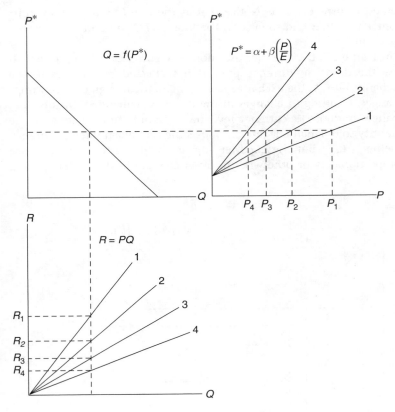

Figure 2.5 The effect of exchange rate changes on the revenue of an exporter (foreign currency pricing)

change as the exchange rate changes. In the top right-hand part of the diagram, changes in the exchange rate are represented by the rotation of the line $P^* = \alpha + \beta(P/E)$, such that a move from 1 towards 4 represents a lower exchange rate (weaker foreign currency). For various levels of the exchange rate there are corresponding levels of the domestic price, such that a higher level is associated with a higher exchange rate (given that the foreign currency price is constant). With no change in the foreign currency price, the quantity demanded is not affected, which means that changes in domestic currency revenue result only from changes in the domestic currency price. With a constant quantity, a higher level of domestic currency revenue is associated with a higher level of the domestic currency price. Notice that as the line $P^* = \alpha + \beta(P/E)$ shifts from 1 to 2 to 3 and then to 4, the line $R = PQ$ shifts in the opposite direction.

In Figure 2.6 the exporter uses domestic currency pricing, in which case the domestic currency price is not affected by changes in the exchange rate. As the exchange rate changes, the foreign currency price changes, resulting in changes in the quantity demanded. In this case, changes in domestic currency revenue result only from changes in the quantity sold. Finally, Figure 2.7 shows the case when foreign currency pricing is used but the exporter adjusts the domestic currency price (proportionately or otherwise) to offset changes in the exchange rate.

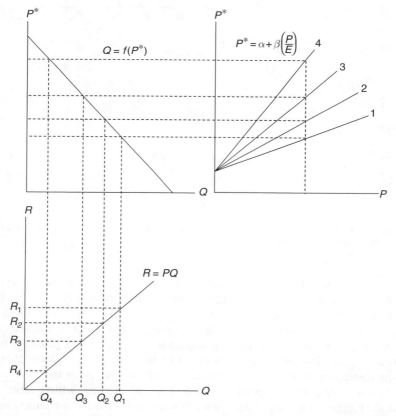

Figure 2.6 The effect of exchange rate changes on the revenue of an exporter (domestic currency pricing)

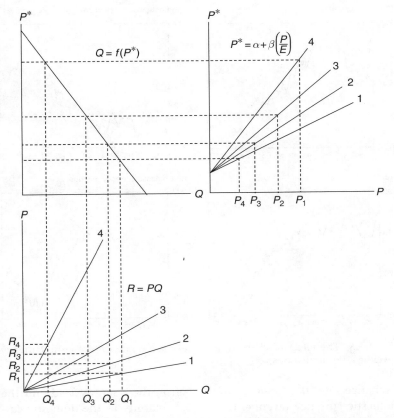

Figure 2.7 The effect of exchange rate changes on the revenue of an exporter (foreign currency pricing with domestic price adjustment)

In this case changes in domestic currency revenue result from changes in both the domestic currency price and the quantity sold.

What is important to realize from these diagrams is that fluctuations in the exchange rate cause fluctuations in domestic currency revenue irrespective of the pricing strategy used by the exporter. We can demonstrate the effect of the exchange rate on the domestic currency revenue by using a simple simulation exercise for the case of domestic currency financing. Let $P = 10$, so that $P^* = 1.2(10/E)$ and $Q = 100 - 2.5P^*$. If E starts with a value of 2 at $t = 1$, changes over the period $t = 2$ to $t = 100$ can be generated from a normal distribution. The results of simulation are shown in Figure 2.8, which plots 100 simulated observations of the

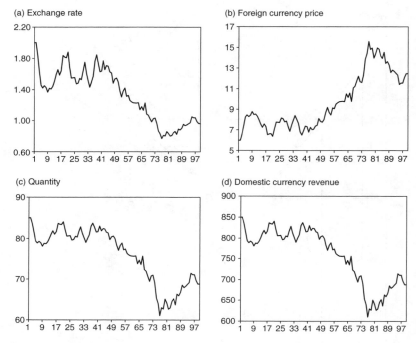

Figure 2.8 The effect of changes in the exchange rate on domestic currency revenue (100 simulations)

exchange rate, the foreign currency price, the quantity sold and the domestic currency revenue. Obviously, volatility in the domestic currency revenue is associated with exchange rate volatility.

The balance of payments and the exchange rate

One of the arguments for flexible exchange rates and against fixed rates pertains to the balance of payments adjustment mechanism under the two regimes. Therefore, it is worthwhile examining in detail the relationship between the balance of payments and the exchange rate.

This relationship arises because the transactions involving trade and capital flows, which are recorded on the balance of payments, give rise to demand for and supply of currencies. Transactions in the market for goods and services, such as imports and exports, give rise to demand for and supply of foreign exchange respectively. Equivalently, these transactions lead to the supply of and demand for the domestic currency respectively.

Transactions in financial markets, which are recorded on the capital account, also lead to demand for and supply of currencies. The sale of domestic securities and the purchase of foreign securities give rise to demand for foreign exchange (supply of domestic currency). Conversely, the purchase of domestic securities and the sale of foreign securities give rise to demand for the domestic currency (supply of foreign exchange).

The relationship between the balance of payments and the foreign exchange market is, therefore, obvious. For each transaction on the foreign exchange market there is a corresponding entry on the balance of payments. For the purpose of illustrating this relationship further we will examine the foreign exchange market from the perspective of the foreign currency, such that the exchange rate, E, is measured as the domestic currency price of one unit of the foreign currency. Three possible cases are illustrated in Figure 2.9, which shows the demand for and supply of foreign exchange curves (D and S respectively). In Figure 2.9(a), the foreign exchange market is in equilibrium at the exchange rate E_0, at which the supply of and demand for foreign exchange are equal. This is equivalent to saying that the balance of payments is in equilibrium. In Figure 2.9(b), there is excess demand for foreign exchange at the exchange rate E_1, which is below the equilibrium exchange rate. This excess demand is equivalent to a deficit on the balance of payments. Finally, Figure 2.9(c) shows the case when there is excess supply of foreign exchange, which is equivalent to a surplus on the balance of payments. This occurs at the exchange rate E_2.

Let us for simplicity concentrate on the current account of the balance of payments by assuming that exports and imports are the sources of, supply of and demand for foreign exchange. Given this simplifying assumption about its structure, the relationship between the balance of payments and the foreign exchange market can be restated by examining the demand for and supply of imports and exports as represented in Figure 2.10. Since we are still examining the relationship from the perspective of the foreign currency, the prices of imports and exports, P_m^* and P_x^* respectively, are expressed in foreign currency terms. Figure 2.10(a) shows the supply and demand curves for imports, S_m and D_m, both of which are drawn as linear functions relating the quantity of imports, Q_m, to the foreign currency price of imports. The area of the rectangle defined by the axes and the point of intersection of the supply and demand curves represents the amount of foreign exchange spent on imports (that is, import expenditure). Recalling that the demand for imports leads to demand for foreign exchange, import expenditure should be equivalent to the demand for foreign exchange. Likewise,

40

(a) Balance of payments equilibrium

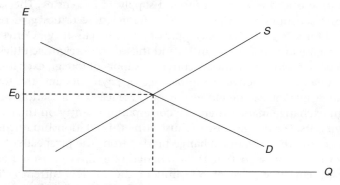

(b) Balance of payments deficit

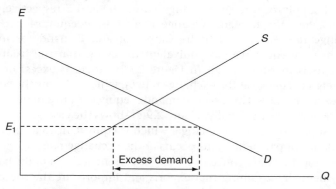

(c) Balance of payments surplus

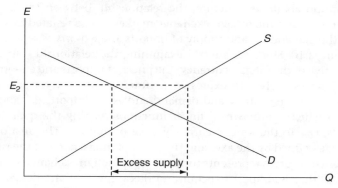

Figure 2.9 The relationship between the balance of payments and the exchange rate

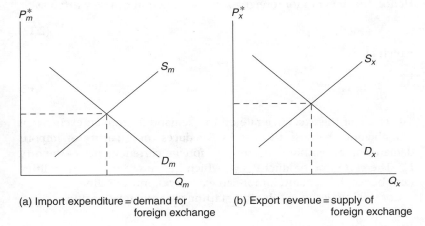

(a) Import expenditure = demand for foreign exchange

(b) Export revenue = supply of foreign exchange

Figure 2.10   Import expenditure and export revenue

the rectangle in Figure 2.10(b) defines export revenue and hence the supply of foreign exchange. Bearing these points in mind, we can proceed to derive the demand for and supply of foreign exchange curves by considering what happens to import expenditure and export revenue as the exchange rate changes.

Consider the demand side first. It is important to remember that imports are foreign goods consumed in the home country. Domestic consumers base their decision concerning the amount of imports they choose to consume on the domestic currency price of imports. For simplicity we assume that this price can be obtained by converting the foreign currency price at the current exchange rate, by using the equation

$$P_m = EP_m^* \tag{2.8}$$

where P_m and P_m^* are the domestic currency and foreign currency prices of imports respectively. Let us now specify the demand for imports as a function of the domestic currency price. The import demand function may be written as

$$Q_m = \alpha_0 - \alpha_1 P_m \tag{2.9}$$

where α_0 and α_1 are positive constant parameters and Q_m is the quantity of imports demanded. By substituting equation (2.8) into equation (2.9), we obtain

$$Q_m = \alpha_0 - \alpha_1 EP_m^* \tag{2.10}$$

Hence, the demand for foreign exchange function can be written as

$$Q_f = \alpha_0 P_m^* - \alpha_1 E P_m^{*2} \tag{2.11}$$

which gives

$$\frac{\partial Q_f}{\partial E} = -\alpha_1 P_m^{*2} \tag{2.12}$$

The effect of the exchange rate on the demand for foreign exchange is unambiguous because the rise in E reduces the quantity of imports demanded, Q_m, without affecting the foreign currency price of imports, P_m^*. Therefore, the product $P_m^* Q_m$, which measures import expenditure (and hence the demand for foreign exchange), must decline.

Consider now the supply side, starting with the relationship

$$P_x^* = \frac{P_x}{E} \tag{2.13}$$

where P_x and P_x^* are the domestic currency price and foreign currency price of exports respectively. Since exports are domestic goods that are consumed abroad, the demand for exports is specified as a function of the foreign currency price. Hence, the export demand function takes the form

$$Q_x = \beta_0 - \beta_1 P_x^* \tag{2.14}$$

where β_0 and β_1 are positive constant parameters and Q_x is the quantity of exports demanded. From equations (2.13) and (2.14), we can see that a rise in E reduces the foreign currency price, leading to an increase in the quantity of exports demanded. Because the price and quantity move in opposite directions, the net effect on export revenue, and hence on the supply of foreign exchange, is ambiguous. It could rise, fall or stay at the same level. The supply of foreign exchange function is then

$$Q_f = \beta_0 P_x^* - \beta_1 P_x^{*2} \tag{2.15}$$

By combining (2.15) and (2.13) we obtain

$$Q_f = \frac{\beta_0 P_x}{E} - \frac{\beta_1 P_x^2}{E^2} \tag{2.16}$$

Hence, the slope of the supply curve is

$$\frac{\partial Q_f}{\partial E} = -\frac{\beta_0 P_x}{E^2} + \frac{2\beta_1 P_x^2}{E^3} \tag{2.17}$$

which may be positive or negative, depending on the level of the exchange rate (positive at low exchange rates and vice versa). In fact the supply curve will be backward-bending, having a positive slope at low exchange rates.

Figure 2.11 shows the downward-sloping demand curve and the backward-bending supply curve. Because the supply curve is backward-bending, the equilibrium exchange rate may not be unique. In Figure 2.11, it is shown that there are three equilibrium values for the exchange rate: E_1, E_2 and E_3. Multiple equilibria create several problems, the first of which is that some equilibrium exchange rate values are unstable. It is typically the case that each unstable equilibrium is bounded by two stable equilibria. When the exchange rate is above E_2, it tends to move to E_3, and when it is below E_2 it tends to move to E_1. The second problem is that the equilibrium values of the exchange rate are ranked differently by the two countries involved in the bilateral exchange rates. For example, one country may prefer E_1 while the other prefers E_3. A situation like this could lead to conflict in the economic policies of the two countries.

The third problem is that speculation as well as balance of payments disturbances may cause sharp fluctuations in the exchange rate, which lead to an unnecessary and wasteful reallocation of resources. For

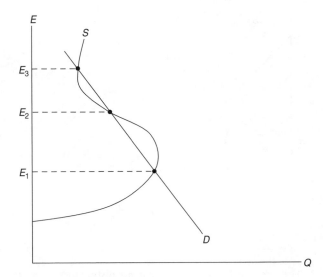

Figure 2.11 Multiple equilibria in the foreign exchange market

example, if the exchange rate rises slightly above E_1, speculators will start buying the foreign currency, thinking that it will rise further. The exchange rate will rise beyond the unstable level E_2, all the way to the stable level E_3. When it reaches E_3, speculators sell the foreign currency, causing the exchange rate to fall all the way to E_1. The effect of a balance of payments disturbance is illustrated in Figure 2.12. A fall in the demand for foreign exchange is represented by a shift in the demand curve, and the equilibrium exchange rate falls from E_1 to E_2. This big drop is caused by the backward-bending nature of the supply curve. Changes in the exchange rate would be less dramatic under a normal upward-sloping supply curve.

The effect of the exchange rate on the current account of the balance of payments emanates from the effect of changes in the exchange rate on prices and, therefore, the demand for domestic and foreign goods (exports and imports). When the exchange rate rises (the domestic currency depreciates), prices of exports in foreign currency terms fall while prices of imports in domestic currency terms rise. If the elasticities of the demand for exports and imports are sufficiently high, then the demand for imports falls and the demand for exports rises, leading to improvement in the current account. This chain of reasoning is the basis of using devaluation to correct a balance of payments deficit.

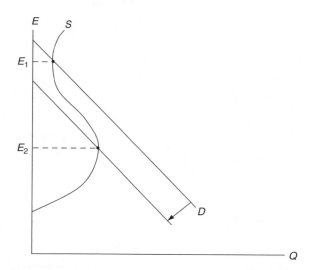

Figure 2.12   The effect of a balance of payments disturbance when the supply curve is backward-bending

Figure 2.13 illustrates the effect of devaluation of the domestic currency (a higher exchange rate) on the current account. In Figures 2.13(a) and 2.13(b), devaluation is ineffective because the elasticities of demand for imports and exports are low. In this case, devaluation results in a small reduction in import expenditure, as shown by Figure 2.13(a), and a fall, rather than a rise, in export revenue, as shown by Figure 2.13(b). The latter occurs because devaluation in this case reduces the foreign currency price of exports by more than the increase in the quantity of exports demanded. Hence, devaluation may lead to deterioration rather

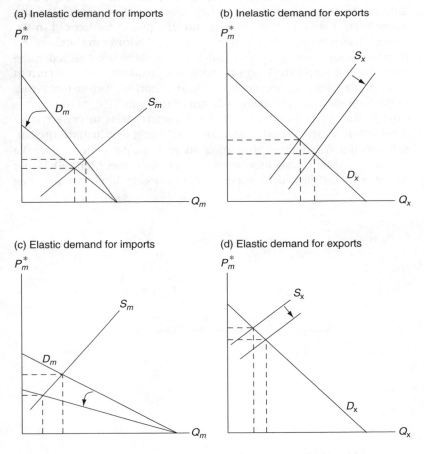

Figure 2.13 The effect of devaluation when elasticities are high and low

than improvement in the current account. In Figure 2.13(c) and 2.13(d), on the other hand, demand is elastic. Hence, devaluation causes a significant reduction in import expenditure and a rise, not a fall, in export revenue. The result is improvement in the current account.

This type of analysis is referred to as the elasticities approach to the balance of payments. The core of this approach is the Marshall–Lerner condition, which tells us that devaluation will have a favourable effect on the current account if the sum of the absolute values of the elasticities of demand for exports and imports is greater than unity. This approach has an important implication for the dynamic response of the current account to devaluation (or depreciation). The response is different in the short run (the period immediately following devaluation) than it would be in the long run (the period further out in the future). This is because the elasticity of demand is lower in the short run than in the long run. If the Marshall–Lerner condition is satisfied in the short run but not in the long run, there is a possibility that the current account may deteriorate even further in the short run before recovering in the long run. This behaviour is described in Figure 2.14. At time t_1, the current account is in deficit, and a decision is taken to correct it by devaluation. In the period immediately following devaluation, the current account deteriorates, registering an even greater deficit. With the passage of time, elasticities increase and once the Marshall–Lerner condition is satisfied, the current account starts to improve. At t_2, the

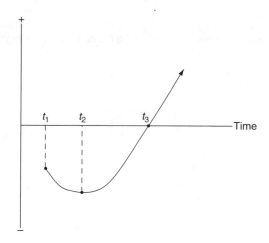

Figure 2.14   The J-curve effect

deficit reaches its highest value, and from then onwards it starts to shrink. At t_3, the deficit is eliminated, and this is followed by the achievement of a surplus. The time path of the current account position resembles the letter J, and this is why this process is called the 'J-curve effect'.

Another approach is the absorption approach associated with Alexander (1952). The starting point is the national income identity, which can be written as

$$Y = C + I + G + (X - M) \tag{2.18}$$

where Y is national output or income, C is consumption, I is investment (capital formation), G is government expenditure, X is exports and M is imports. Equation (2.18) can be written as

$$X - M = Y - A \tag{2.19}$$

where absorption, A, is given by

$$A = C + I + G \tag{2.20}$$

Thus, if $Y > A$, the current account is in surplus, whereas if $Y < A$, it is in deficit. The absorption approach can be illustrated as follows. First, define consumption as the difference between income and saving, which gives

$$C = Y - S \tag{2.21}$$

where S is saving. By ignoring G and substituting equation (2.21) into equation (2.20) we obtain

$$Y - A = S - I \tag{2.22}$$

Hence, the equilibrium condition may be written as

$$S - I = X - M \tag{2.23}$$

The difference between the elasticities and the absorption approaches is that while the former focuses on the X–M schedule (which makes it a partial approach), the latter combines this schedule with the S–I schedule to obtain an equilibrium condition.

Figure 2.15 shows that the S–I schedule is upward-sloping because saving, S, is an increasing function of income, Y, whereas I can be assumed to be independent of Y. Thus, as Y rises, S–I rises. This schedule shows the excess of domestic saving over domestic investment (or otherwise) at any level of income. The X–M schedule, which shows the

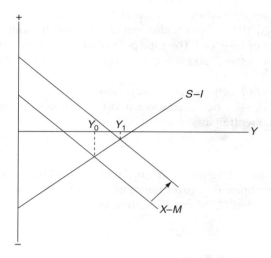

Figure 2.15   The absorption approach to the balance of payments

current account position for each level of income, slopes downwards because M is an increasing function of Y while X is independent of it. Initially, the current account is in deficit at Y_0. If the Marshall–Lerner condition is satisfied, devaluation (or depreciation) leads to a shift in the X–M schedule. If the level of income is unchanged at Y_0, as implicitly assumed by the elasticities approach, the current account registers a surplus. However, an increase in net exports is bound to have an expansionary effect on the economy, leading to a rise in the level of income to Y_1, at which the current account is still in deficit, albeit smaller than before. The explanation of this result is simple: the rise in income leads to a rise in imports, reducing the extent of the rise in net exports resulting from devaluation. Thus, the satisfaction of the Marshall–Lerner condition is not sufficient for devaluation to have a favourable effect on the current account. While the elasticities approach is based exclusively on the price adjustment mechanism, the absorption approach takes into account the income adjustment mechanism as well.

Central bank intervention in the foreign exchange market

The issue of central bank intervention in the foreign exchange market is crucial and highly relevant for the issue of exchange rate regime choice. Under a fixed exchange rate regime, the central bank maintains (or tries to maintain) the fixed exchange rate against pressure from market forces by imposing capital controls or by buying and selling currencies. Intervention by buying and selling currencies is required also under a system of managed floating, but not under a system of free or clean floating.

If flexible exchange rates are as good as Friedman claims, why is it that central bank intervention is an undisputable fact of life? In other words, what is the rationale for central bank intervention? A typical answer to this question is that 'intervention is required to smooth out excessive fluctuations in exchange rates in order to avoid the adverse effects of these fluctuations on economic activity'. This kind of justification was presented, for example, for the Plaza Accord of September 1985, whereby the central banks of the five largest industrial countries (G5) agreed to carry out concerted intervention to bring down the US dollar, which had been appreciating relentlessly for the previous four years or so.

But if the foreign exchange market was efficient, all the information relevant to the determination of the equilibrium rate would be reflected in the actual exchange rate by the activities of rational market participants. In this case, the market would always be in equilibrium such that market participants would always act in a manner that is conducive to market stability, which precludes any scope for intervention. However, trading behaviour may not be consistent with the efficient-market hypothesis, and this can lead to changes in sentiment, producing highly volatile and misaligned exchange rates. This situation may justify intervention, implying that it is warranted by dissatisfaction with flexible exchange rates. Signatories of the 1985 Plaza Accord were very critical of the status quo, as they declared the following:

> The ministers and governors [of the G5 countries] agreed that the exchange rates should play a role in adjusting the external imbalance. In order to do this, exchange rates should better reflect fundamental economic conditions than has been the case. They believe that agreed policy actions must be implemented and reinforced to improve the fundamentals further, and that in view of the present prospective changes in fundamentals, some further orderly appreciation of the main non-dollar currencies against the dollar is desirable. They stand ready to co-operate more closely to encourage this when to do so would be helpful. (Cited in Carew and Slatyer, 1989, p. 112)

The signatories of the Louvre Accord of 1987 expressed their pleasure at the developments that took place following the implementation of the Plaza Accord. Hence:

> Further substantial exchange-rate shifts among [these] currencies could damage growth and adjustment prospects in [these] countries. In current circumstances, therefore, [ministers and governors] agreed to co-operate closely to foster stability of exchange rates around current levels. (Cited in Carew and Slatyer, 1989, p. 112)

There are, in general, three arguments for central bank intervention: (i) exchange rate fluctuations can be excessive; (ii) exchange rate fluctuations have a substantial adverse effect on economic activity; and (iii) central banks can, in practice, smooth out exchange rate fluctuations through the purchase and sale of currencies in the foreign exchange market. The problem with the first argument is that it is not straight forward to draw a line between 'excessive' and 'normal' or 'acceptable' exchange rate fluctuations. The second argument is theoretically plausible, and there is some evidence for the hypothesis that exchange rate fluctuations discourage international trade (for example, Cushman, 1986, 1988; Pozo, 1992; Arize, 1995). The third argument leads to two questions: (i) how do central banks determine the timing of intervention?, and (ii) are they capable of reversing or even slowing down a market trend? If it turns out that central banks are incapable of determining the timing of intervention or affecting the time path of the exchange rate, a strong argument would arise for letting the market do the work without intervention, which means adopting a system of perfectly flexible exchange rates. We start with the first question.

The consensus view on timing is that central bank intervention should not take the form of interfering with a fundamental adjustment of the exchange rate (that is, a change in the equilibrium value of the exchange rate as warranted by the underlying economic fundamentals). If the central bank cannot distinguish between temporary fluctuations (resulting, for example, from a destabilizing speculative action) and a fundamental change, then there is a problem. This problem is illustrated with the aid of Figure 2.16. The exchange rate initially fluctuates around its equilibrium value, $\bar{E}_1$. At time t_1, there is a temporary jump in the exchange rate resulting from a speculative bubble that takes it to E_3. Without central bank intervention the bubble would eventually burst, leaving the exchange rate to resume its fluctuations around the equilibrium level $\bar{E}_1$. If the central bank intervenes by selling the foreign

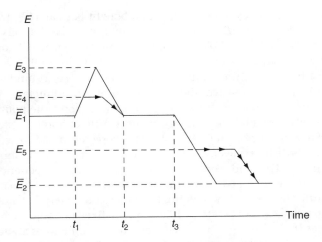

Figure 2.16 Stabilizing and destabilizing central bank intervention

currency at E_4, the exchange rate will be prevented from reaching the level E_3. It will be confined to the level E_4, from which it goes back to fluctuating around $\bar{E}_1$ at t_2 and subsequently (the behaviour of the exchange rate with central bank intervention is indicated by the arrowed lines). Thus, central bank intervention is stabilizing in this case. At t_3, a fundamental change takes place, forcing the exchange rate to a new equilibrium level, $\bar{E}_2$. Not knowing that this is a fundamental change and mistaking it for a temporary swing, the central bank intervenes by buying the foreign currency (selling the domestic currency) at E_5. In this case, the exchange rate will be prevented from going to the new equilibrium level, $\bar{E}_2$, only if the central bank maintains its intervention. Eventually, the central bank gives up and the exchange rate goes down, fluctuating around the new equilibrium level, $\bar{E}_2$.

In his defence of flexible exchange rates, Friedman (1953) did not object to central bank intervention, provided that the objective of intervention was to smooth out temporary fluctuations and not to interfere with fundamental adjustment. Whether or not the central bank has this objective depends on whether intervention turns out to be profitable or otherwise. In essence, therefore, Friedman put forward the proposition that stabilizing intervention is profitable, which can be illustrated using Figure 2.16. In the case of stabilizing intervention, the central bank sells the foreign currency at E_4 and buys it back (to replenish reserves) at $\bar{E}_1$, which is profitable, since $E_4 > \bar{E}_1$. In the case of destabilizing intervention, the domestic currency is sold at $1/E_5$ and bought back at $1/\bar{E}_2$, which is not profitable, since $1/E_5 < 1/\bar{E}_2$. Obviously, central bank intervention against a speculative bubble is profitable, but not when it is directed against a fundamental change. The best real-life example on losing money through central bank intervention against a fundamental change is what happened during the European Monetary System (EMS) crisis of September 1992. In its efforts to support the pound, the Bank of England sold billions of dollars worth of foreign exchange reserves to achieve nothing. The bill for that operation had to be picked up by the British taxpayers. In the second half of 1997, the monetary authorities of Thailand went through the same bitter experience. It is this kind of event that has led to the emergence of the bipolar view, postulating the optimality of going for either completely fixed or completely flexible exchange rates, while avoiding fixed but adjustable rates.

As far as the second question is concerned, it is sometimes argued that the sums available for intervention are so small relative to the market size that intervention cannot be effective. However, some economists argue that although the amounts available to central banks are relatively small, operations can be effective because the market watches the central bank, which can use the signalling effect with or without actual currency sales. This point can be explained with reference to Figure 2.17. An increase in the demand for foreign exchange takes the exchange rate

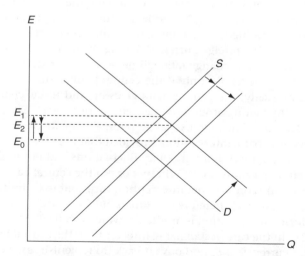

Figure 2.17 Central bank intervention with signalling effect

from its initial level at E_0 to E_1, which the central bank believes to be too high. The central bank intervenes by selling foreign exchange, which brings the exchange rate down to E_2. The signalling effect takes the form of passing the information that E_1 is not an acceptable level of the exchange rate, and this becomes more credible if it is coupled with currency sales as in this case. Currency traders will then sell foreign exchange, bringing the exchange rate back to its original level.

Dominguez and Frankel (1993) argue that the signalling hypothesis is one example of how expectations act to determine the exchange rate. If intervention to support a currency is interpreted as new information that monetary policy will be more restrictive in the near future, the currency will appreciate. However, there is little evidence supporting the proposition that central bankers consistently seek to communicate their monetary policy initiatives through intervention. They also argue that the signalling hypothesis can explain how intervention could affect expectations. For example, market participants may expect the monetization of an intervention operation in the distant future even if the authorities are not deliberately signalling monetary ease in the short run.

Yet, there are strong views casting doubt on the effectiveness of intervention, even among central bank economists. Such views were expressed at a meeting of central bank economists at the Bank for International Settlements (BIS) in November 1987. Ralph Smith and Brian Madigan of the Federal Reserve System expressed the view that

> It is doubtful whether the experience with large-scale co-ordinated intervention under the Plaza Agreement and the Louvre Accord has changed the general view of the effectiveness of intervention... that [it] can be useful in the short-run in certain circumstances, but that it does not appear to have a significant, lasting effect on the level of the exchange rate. (Cited in Carew and Slatyer, 1989, p. 119)

Similarly, Anthony Coleby and John Ryding of the Bank of England expressed the view that

> Present day exchange markets are characterized by massive turnover stemming particularly from short-term position taking. All this leads to increased volatility and/or bandwagoning in exchange rates. In these conditions the role of intervention is bound to be limited. Nevertheless, we regard the co-ordinated intervention undertaken in recent years as modestly successful. (Cited in Carew and Slatyer, 1989, p. 120)

While these views may not represent the official stances of the Federal Reserve System and the Bank of England respectively, the official view of the former German Bundesbank seems to be more assertive about this issue. The 1980 Annual Report of the Bundesbank stated that

> the experience gained in 1980 demonstrates in the final analysis that interventions in the foreign exchange market are just as powerless against interest-rate induced capital movements...as against one-sided market expectations.

The apparent weakness of central bank intervention in the absence of capital controls is sometimes viewed as a reason for the shift away from fixed exchange rates. A common view is that capital markets have grown so big that the task of maintaining a fixed exchange rate has become a hazardous endeavour. Currently, the daily volume of foreign exchange transactions exceeds one trillion dollars, which is greater than the reserves of any central bank or most central banks put together. However, Obstfeld and Rogoff (1995) argue that this is not a problem and that most central banks have access to sufficient foreign exchange resources to beat a speculative attack of any magnitude, provided that they are willing to subordinate all other objectives of monetary policy. To defend a fixed exchange rate, they argue, the monetary authorities only need enough resources to buy back the monetary base, or a large part of it. By doing that, the central bank raises interest rates to a level so high that speculators will find it prohibitively expensive to go short on the domestic currency.

But if this argument is valid, why is it that the Bank of England failed miserably to defend the pound in 1992 (this is just an example of many)? The answer to this question is that central banks have other objectives apart from targeting or defending the exchange rate. Moreover, unanticipated sustained increases in interest rates are rather costly, adversely affecting the banking system, which typically borrows short and lends long. Over the long run, high interest rates have adverse effects on investment, unemployment, the budget deficit and the distribution of income. A government pledge to ignore these side effects is unlikely to be credible, and the lack of credibility in turn makes a fixed exchange rate regime more vulnerable to speculative attacks.

The objectives of central bank intervention are neatly related to the question of exchange rate policy. The following objectives can be identified: (i) reducing volatility, (ii) stabilization of the nominal effective exchange rate, (iii) stabilization of the real effective exchange rate,

(iv) smoothing the pace of depreciation, and (v) smoothing the pace of appreciation. Reducing volatility is a possible reason for adopting dirty floating, which involves heavy central bank intervention. By contrast, stabilization of the nominal effective exchange rate requires pegging to a basket of currencies. Countries may be more concerned about the stabilization of the real effective exchange rate because it is the macro-economic relative price guiding the composition of production and absorption between traded and non-traded goods. Smoothing the pace of appreciation and depreciation amounts to smoothing changes in the domestic currency price of imports and the foreign currency price of exports.

Multiple exchange rates

A system of multiple exchange rates exists when different exchange rates are used to settle transactions involving items with different degrees of importance for the country using the system. If such a system is used to settle import transactions, then the most favourable exchange rate will be assigned to the most important import item, and so on. Reinhart and Rogoff (2004) point out that dual or multiple exchange rates were the norm in the 1940s and the 1950s, lasting until much later in some cases. Some important countries clung to dual or multiple rates (for example, the UK until the 1970s, Italy until the 1980s and Belgium until the 1990s).

While multiple exchange rates are likely to create waste, they represent a means of affecting resource allocation and income distribution in the domestic economy. By interfering with free market prices a government can reallocate resources, direct resources into alternative uses, and affect the real incomes of different sectors and those of the factors of production. A special exchange rate may have the same effect as tariffs and other instruments for reallocating resources. If an industry is to be protected against foreign competition, a tariff can do the job but so can a high exchange rate for this particular type of good. Consider, for example, three sectors of the economy: A, B and C, all of which import the same commodity from the same source at the same foreign currency price. If the three sectors are of different importance for the domestic economy, such that A is the most important and C is the least important, sector A may be given a more favourable rate to settle its imports than B, which in turn is assigned a more favourable rate than C. In Figure 2.18 it is shown that for the same foreign price level, $\bar{P}^*$, sector A pays the lowest domestic currency price for the imported item, P_A,

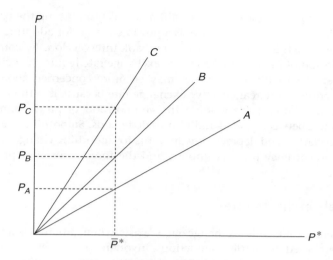

Figure 2.18 The effect of multiple exchange rates when assigned to different importers

where $P_A < P_B < P_C$. This is like subsidizing sector A more heavily than sector B and leaving sector C without any subsidy if this sector uses the free-market rate.

Special exchange rates for particular groups of imports involve two separate issues: (i) the purchasing power of wages, and (ii) industrialization. The problem is that across-the-board increases in import prices have adverse political consequences: increased prices of imported goods reduce the purchasing power of wages, creating political problems. Governments therefore look for a more selective way to ration foreign exchange, which can be done by distinguishing between 'essential' and 'non-essential' imports. For essential imports, the exchange rate is held constant but for non-essential imports it is raised sharply to reduce foreign exchange outlays and solve the trade deficit problem. By using this policy, the purchasing power of wages in terms of essential goods stays unchanged, but it declines sharply in terms of other goods. The poorest group in the economy might be protected but the middle class will be hurt.

The other main argument for using multiple exchange rates to settle import transactions is industrialization, which is the case if the government feels that domestic industry should be protected. This policy is often at odds with trade-oriented growth. A firm in a protected industry can charge higher prices and can afford to produce at a cost that is higher than the world market's. If they keep doing that they will enjoy protection at the expense of consumers and the cost of a waste of resources.

Special exchange rates may be used to settle export transactions for at least two reasons, the first of which is the desire to encourage industrialization. Particular export industries, such as manufacturing and non-traditional export industries, are given an implicit subsidy that allows them to sell at world prices. This situation is illustrated in Figure 2.19, which assumes the simple relationship $P = EP^*$. Suppose that the world price is P_W^*, which the exporting firm cannot match at the market exchange rate, E_M, if the minimum domestic currency price the firm can charge is $\bar{P}$. If this firm is granted a preferential exchange rate $\bar{E}$, such that $\bar{E} > E_M$, then the firm can afford to sell at the world price if $P_W^* = P/\bar{E}$. Typically, this policy is applied to manufacturing or non-traditional export industries.

The second reason for applying special exchange rates to exports pertains to traditional export industries (for example, oil and agriculture). A government may believe that these industries should not enjoy a windfall gain from domestic currency depreciation because their output is not that responsive to changes in the exchange rate. Thus the

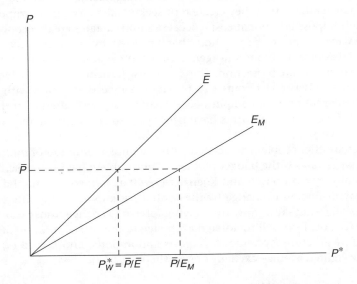

Figure 2.19 Subsidizing an exporter through a preferential exchange rate

government may use a special exchange rate to tax any windfall profits away from these industries. This argument is more attractive when it is applied to foreign oil companies.

However, there is no free lunch. The desirability of multiple exchange rates must be judged against the costs of implementing them. The first adverse effect of multiple exchange rates is the misallocation of resources. In an economy that allocates resources efficiently, the marginal cost of an extra unit of output is equal to the price a firm receives, which is equal to the value a buyer places on an extra unit of output (marginal cost pricing). When this equality prevails, there is no way of reshuffling productive resources so as to make one person better off without making anyone else worse off (Pareto optimum). Multiple exchange rates interfere with the optimal allocation of resources as defined here because different sectors pay or receive different amounts of the domestic currency for one unit of the foreign currency. Resources can be reshuffled by going on unified rates to reduce the resource cost of earning foreign exchange and to spend the foreign exchange earned in a better way. Governments often believe (perhaps erroneously) that the resource allocation effects of a distortionary exchange rate regime are small because resources do not easily move across industries and because consumers are relatively unresponsive to price changes. This is not necessarily the case.

A major problem resulting from the implementation of multiple exchange rates is that they create rent-seeking, red tape and corruption, which impose additional costs. Because multiple rates create economic rents for factors of production that are used by activities receiving special attention, economic agents will devote real resources to obtaining exchange rate protection. These agents will spend time on lobbying, which involves real resource costs. The red tape that comes with the implementation of a complicated exchange rate system adds to these costs (for example, all firms have paperwork to show compliance with the system).

Yet another problem associated with the implementation of multiple exchange rates is the budget problem. This problem has been described formally by Dornbusch and Kuenzler (1993) as follows. Define the net outlay of foreign exchange by the central bank (*NO*) as the difference between outlays resulting from buying foreign exchange from exporters and receipts from selling foreign exchange to importers. If X and M are the foreign currency values of exports and imports, and E_x and E_m are the weighted average exchange rates, then

$$NO = E_x X - E_m M \qquad (2.24)$$

By adding and subtracting $E_m X$, we obtain

$$NO = X(E_x - E_m) + E_m(X - M) \tag{2.25}$$

If $X = M$ then

$$NO = X(E_x - E_m) \tag{2.26}$$

If $E_x > E_m$, the central bank will be making losses on its foreign exchange transactions. To finance its losses, the central bank resorts to printing currency, which is an inflationary process.

Black foreign exchange markets

Black markets for foreign exchange exist for a number of reasons:

- The rationing of foreign exchange by quotas, licences, absolute restrictions or special exchange rates gives rise to demand for foreign exchange to finance illegal imports.
- Portfolio demand for foreign exchange that needs to be satisfied if the government does not sell foreign exchange for that purpose when economic agents want to hold foreign assets.
- If the black market rate exceeds the official rate (which is invariably the case), exporters have an incentive to underreport their true exports and surrender their foreign exchange to the black market rather than the central bank. Likewise, firms may overstate the size of authorized imports, surrendering part of the foreign exchange obtained at the official rate to the black market.

Figure 2.20 illustrates the determination of the black market rate and therefore the black market premium (the difference between the black market rate and the official rate, P). In the official market the official rate is fixed at E_O, whereas the fixed amount supplied at this rate is indicated by a vertical supply curve. Given a normal downward-sloping demand curve, there is obviously a shortage of foreign exchange at the official rate. Let us assume that the only source of supply of foreign exchange in the black market is what black market participants (sellers) can raise on the official market. This amount is then transferred to the black market and sold at the black market rate, which depends on how much of the supply in the official market is transferred to the black market. If the whole amount is transferred, as shown in Figure 2.20, the black market rate would be equivalent to the rate determined by the

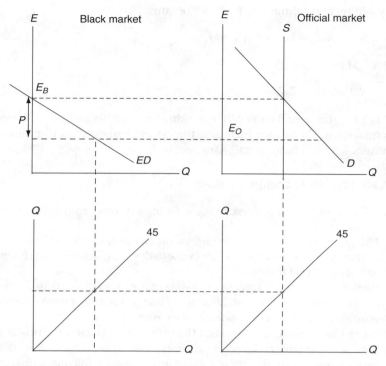

Figure 2.20   Determination of the black market rate (1)

intersection of the supply and demand curves in the official market. It can be seen that the black market rate, E_B, clears the black market (zero excess demand, *ED*). The lower parts of the diagram are merely 45-degree lines that are used to trace out quantity from the official market to the black market.

If the black market rate is lower than E_B, only part of the amount traded on the official market will be transferred to the black market, and if the black market rate is equal to the official rate there will be no dealing in the black market. Naturally, we cannot expect the entire amount traded in the official market to be transferred to the black market, and there is the possibility that extra supply may come from other sources. Consider Figure 2.21, which demonstrates the case when only about half the amount of foreign exchange supplied to the official market is transferred to the black market. Here, the black market rate

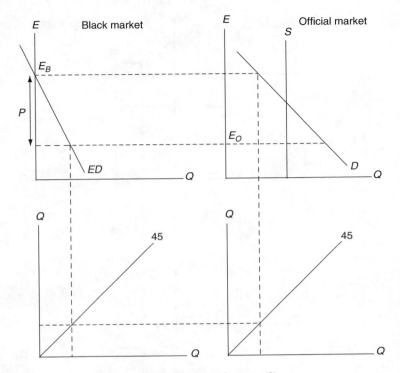

Figure 2.21 Determination of the black market rate (2)

will be higher than in the previous case. At the same official rate the premium will also be higher (to maintain the premium at the same level as in the first case, the official rate must be raised).

With no change in the official rate the black market premium may change for a number of reasons. Figure 2.22 shows what happens when supply in the official market declines, as represented by a leftward shift in the supply curve. If the official rate is maintained at the same level, the excess demand function in the black market will shift as shown. As a result, the black market rate and the premium will rise.

In general, Dornbusch and Kuenzler (1993) identify the following factors that lead to changes in the black market rate/premium:

- Higher foreign interest rates and expectation of domestic currency depreciation lead to increase in demand in the black market, resulting in a higher black market rate/premium.

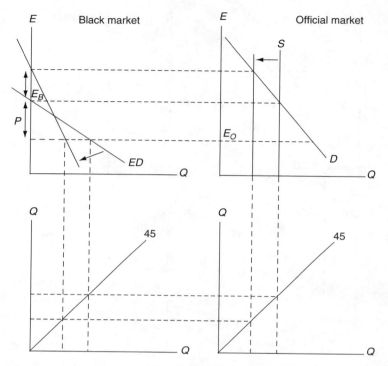

Figure 2.22   The effect of a decrease in supply in the official market

- Likewise, an increase in trade restrictions leads to increasing demand in the black market.
- A greater ease in supplying the black market by misinvoicing results in a higher black market rate/premium.

3
Fixed versus Flexible Exchange Rates: The Everlasting Debate

Introduction

The origin of the debate on fixed versus flexible exchange rates in its modern form is arguably Friedman's (1953) piece 'The Case for Flexible Exchange Rates'. Friedman strongly rejected the conventional wisdom of the time, arguing that flexible exchange rates are 'absolutely essential for the fulfillment of our basic economic objectives: the achievement and maintenance of a free and prosperous world community engaging in unrestricted multilateral trade'. On the other hand, he argued against fixed exchange rates by asserting that 'there is scarcely a facet of international economic policy for which the implicit acceptance of a system of rigid exchange rates does not create serious and unnecessary difficulties'. It must be emphasized, however, that Freidman distinguished between 'flexible' and 'unstable' exchange rates. In this sense, he advocated as the 'ultimate objective' what he described as 'a world in which exchange rates, while free to vary, are in fact highly stable'. However, he argued that the elimination of exchange rate instability by 'administrative freezing' of exchange rates cures none of the underlying difficulties and only makes adjustment to them more painful.

Friedman proceeded to defend flexible exchange rates by considering the arguments that (i) flexible exchange rates are unstable, (ii) they result in uncertainty surrounding the domestic currency values of payments and receipts, (iii) there is the tendency for destabilizing speculation under flexible rates, and (iv) they result in increased uncertainty in the internal economy.

As far as the first argument is concerned, Friedman pointed to the confusion of symptom with illness. The mere fact that rigid exchange rates do not change whereas flexible exchange rates do, is no evidence that the former produce greater stability in any sense. To the second argument, Friedman responded by saying that traders could almost always protect themselves against exchange rate fluctuations by using futures contracts. In response to the third argument, he put forward the view that speculation is indeed stabilizing under flexible exchange rates. This is because profitable speculation requires buying low and selling high, which is what it takes to make speculation stabilizing. Finally, Friedman undermined the fourth argument, which implies that domestic currency depreciation is taken as a signal of future inflation, by arguing that fear of inflation has little or no chance of producing inflation, except in a favourable monetary environment. At around the same time, Meade (1951) put forward a case for flexible exchange rates based on the difficulty of adjustment with a fixed rate when wages and prices are inflexible. However, he qualified his argument by stating that flexible exchange rates are not a panacea, and that there are indeed circumstances where they may not help to accommodate disturbances.

Friedman put forward his forceful arguments in the early 1950s following the establishment of the Bretton Woods system of fixed but adjustable exchange rates in 1944. This system was designed in an attempt to combine the advantages of fixed exchange rates with the advantages of flexible exchange rates, given that the world had experimented with both of these arrangements under the gold standard and during the interwar period. It is arguable, however, that what the Bretton Woods system achieved was a combination of the disadvantages of both fixed and flexible exchange rates. But it may sound strange that Friedman was so forceful in his defence of flexible exchange rates when the world economy performed much better under the fixed exchange rate system of the gold standard than under the flexible exchange rates of the interwar period. However, we cannot be certain about attributing the prosperity that prevailed under the gold standard and the misery of the interwar period to the exchange rate regime in operation at that time. Let us not forget that the world economy entered the Great Depression under the fixed exchange rates of the gold exchange standard of the interwar period.

On exactly the opposite extreme to Friedman was Einzig (1970), who wrote a detailed account of his opposition to flexible exchange rates at a time when support for flexibility was at its peak. Einzig talked about discrediting the case for 'gnomocracy', which he defined as a 'system under which the determination of exchange rates would be left to the mercy of speculators as a result of the adoption of floating exchanges'. He argued strongly for his contention that the theoretical arguments for flexible rates are 'utterly fallacious' and that 'its supporters completely ignore the grave practical consequences of its adoption'. He went as far as describing the proponents of flexible exchange rates as 'idealist dogmatists' and 'self-seeking demagogues who want to outbid their political rivals'. Most of his case against floating rates rests on what he called the 'myth of the equilibrium level of the exchange rate', as he argued that those who believe or profess to believe in the existence of the equilibrium level overlook or disregard the 'self-aggravating character of exchange movements and the variety of conflicting influences that are liable to divert exchange rates from their equilibrium level'. These arguments are in line with Nurkse's (1944) contention that flexible exchange rates are destabilizing because market psychology generates periods of 'overreaction and bandwagon effects'. It is this contention that helped establish the conventional wisdom that Friedman attacked.

Friedman might have been vindicated by the shift to flexible rates in the 1970s. But even then, dissatisfaction with flexible rates led European countries to resort to fixed rates, starting with the Snake in the Tunnel, passing through the European Monetary System (EMS) and ending with the European Monetary Union (EMU) that has been in operation since 1999. It is interesting to note that Friedman once predicted the eventual collapse of the EMS. That was an accurate prediction, but the EMS has been replaced by the EMU, which is a move from fixed but adjustable rates to completely fixed rates. The lessons learnt from the European move seem to be largely based on the argument for fixed exchange rates that can be found in the literature on optimum currency areas, which sets out to address the question of which areas or countries adopt genuinely fixed exchange rates amongst themselves, while allowing variability of their exchange rates in relation to other currency blocs. This literature began with the classic article by Mundell (1961), who suggested that the extent of factor mobility is the principal criterion for determining the domain of an optimum currency area. Likewise, McKinnon (1963) and Kenen (1969) advocated fixed exchange rates in an optimum currency area framework on the basis of the criteria of openness and product diversification in trade, respectively.

In the early days of the debate, and prior to the shift to flexible exchange rates, the case for flexibility was generally based on hopes of what would happen (for example, policy autonomy), whereas the case against flexibility was based on the fear of what might happen (for example, the effect of shocks). However, Artus and Young (1979) argued that following the adoption of floating, few would advocate flexible rates on the grounds that they permit countries to take advantage of a long-term trade-off between employment and wage increases. They also argued that the envisaged role of flexible exchange rates in external adjustment was rather exaggerated and so was the view that flexible rates would insulate countries from external influence, leaving them free to pursue domestic objectives via domestic policies. However, the advocates of flexible exchange rates believe that the drawbacks of flexibility are less damaging than their intellectual opponents claim.

Murray (2003) suggests that the advantages of fixed exchange rates, such as the reduced transaction costs associated with converting and hedging currency positions, are largely microeconomic. Other advantages are related to reduced uncertainty and improved decision-making. They also improve the operation of the price system and enhance the usefulness of money as a medium of exchange, unit of account and store of value. Against these microeconomic benefits comes the macroeconomic cost of readjusting after a shock. Under fixed exchange rates, the burden of adjustment falls on other variables, but the problem is that wages and prices are sticky and the factors of production are not highly mobile. The result would be greater variability in output and employment.

It may be useful to note that systems of fixed and flexible exchange rates may overlap, and this may arise under two sets of circumstances. The first case is when the fixed exchange rate system requires the monetary authorities to announce buying and selling rates for its currency in terms of a foreign currency and promises to trade in unlimited amounts at that rate. The buying and selling rates could be identical, but in most systems they differ, which gives rise to (usually narrow) bands within which exchange rates may fluctuate. As the official buying and selling rates move further apart, the exchange rate arrangement approaches a free float. The second case is when a fixed exchange rate is allowed to move within a band. Again, if the band is wide then it will behave like a flexible rate. For example, when the exchange rates in the EMS were allowed to move within a band of ±2.5 per cent, it was something like a fixed exchange rate system. But in 1993, the band was widened to ±15 per cent, which made it a *de facto* flexible exchange rate system.

The arguments for and against fixed and flexible exchange rates will be presented with some degree of elaboration in the following sections, and so will the criteria used to choose between fixed and flexible exchange rates. The arguments for and against fixed exchange rates may be taken literally to mean arguments against and for flexible exchange rates and vice versa, but this may not necessarily be the case.

It must be emphasized here that the points raised in the 'duel' between fixed and flexible exchange rates may have significant overlapping.

Arguments for fixed exchange rates

In this section the following arguments for fixed exchange rates are presented:

- Fixed exchange rates produce low inflation and boost credibility.
- They are a conduit to economic growth.
- They are suitable for countries that satisfy the optimum currency areas criteria.
- They are suitable for a small economy.
- They produce fiscal discipline.
- Fixed exchange rates reduce the cost of access to international financial markets, reduce interest rates, facilitate disinflation and make it difficult to monetize the fiscal deficit.

These points will be discussed in turn.

Fixed exchange rates as a conduit to low inflation and credibility

If the fixed exchange rate takes the form of pegging the domestic currency to the currency of a low-inflation country, domestic inflationary pressures will be restrained irrespective of whether they originate from excessive government budget deficits or from the wage- and price-setting decisions of the private sector. This discipline argument comes in many shapes and forms but the basic idea is simple: an announced policy of pegging the exchange rate may serve as a commitment that allows the government to resist and even forestall subsequent temptations to follow excessively expansionary macroeconomic policies. Berger *et al.* (2001) argue that fixed exchange rates provide the benefit of nominal stability and that high inflation can be brought down by 'piggy-backing' on the monetary policy of a disciplined anchor country. It is also argued that fixed exchange rates are particularly useful for countries disinflating after periods of price instability. For such countries, fixed rates have the attraction of anchoring price inflation for internationally traded goods and that of providing a guide for private sector inflationary expectations (Bruno, 1991).

Little *et al.* (1993) do not seem to be sure about the direction of causation by postulating that the relationship between exchange rate regimes and inflation can go two ways. On the one hand, a country committed to an exchange rate that is pegged to the currency of a low-inflation country might be reluctant to monetize its fiscal deficit, which inhibits inflation. In this case the exchange rate is the nominal anchor in the sense that it anchors the price level. On the other hand, some countries have been able to maintain fixed exchange rates because they wanted and achieved low inflation.

Fixed exchange rates and economic growth

The second argument for fixed exchange rates is that they provide a stable economic environment that boosts economic growth. This argument is normally applicable to hard pegs, as happens in a currency union. The growth effect works through two channels, the first of which is advocated by Dornbusch (2001) who emphasizes the channel of lower interest rates, higher investment and faster growth. The second channel is that by eliminating exchange rate volatility, fixed exchange rates encourage international trade and hence faster growth. Rose and van Wincoop (2001), among others, have emphasized the trade channel within the context of currency unions. Klein and Shambaugh (2004) found a significant effect of fixed exchange rates on bilateral trade between an anchor country and a country that pegs to it. Other economists have shown that the pre-First World War gold standard had an important role in promoting trade and that its demise contributed to the reduction in world trade in the interwar period (see, for example, Estevadeordal *et al.*, 2003; Lopez-Cordova and Meissner, 2003).

The optimum currency areas argument for fixed exchange rates

If a group of countries have some characteristics that allow them to form an optimum currency area, then this necessarily means that fixed exchange rates are more suitable for these countries. The theory of optimum currency areas sets out to address the question of which group of countries should adopt genuinely fixed exchange rates among themselves, allowing variability of their exchange rates in relation to other countries. When the exchange rates between major currencies are floating, a peg by a country to one of the major currencies gives rise to what can be considered a currency area.

The literature on optimum currency areas began with the classic article of Mundell (1961), who suggested that the extent of factor mobility is the principal criterion determining the domain of an optimum currency area. McKinnon (1963) advanced the criterion of the openness of the economy, whereas Kenen (1969) argued that product diversification in trade should be considered a major determinant of whether or not a country should opt for a currency area. Other contributions to the literature on optimum currency areas have suggested additional criteria, such as the similarity of inflation rates and the degree of policy coordination.

Fixed exchange rates and economic size

Small open economies often encounter a situation requiring choice between issuing their own floating currencies and the alternative of having fixed exchange rates by being part of a currency union. McKinnon (1963) has argued that if a small open economy issues its own currency and allows the currency to float against those of its trading partners, the likely amplitude of fluctuations in the exchange rate tends to undermine the domestic currency in performing its monetary functions, encouraging agents in the economy to substitute foreign currency for the domestic currency. In such an economy, which is highly open in terms of the ratio of traded to non-traded goods, the variability of a floating exchange rate would cause corresponding fluctuations in the domestic currency price of traded goods. With monetary policy capable only of affecting the price of non-traded goods, the result would be considerable variability in both the price level and relative prices. This volatility would make the real rate of return on the domestic currency uncertain compared with that of the foreign currency. It would also make the latter preferable as the numeraire in domestic accounts and contractual obligations. This is the currency substitution argument for fixed exchange rates.

Leaving the currency substitution argument aside, it is still arguable that fixed exchange rates are more suitable for a small economy, which is typically a price-taker in world markets. If this is the case, a small country cannot respond to an adverse exchange rate movement by changing prices. Hence, a small country might as well avoid exchange rate fluctuations altogether by adopting fixed exchange rates.

Fixed exchange rates and fiscal discipline

It is arguable that fixed exchange rates provide more fiscal discipline than flexible exchange rates. The rationale for this argument is that lax fiscal policies eventually lead to a collapse of the peg, giving rise to significant political and economic costs, which means that a lax fiscal policy at present leads to punishment in the future. This potential punishment forces the government to have fiscal discipline. Canavan and Tommasi (1997) argue that an exchange rate anchor provides discipline because it is much easier for the public to monitor the nominal exchange rate than other variables.

This argument does not go without challenge, however. Tornell and Velasco (1995, 1998) point out that by delaying the inflationary consequences of fiscal laxity, a fixed exchange rate regime can actually induce impatient policy-makers to spend more. The empirical evidence on this issue is mixed. Gavin and Perotti (1998) find significant correlation between fixed exchange rates and budget deficits in Latin American countries, but not in developing countries, whereas Hamman (2001) could not support the hypothesis that fiscal discipline is enhanced by adopting an exchange rate-based stabilization policy. Fatas and Rose (2001) found currency boards to be associated with fiscal restraint but that is not the case for members of a currency union. Sun (2003) found that future punishment against fiscal laxity exists under both fixed and flexible exchange rate regimes and that fixed rates induce more fiscal discipline only if the future punishment is sufficiently greater under flexible rates.

Other advantages of fixed exchange rates

Poirson (2001) adds the following advantages of fixed exchange rates, which are not necessarily stated explicitly above:

- Fixed exchange rates reduce the cost of access to international financial markets by lowering the risk premium.
- They also reduce domestic interest rates by reducing the spread with the 'world interest rate'.
- Fixed exchange rates facilitate disinflation.
- They make it more difficult to monetize the fiscal deficit (see a case study of Iraq in Chapter 9).

In addition to these advantages, Frankel (2003) argues that one advantage of fixed exchange rates is that they preclude speculative bubbles of the sort that pushed up the dollar in 1985 and the yen in 1995.

Arguments against fixed exchange rates

The following arguments against fixed exchange rates will be discussed in turn in this section:

- Fixed exchange rates lead to the loss of policy autonomy.
- Fixed exchange rates are not capable of dealing with most shocks.
- With fixed exchange rates, real appreciation (which may have adverse consequences for the balance of payments) may result from changes in prices.

- They make adjustment costly in the case of a crisis.
- Fixed exchange rates are crisis-prone.

Fixed exchange rates as a cause for losing policy autonomy

Typically, the most serious problem with fixed exchange rates is claimed to be the loss of policy autonomy. Under fixed exchange rates the domestic authorities import (on a secular basis) the monetary policy of the country of the anchor currency. Furthermore, the control of the domestic money supply may be largely subordinated to the balance of payments constraint.

The key lesson arising from this discussion is that a government that fixes its exchange rate loses control of the domestic money supply. Any attempt to increase the money supply via open-market purchases of domestic securities would fail because the acquisition of domestic securities is exactly offset by foreign exchange reserve losses. A government that is committed to a fixed rate has no choice but to allow reserve losses, because the domestic currency will otherwise appreciate. Therefore, it can be stated that the fundamental problem with fixed exchange rates is that the government must be prepared to forgo completely the use of monetary policy for stabilization purposes.

Fixed exchange rates as a (bad or incapable) shock absorber

Consider the problem faced by a country experiencing a sudden and permanent fall in the demand for its exports. Even in a flexible-price world, such a shock would make the country worse off. But with a fixed exchange rate and temporary rigidity in nominal prices and wages, the harm is magnified. With no way for the relative prices of exports and imports to adjust in the short run, domestic employment and output must fall. The government cannot in this case lower interest rates to stimulate short-run demand because of the combination of a fixed exchange rate and open capital markets. The issue of shocks, however, is not that straightforward as the suitability of fixed or flexible exchange rates (and the desired degree of flexibility in general) depends on the kind of shock that hits the economy: real, nominal, external, internal or a combination thereof. Obviously, the example above pertains to a real external shock. We will elaborate on this point in the following section.

Three more disadvantages

Fixed exchange rates have three more disadvantages. The first is that real appreciation is more likely to result from changes in domestic and foreign prices. Since $R = E(P^*/P)$, a fall in P^*/P while E is fixed leads to a fall in R, which is real appreciation of the domestic currency. One of the consequences would be deterioration in the current account. The second of the 'three more disadvantages' is that adjustment may be too costly in the case of a crisis.

The third disadvantage, which is related to the second, is that fixed exchange rate regimes are more crisis-prone. Bubula and Otker-Robe (2003) concluded that fixed exchange rate regimes have been characterized by a higher incidence of crises than floating regimes. Razin and Rubenstein (2004) point out that almost every international economic crisis since 1990 'has been rooted in rigid exchange rates'. Fischer (2001) makes the observation that each of the major international crises 'has in some way involved a fixed or pegged exchange rate regime'. Among the recent studies of the vulnerability of fixed exchange rate regimes are Calvo *et al.* (1995), Obstfeld and Rogoff (1995), Chang and Velasco (2000) and Ghosh *et al.* (2000).

Arguments for flexible exchange rates

In this section we present the following arguments for flexible exchange rates:

- Flexible exchange rates are market-determined, distortion-free prices.
- External adjustment is smoother under flexible rates.
- Flexible rates provide policy autonomy.
- They boost economic growth.
- They act as shock absorbers.
- They neutralize the effect of inflation on competitiveness.

The exchange rate as a free-market price

A simple *laissez-faire* view is that exchange rates should be determined by the forces of supply and demand in a free market without government intervention for the same reason that any other price should be determined in a free market. Changes in exchange rates result from changes in supply and demand: if these changes are permanent, intervention merely postpones the needed adjustment. If they are temporary, intervention transfers the burden of uncertainty to someone else in the economy. A parallel view is that it is easier to adjust the exchange rate to respond to new developments in the economy than to adjust wages and prices.

The balance of payments adjustment under flexible exchange rates

The second argument for flexible exchange rates and against fixed rates pertains to the mechanism of adjustment in the balance of payments. Flexible exchange rates move continuously and in small doses to restore equilibrium, which makes the balance of payments adjustment process smoother and less painful than that provided by fixed exchange rates. Under flexible exchange rates, a deficit can be eliminated by depreciation in the domestic currency (assuming that the Marshall–Lerner condition is satisfied). Under fixed exchange rates, on the other hand, if devaluation is not allowed, a deflationary policy must be adopted. This policy is painful in the sense that the cost of eliminating the deficit is the onset of recession and the rise of unemployment. This cost can be rather severe and politically unacceptable.

It is also argued that, since flexible exchange rates move continuously in reaction to disequilibria in the balance of payments, large and persistent deficits will not develop. This will in turn boost confidence in the international monetary system, resulting in fewer attempts to readjust currency portfolios, and this can only result in calmer foreign exchange markets. It is also claimed that liquidity problems do not arise (or at least they are not as acute) under flexible exchange rates, because central banks do not need to hold foreign exchange reserves for market intervention. But this is not as simple as it sounds. Calvo and Mishkin (2003) point out that many large emerging-market economies with floating rates (such as Mexico and Brazil) hold sizeable international reserves. This is because these countries 'float with a large life jacket', which can be explained in terms of the ability of reserves to provide collateral for public bonds issued in connection with open-market operations. Another argument is that flexible exchange rates are more conducive to achieving free international trade. The reasoning is simple: because this system maintains equilibrium in the balance of payments, tariffs and other trade impediments will not be imposed.

Artus and Young (1979) point out that flexible exchange rates are not 'an instant cure' for all external adjustment problems, recognizing the fact that protracted imbalances inherited from the fixed rate period could not be eliminated outright following the general shift to floating in the 1970s. For example, Germany and Japan had significant balance of payments surpluses in the 1970s despite the appreciation of their currencies, an indication that the adjustment process in the goods market has not worked well. Artus and Young conclude that 'the argument that flexible rates would remove the balance of payments motive for restrictions on international trade has clearly not been validated'.

Flexible exchange rates and policy autonomy

One of the benefits of flexible exchange rates is that they allow the achievement of monetary independence, which is the ability to choose the inflation rate independently (see, for example, Johnson, 1972). The pursuit of domestic monetary policy that yields a lower secular inflation rate than that prevailing in the rest of the world would allow the country to have a more efficient medium of exchange and unit of account, thereby achieving a better intertemporal allocation of resources. The more important argument is that a country would have the freedom to choose an optimum point on its Phillips curve.

Flexible exchange rates as a conduit to stable growth

Some advocates of flexible exchange rates argue that they make it easier to achieve more stable economic growth. This argument is based on three propositions: (i) flexible rates insulate domestic economic activity from foreign business cycles; (ii) flexible rates boost control over the domestic money supply, making it possible to use monetary and fiscal policies to influence economic activity; and (iii) they enhance the efficacy of monetary policy. Artus and Young (1979) argue that all of these propositions are questionable (for one thing, the degree of economic interdependence seems to have been greater since 1973).

Flexible exchange rates as a (good) shock absorber

A strong argument in favour of exchange rate flexibility in response to certain shocks has been put forward by Flanders and Helpman (1978). They consider exchange rate policy for an economy that is a price-taker for traded goods but also produces non-traded goods. The case for flexible exchange rates rests on the assumption of the familiar argument of downward inflexibility in domestic wages and the prices of non-traded goods. Flanders and Helpman show that, for a foreign price shock, exchange rate flexibility ensures full employment in their model. For a fall in the foreign currency price of traded goods, the effect on the domestic price of traded goods and relative prices is offset by a change in the exchange rate. Exchange rate flexibility counters the rigidity in the domestic price of non-traded goods, thereby permitting the equilibrium relative price ratio and full employment to be maintained.

Under fixed exchange rates, however, a downward foreign price shock causes a fall in the domestic price of traded goods and a conflict between the internal and external balances. If monetary policy is consistent with the external balance, unemployment will arise. Full employment may be attainable only at the cost of a balance of payments deficit (which is not sustainable). If domestic relative price disturbances take place, the outcome depends on whether preferences shift in favour of or against non-traded goods. The general proposition here is that domestic monetary policy can be adjusted in the model under a flexible exchange rate so as to attain full employment. Hence, a flexible exchange rate regime is always as good as or better (in dealing with shocks) than a fixed exchange rate regime in the presence of downward price and wage rigidities.

Although Flanders and Helpman concentrate on the effects of particular types of shocks on the level of output and employment, Black (1976) emphasized the stability of domestic relative prices and the structure of production and consumption. He maintained that the optimal exchange rate policy depends on the type and nature of shocks. A fall in the world price of traded goods reduces the domestic price of traded goods with a fixed exchange rate, leading to a departure of relative prices from the initial equilibrium ratio and to money market disequilibrium. These effects and the resultant process of internal and external adjustment can be avoided if the exchange rate changes as foreign prices fall to offset the fall in domestic prices. For a domestic supply shock, Black believes that the optimal policy is to fix the exchange rate, thus providing some insulation to the domestic economy. This degree of insulation will reduce the incidence of domestic relative price movements and resource shifts compared with those required under flexible exchange rates.

Lipschitz (1978) found that for a domestic supply (output) shock, fixing the exchange rate is superior for stabilizing absorption, because absorption will be constrained to output under flexible exchange rates. With a fall in real output, absorption can only be prevented from falling if real resources are forthcoming from abroad, which (according to the model) requires a balance of payments deficit financed by the monetary authorities dishording or borrowing at the fixed exchange rate. A money demand shock, however, will have no effect on absorption under flexible exchange rates, but under fixed exchange rates it will cause a departure from the internal and external balance unless the authorities have perfect foresight and can appropriately manipulate the domestic component of the monetary base. The conclusion that can be reached is that optimal exchange rate policy depends on the type of disturbance likely to be encountered. In the Lipschitz model, the exchange rate policy is to allow the exchange rate to correct for domestic money demand shocks but not for temporary supply shocks. The effects of transitory domestic supply shocks can be cushioned via fixed exchange rates. Domestic supply shocks are of particular concern to some developing countries that produce exportable or importable primary agricultural products subject to variable harvest conditions.

The problem is that there is no room in Lipschitz's simple model to analyse the interaction between various types of shocks, relative prices and exchange rates. This may weaken the case put forward for exchange rate flexibility in response to domestic monetary disturbances. In Black's (1976) model, in contrast, monetary or price disturbances (nominal shocks) at home and abroad manifest themselves in domestic relative price changes at a fixed exchange rate, and it is the undesirability of these relative price changes in terms of the internal and external balance that make flexible exchange rates more desirable.

Friedman (1953) has also expressed the view that flexible exchange rates put the economy in a better position to adjust in response to external shocks. Obstfeld and Rogoff (1995) examine the issue through the concept of the real exchange rate by stipulating that real external shocks, including terms of trade and real interest shocks, result in changes in the equilibrium real exchange rate. If the nominal exchange rate is fixed, the adjustment in the equilibrium real exchange rate will take place through changes in domestic nominal prices and wages. As Meade (1951, pp. 201–2) argued, this adjustment will be difficult in countries with a fixed rate and inflexible money wages. According to Meade, the economy is likely (in the presence of these rigidities) to benefit from what he called a 'variable exchange rate' regime. However, he was careful to note that flexible exchange rates are not a panacea, and that there are indeed circumstances where they may not help to accommodate external disturbances. This would be the case if, for example, real wages are inflexible due to indexation or other mechanisms. Indeed, Meade (1951, p. 203) put forward the explicit argument that 'for the variable-exchange-rate mechanism to work effectively there must be sufficient divorce in movements in the cost of living and movements in money wage rates'.

The general conclusion that has been drawn from these and other simple theoretical models is that the optimal exchange rate regime in the face of various types of disturbances may be one intermediate between fixed and fully flexible exchange rates. The policy problem is, therefore, to determine the appropriate degree and type of exchange rate management consistent with the amount and kind of information available and with the administrative abilities of the authorities. A consensus is also that flexible exchange rates are more suitable for one kind of shock, whereas fixed rates are more suitable for another. Hausmann *et al.* (2001) point out that if shocks are mostly nominal then fixed rates are preferable, but if they are real, then flexibility is important to stabilize output. Guitian (1994) distinguishes between external nominal shocks, domestic nominal shocks and domestic real shocks. Flexible exchange rates are more appropriate to deal with external nominal shocks because 'whatever effects the shocks could have had on the foreign price level have been countered by compensating changes in the exchange rate, shielding the domestic economy from the disturbance'. He stresses, however, that domestic nominal shocks (such as those originating from money market imbalances) are best handled by fixed exchange rates. In contrast, domestic real shocks (such as those arising from imbalances in the goods markets) are best handled through flexible exchange rates.

Therefore, it seems that the 'shocks argument' cannot be used exclusively in favour of flexible exchange rates as one may initially think. Consider the following examples of a domestic nominal shock and a domestic real shock. Suppose first that the domestic shock takes the form of excess domestic money supply. This leads to a balance of payments deficit that, under fixed exchange rates, restores balance to the money market through international reserve losses. The shock does not spill over to the real economy, which is protected by the fixed exchange rate regime. If the real shock takes the form of imbalance in the goods market, then under flexible exchange rates a domestic demand shock leads to changes in the exchange rate that bring about offsetting movements in foreign demand so that domestic output is not severely affected. Guitian (1994) argues that although economies confront both nominal and real shocks, a shift in the exchange rate regime in response to the nature of the shock is not a workable proposition. He rejects the view put forward by Flood and Marion (1991) that the best choice is an exchange rate regime that exhibits an intermediate degree of flexibility. This debate shows one thing: the 'shocks argument' cannot be used exclusively (but it can be used predominantly) in favour of flexible exchange rates.

Neutralization of the effect of inflation

One of the advantages of flexible exchange rates is arguably their ability to neutralize the effect of inflation on export competitiveness. However, the ability of flexible rates to perform this function depends on whether or not PPP holds. Given that competitiveness depends on the real exchange rate, a rise in the domestic inflation rate will be matched (under PPP) by a proportional depreciation of the domestic currency, leaving the real exchange rate (and hence competitiveness) unchanged. One has to remember, however, that large and persistent deviations from PPP are the rule rather than the exception. Dominguez and Frankel (1993, p. 31) argue that it is easy to dispose of the simplistic argument that movements in the nominal exchange rate would offset movements in prices, and thus no real effects would arise. On the contrary, they argue, a very small fraction of movements in the nominal exchange rate are offset by movements in prices. Movements in nominal rates translate almost fully into movements in real exchange rates.

Arguments against flexible exchange rates

The list of arguments against flexible exchange rates seems to be longer than any of the three lists that we have gone through so far. This list contains the following arguments:

- Flexible exchange rates create an atmosphere of uncertainty.
- Flexible exchange rates tend to undermine the currency of a small open economy due to currency substitution.
- Speculation is destabilizing under flexible exchange rates.
- Flexible exchange rates are not suitable for developing economies.
- Flexible exchange rates are unstable.
- Flexible exchange rates may lead to adverse changes in real exchange rates.
- Flexible exchange rates are not suitable in the presence of a large element of exchange rate pass-through.
- They produce imported inflation.
- They reduce anti-inflationary discipline.
- They are a source of strains on the monetary authorities.
- They may lead to harmful competitive depreciation and the postponement of structural adjustment.

These arguments will be examined in turn.

Flexible exchange rates and uncertainty

The volatility of flexible exchange rates can inflict damage on businesses and economies at large. Although the associated costs have not been quantified rigorously, many economists believe that exchange rate uncertainty reduces welfare-enhancing international trade, discourages investment and compounds the problems people face in assessing their human capital in incomplete asset markets. Furthermore, workers and firms hurt by protracted exchange rate swings may often demand import protection from their governments.

The effect of exchange rate volatility on international trade has been examined in a number of empirical and theoretical papers. The empirical studies include Kenen and Rodrik (1986), Qian and Varangis (1994), Lee (1999) and Doyle (2001). The theoretical studies include Ethier (1973), Hooper and Kohlhagen (1978), Baldwin and Krugman (1989) and Viaene and de Vries (1992). A survey of the literature is provided by McKenzie (1999). The evidence for industrial countries is mixed: Chowdhury (1993), Arize (1995) and Choudhry (2001) report a negative impact, whereas Qian and de Varangis (1994) found a negative effect for some countries and a positive effect for others. Frankel and Wei (1992) examined the effect of exchange rate volatility on trade by using data on 1,953 pairs of trading partners, finding a small but statistically significant effect.

Artus and Young (1979) identify the following effects of exchange rate variability: (i) reduction in foreign trade, (ii) decline in foreign investment, and (iii) adverse effect resulting from changes in the value of reserve currencies. Proponents of flexible exchange rates argue that foreign exchange risk can be eliminated by using forward contracts, but then a forward contract that eliminates transaction exposure to foreign exchange risk may not eliminate economic exposure (Moosa, 2003). One has to remember also that forward hedging is not cost-free, as the cost is measured by the bid-offer spread. Furthermore, contracts cannot be used to hedge the risk arising from the instability of long-term investment flows.

Flexible exchange rates and currency substitution

Through a broad general appeal to the arguments of openness and currency substitution, Branson and Katseli-Papaefstratiou (1981) and Connolly (1982) believe that flexible exchange rates may not be feasible for many developing countries. A floating rate would undermine the domestic currency, as domestic residents would want contracts effectively denominated in a foreign currency, in which case there would be no basis for the demand for local currency. As openness increases, it becomes more likely that a flexible rate regime would lead to the erosion of the demand for the domestic currency.

Destabilizing speculation under flexible exchange rates

Destabilizing speculation occurs when traders sell a currency when it is weak (thinking that it will depreciate further) and buy it when it is strong (thinking that it will appreciate further). We have already seen Friedman (1953) arguing that this line of reasoning is inconceivable because it implies that traders indulge in loss-making operations. Instead, he showed that profit maximization behaviour implies stabilizing speculation as traders buy low and sell high. On the other hand, it is argued that speculation is destabilizing under fixed exchange rates. When a currency is under pressure and reserves are low, there is only one way it can go: downwards (or south, as foreign exchange dealers like to say).

The suitability of flexible exchange rates for developing economies

Freely floating exchange rates are not appropriate for developing countries because they tend to be highly volatile and can easily move beyond what economic fundamentals dictate, exerting harmful impact on trade, investment and growth. Developing economies have limited ability to absorb large exchange rate fluctuations. In developed economies, floating exchange rates are less harmful because financial markets are deeper, hedging instruments are more developed, and economic systems are more resilient.

Black (1976) and Branson and Katseli-Papaefstratiou (1981) argued that whereas the potential benefits of floating exchange rates are not necessarily limited to developed countries, certain characteristics found in many developing countries rule out floating as a feasible or realistic option. One important factor stressed as precluding floating as a viable policy option is the inadequate development of domestic financial markets. In the Branson and Katseli-Papaefstratiou analysis, there are two conditions for the success of flexible exchange rates: (i) domestic financial markets of some minimum depth must exist, and (ii) domestic and foreign assets must be substitutes in the private portfolios of wealthholders. Branson and Katseli-Papaefstratiou argue that if these conditions are satisfied then the exchange rate will (in the short run) be determined by equilibrium conditions in financial markets, which makes the stability of the exchange rate dependent on the overall stability of these markets. Countries with integrated financial markets can expect a flexible rate to be stable in the short run. This is an application of the asset market approach to exchange rate determination, in which the exchange rate is determined in the short run by the relative demands for and supplies of domestic and foreign financial assets. If markets are not integrated the exchange rate will be determined by current account flows (that is, by the demand for and supply of foreign exchange emanating from the goods markets). In this case, the short-run stability of the foreign exchange market depends on the Marshall–Lerner condition on trade elasticities. The problem is that there is ample evidence that the Marshall–Lerner condition is not satisfied in the short run.

Black (1976) examined the characteristics of developing countries' exchange and financial markets in comparison with those found in developed countries. The features of an advanced financial system are the presence of institutions that efficiently and competitively intermediate the demand for and supply of various financial assets on behalf of the residents of the countries concerned. Financial markets in developing countries, Black argues, typically do not have similar breadth and depth or such a range of institutional development. Forward exchange facilities are typically absent, and markets for common stocks, securities and bills are often poorly developed or thin, or they do not exist. The predominant source of financial intermediation is a limited banking system that offers a small range of financial instruments. In some developing countries, there may indeed be insufficient participation to ensure the effective functioning of competitive markets for foreign exchange and for domestic financial assets.

Relatively low levels of financial and associated institutional development are often found in conjunction with restrictions on current and capital account transactions as well as controls on the yields from available financial instruments. Black argues that the successful introduction of floating rates would require substantial commitment of real resources to the development of adequate financial markets, as well as willingness by the authorities to eschew exchange and payment restrictions and devices used to intervene in domestic financial markets. The development of an active forward market depends heavily on allowing free movement of short-term capital. McKinnon (1979) postulates that, for a competitive and unified foreign exchange market to emerge, substantial freedom must be afforded to non-bank residents to make and receive payments on the current account, whereas financial institutions must be in a position to intermediate efficiently.

More recently, the theory of 'fear of floating' has surfaced. Calvo (1999), Reinhart (2000) and Calvo and Reinhart (2002) argue that in a world that is characterized by high capital mobility, incomplete information, fads, rumours and dollar-denominated liabilities, the monetary authorities in developing countries are severely haunted by the fear of floating. This is because any significant depreciation of the domestic currency produces negative effects on inflation and on foreign currency debt.

Instability of flexible exchange rates

It has been established that if the Marshall–Lerner condition is not satisfied then exchange rates will be unstable. No one has put forward this argument as forcefully as Einzig (1970), who asserted that even if the foreign exchange market were confined to transactions arising from international trade, it would be quite inconceivable for exchange rates to settle at the level at which the supply and demand originating from trade would necessarily balance. In an implicit reference to the Marshall–Lerner condition, he referred to a 'wide variety of incalculable elasticities' that influence the effect of changes to exchange rates on the volume and value of imports and exports. He argued that unless these effects cancel each other out (which is highly unlikely), they would divert exchange rates from their equilibrium level. He added that the 'effect on the terms of trade is anybody's guess'.

The real exchange rate as a proxy for the distribution of income

If PPP is not valid (which is invariably the case in the short run) then real and nominal exchange rates tend to be highly correlated, which means that changes in the nominal rates are matched by corresponding changes in the real rates. One line of argument against flexible exchange rates is based on introducing the real exchange rate directly into the authorities' objective function. The real exchange rate may be a proxy for the distribution of income among workers in the traded and non-traded goods sectors. Although the significant appreciation of the dollar in the mid-1980s did not lead to a severe recession due to expansionary fiscal policy, its immediate impact was the large-scale dislocation of the US manufacturing industry.

Flexible exchange rates in the presence of large foreign currency liabilities

A number of economists argue that flexible rates are not effective in countries where the private and public sectors have large foreign currency-denominated liabilities (Eichengreen and Hausmann, 1999). In this case, it is even possible that a flexible exchange rate regime will amplify the negative effects on the terms of trade. The reason for this is that, in the presence of 'balance sheet effects', currency depreciation generated by an external shock produces (large) increases in the domestic currency value of debt. This in turn may trigger bankruptcies, lead to public sector insolvency and result in a reduction in the growth rate (Calvo, 2001).

Recent models proposed by Aghion *et al.* (1999, 2000) and Bacchetta (2000) suggest that when firms hold a large fraction of their debt in foreign currency, monetary policy becomes increasingly complex. This is due to the fact that while reducing interest rates can have expansionary effects through a credit channel, the depreciation brought about by lower interest rates can be contractionary through a balance sheet channel. Hence, as the importance of foreign currency debt increases, the central bank optimally chooses less exchange rate flexibility. Cespedes *et al.* (2000), however, find that while balance sheet effects are in fact important, they do not change the basic Mundell–Fleming implication that flexibility is better in the presence of external real shocks. The existence of important currency mismatches in the economy may force the central bank to limit exchange rate volatility, as depreciation can hurt those exposed to foreign currency liabilities (thus, adversely affecting output). If the mismatches are important, depreciation may generate widespread bankruptcies (if currency mismatches are in the public sector) or result in serious fiscal consequences (if mismatches are in the private sector) or both.

Flexible exchange rates in the presence of significant exchange rate pass-through

Countries that decide to adopt a floating regime should use monetary policy to target inflation. Svensson (1997) has formally shown the optimality of inflation targeting implemented through a Taylor rule in which interest rate adjustment depends on changes in inflation and output. However, Ball (1999) has shown that while inflation targeting and a standard Taylor rule are appropriate for closed economies, this may not be the case for open economies in which pass-through from exchange rates to prices is high. A high level of exchange rate pass-through may lead the central bank to be more concerned about exchange rate movements.

Countries care about the exchange rate, particularly when the pass-through from exchange rates to prices is large. Attention to the exchange rate should be less in countries where the effect of exchange rate changes on prices is small, or when the effect of pass-through takes a long time to materialize. Hausmann *et al.* (2001) find strong negative correlation between pass-through and flexibility. Exchange rate pass-through has a role in explaining the degree to which policy-makers intervene in foreign exchange markets, but the impact of pass-through disappears once allowance is made for the role of foreign exchange liabilities.

Flexible exchange rates as a source of imported inflation

It has been recognized that prices are sticky downwards. As a result, the upward movement in domestic prices caused by depreciation is larger than the downward movement caused by appreciation of equal magnitude. Dominguez and Frankel (1993) argue that little empirical evidence supports this hypothesis.

Flexible exchange rates and anti-inflationary discipline

Floating exchange rates can reduce anti-inflationary discipline. Since no visible payments deficits emerge, the political will to resist money supply increases is blunted. If there are strong trade unions and the money supply becomes passive, a depreciation–inflation spiral could develop. Nominal depreciation cannot be translated into real depreciation.

The proposition that flexible exchange rates are inflationary is, according to Artus and Young (1979), a variant of the notion that it is harder to maintain the discipline of prudent monetary and fiscal policies under flexible rates than under fixed rates. As far as this matter is concerned, Artus and Young conclude that it is demand-management policies rather than flexible exchange rates that are the fundamental factor. The case for a positive link between flexible rates and inflation rests on the view that there may be occasions in which the authorities feel constrained to accommodate incipient domestic cost and price increases rather than accept temporary unemployment.

Flexible exchange rates as a source of strains on the monetary authorities

Flexible exchange rates are likely to put special or intolerable strains on the monetary authorities. There is a presumption that this is likely because flexible exchange rates are prone to move by large amounts. If there are capital controls, the foreign exchange market can become unstable because of the lack of speculative activity, since current account shocks are fully transmitted to the exchange rate. If capital movements are free, this too can lead to exchange rate instability.

Two more disadvantages

Flexible exchange rates arguably have two more disadvantages. The first of these can be gleaned from the experience of the interwar period: competitive depreciation, which can be a source of regional instability. Frankel (2003) describes competitive depreciation as an inferior Nash non-cooperative equilibrium, when each country tries in vain to win a trade advantage over its neighbours. The second disadvantage is that flexible rates can lead to the postponement of required structural adjustment.

Factors determining the choice between fixed and flexible exchange rates

So, what determines how a country chooses between fixed and flexible exchange rates? In general, the criteria of exchange rate regime choice fall within three theoretical frameworks: (i) the traditional optimum currency area theory, (ii) political economy theory, and (iii) the fear of floating theory (see Poirson, 2001, Table A4). Sometimes the category of 'other macroeconomic and monetary factors' is added. It is noteworthy that this classification of the determining factors is not unique, as some factors may be classified under more than one category. Moreover, the same factor may be taken to mean more flexibility if it is classified under one category and less flexibility if it is classified under another category. What is presented here is some sort of a consensus view on the effects of the factors that determine exchange rate regime choice. There is more on the classification and effect of these factors in Chapter 8.

The classic view is that exchange rate regime choice should be determined by optimal currency area considerations, as put forward by Mundell (1961). Hence, the extent of factor mobility and the flexibility of relative price adjustment are critical factors. A subsequent view postulates that fixing the exchange rate is a device to create a precommitment to monetary stability threatened by time inconsistency problems, as in Barro and Gordon (1983). In general, countries that trade a lot and have economies that are closely integrated with a large partner are likely to choose fixed exchange rates. The same is true for countries with difficulties in making and maintaining a commitment to monetary stability. Williamson (1991) suggests that when a country does not satisfy the conditions for having a fixed rate system, flexible rates are preferable. These conditions are that: (i) the economy is small and open, (ii) the bulk of trade is undertaken with a major trading partner, (iii) the country wishes to pursue a macroeconomic policy that makes the domestic inflation rate consistent with that of the anchor country, (iv) real shocks are synchronized with those in the anchor country, and (v) the country is prepared to adopt institutional arrangements that will assure continued commitment to fixed exchange rates.

The type of shocks to which the economy is exposed is an important factor. Fixed exchange rates are better in dealing with nominal (or monetary) shocks, which arise from changes in money supply and demand (thus affecting price levels). A monetary shock that causes inflation tends (under flexible rates) to lead to currency depreciation, thus converting a nominal shock into a real shock. Hence, fixed rates provide a mechanism to accommodate these shocks. If shocks are real (such as productivity or terms of trade shocks that affect the relative prices of domestic goods), flexible rates are more suitable. In this case the economy needs to respond to changes in the relative prices of traded and non-traded goods. A shift in the nominal exchange rate offers a speedy way of implementing such a change. Under fixed exchange rates, a downturn in the economy driven by real factors results in a decline in the demand for money, in which case the central bank is forced to absorb the excess money supply, leading to higher interest rates and an increase in the depth of a downturn. The desirability of fixed as opposed to flexible exchange rates also depends on whether the shocks are domestic or external. Depending on the nature of the shock, either system may act as an automatic stabilizer. Flexible exchange rates provide more stability in the face of external shocks, whereas fixed rates are more suitable to deal with internal shocks. In general, the consensus view is that flexible exchange rates are more capable of dealing with foreign nominal shocks and real shocks (foreign or domestic), whereas fixed rates are more capable of dealing with domestic nominal shocks.

Devereux and Engel (1999) examined the role of price-setting in determining the optimality of exchange rate regimes in an environment of uncertainty created by monetary shocks. When prices are set in producer countries' currencies, flexible rates are preferred when the country is large enough, and/or when it is not too risk-averse. On the other hand, they find flexible exchange rates to be preferable when prices are set in consumer countries' currencies because flexible rates allow domestic consumption to be insulated from foreign monetary shocks. They also show that the gains from flexible rates are greater (in this case) in the presence of internationalized production.

Another relevant issue is the connection between the degree of exchange rate flexibility and wage indexation. It has been recognized that the optimal degree of wage indexation depends on the prevailing exchange rate regime. Flood and Marion (1982) showed that a small open economy with fixed exchange rates should adopt a policy of complete wage indexation, whereas an economy with flexible rates should adopt a policy of partial wage indexation. Other economists (for example, Bhandari, 1982) point out that the choice between fixed and flexible exchange rates depends on labour market conditions. Sachs

(1980) and Marston (1982) argue that the choice between fixed and flexible rates should depend on whether wages are indexed or not. Aizenman and Frenkel (1985) extended the analysis by suggesting that the optimal degree of wage indexation and exchange rate intervention are mutually and simultaneously related.

The case for fixed or flexible exchange rates cannot be abstracted from the level of economic development. Crockett and Nsouli (1977) argue that the economic characteristics and institutional realities that differentiate developing from developed countries have important implications for exchange rate regime choice. There are perhaps persuasive theoretical arguments for adopting exchange rate flexibility by large diversified economies but not by small undiversified economies. This is probably why developing countries have traditionally chosen fixed exchange rates. Following the move to general floating in March 1973, a group of ministers representing developing countries issued a communiqué stating that 'a system of stable exchange rates... constitutes an essential element of a satisfactory international monetary order'. Crockett and Nsouli (1977) list the following characteristics of developing countries that may be relevant to the question of exchange rate regime choice:

- A high specialization pattern in production.
- Inability to affect export or import prices in foreign currency terms through their exchange rate policies.
- Inelastic demand for imports and (in the short run) supply of exports.
- Rudimentary financial sectors.
- Capital flows are less responsive to conventional yield considerations.

Furthermore, Aizenman and Hausmann (2000) argue that the choice of an exchange rate regime is intertwined with the financial structure. According to this argument, two factors that lead to preference for fixed exchange rate are: (i) greater reliance on working capital to finance input needs, and (ii) greater segmentation of the domestic capital market. Fixed exchange rates reduce the real interest rate facing producers, thereby boosting output. Likewise, greater integration with the global market reduces the real interest rate benefits derived from exchange rate stability, which means that segmentation leads to preference for fixed exchange rates. Other studies emphasize not only the structure of the foreign exchange and capital markets but also other related factors such as openness of the capital account (for example, Frankel, 1995; Edwards, 1996; Hausmann *et al.*, 2001).

Some economists have tried to relate exchange rate regime choice to various institutional, historical and political characteristics, including independence of the central bank, political stability, whether or not the ruling party has a majority, the number of parties in the coalition and electoral uncertainty (see, for example, Cukierman *et al.*, 1992; Tornell and Velasco, 1995; Edwards, 1996, 1999; Berger *et al.*, 2000; Sun, 2002).

The fear of floating theory has emerged recently to explain why, despite the difficulty of maintaining fixed exchange rates, emerging market economies are reluctant to let their exchange rates float. Calvo and Reinhart (2002) present a simple model showing that the fear of floating arises from a combination of lack of credibility, a high pass-through from exchange rates to prices and inflation targeting. Moreover, fear of floating arises in the Lahiri and Vegh (2001) model because of the output cost associated with exchange rate fluctuations, whereas an inelastic supply of external funds at times of crises is the 'culprit' in the Caballero and Krishnamurthy (2001) model.

In view of this discussion and the previous one, it is possible to summarize the factors that determine exchange rate regime choice as in Table 3.1. It must be stated here that this list is by no means exhaustive. Needless to say, it is rather difficult to match exchange rate regime choice and country characteristics via casual empiricism or rigorous modelling. In fact, Rogoff *et al.* (2004) make it explicit that 'it is difficult to find empirical regularities between potential exchange rate regime determinants and countries' actual regimes that hold consistently across all countries, time periods and regime classification'.

Before closing this chapter, it is probably worthwhile to reconsider the validity of the question of whether fixed exchange rates are better than flexible exchange rates or vice versa. Dehejia and Rowe (2001) and Dehejia (2003) argue that this is a bad, poorly formulated question. Fixed exchange rates may appear to be a well-defined policy (a monetary policy rule that ensures that the value of the nominal exchange rate remains pegged against some other currency at a particular level). But fixed exchange rates come in various shapes and forms, as we are going to see later. Flexible exchange rates come in a variety of shapes, coupled with various monetary policies and degrees of central bank intervention. Flexible exchange rates may be coupled with a policy of monetizing the budget deficit, monetary targeting, price-level targeting, inflation targeting or a Taylor rule. Therefore, the choice between fixed and flexible exchange rates, as described in this chapter, is not well-defined. Dehejia (2003) puts forward the proposition that one should compare a fixed exchange rate of a specific type with a flexible exchange

Table 3.1 Factors determining exchange rate regime choice

Factor	Fixed	Flexible
Size of the economy	Small	Large
Openness of the economy	Open	Closed
International constraints on economic policies	Accepted	Rejected
Economic structure	Less diversified	More diversified
Capital mobility	Low	High
Geographical distribution of trade	Concentrated	Diversified
Sophistication of the financial system	Low	High
Labour mobility	High	Low
Divergence from world inflation	Low	High
Dominant trading partner	Yes	No
Prevalence of foreign nominal shocks	No	Yes
Prevalence of domestic nominal shocks	Yes	No
Prevalence of real shocks (foreign or domestic)	No	Yes
Common policy objectives	Yes	No
Concern about uncertainty	High	Low
Economic/financial development	Low	High
Size of foreign exchange liabilities	Large	Small
Ability to borrow internationally	Low	High
Exchange rate pass-through	High	Low
Wage indexation	Complete	Partial
Reliance on working capital	High	Low
Segmentation of domestic capital markets	High	Low
Credibility of policy-makers	High	Low

rate of a specific type. Ghosh *et al.* (1997) seem to agree with this view, arguing that although it is customary to speak of 'fixed' and 'floating' regimes, actual arrangements are quite diverse. They further argue that 'forcing all regimes into either the fixed or the flexible category may mask important differences'. Likewise, Frankel (1999) argues that 'fixed vs. floating is an oversimplified dichotomy', as there is a 'continuum of flexibility, along which it is possible to place most exchange rate arrangements'. While this argument makes a lot of sense, fixed and flexible exchange rates still have some generic characteristics that can be compared and contrasted.

4

The Taxonomy of Exchange Rate Regimes: Theoretical and Practical Classification Schemes

Introduction

This chapter deals with the theoretical and practical classification schemes of exchange rate arrangements. What we mean by 'theoretical classification' is the theoretical spectrum of exchange rate arrangements falling between the two extremes of perfectly fixed and perfectly flexible exchange rates. The classification is 'theoretical' in two senses, the first of which is that any of the classified arrangements may or may not have been tried in practice. In another sense, the classification is 'theoretical' because the underlying concepts are abstract and generic, unlike what we find in the 'practical' classification. For example, we find the abstract and generic concept of fixed exchange rates in the theoretical classification, but in the practical classification we find the concepts of hard pegs, soft pegs, single-currency pegs and multicurrency pegs, all of which being different kinds of fixed exchange rates that have been tried in practice.

The degree of exchange rate flexibility is not the only criterion that can be used to classify exchange rate regimes. Other criteria include (i) whether the foreign exchange market is unified or segmented, and (ii) the degree of convertibility of the domestic currency (whether foreign exchange is freely available or in restricted supply). There is also the possibility that the degree of flexibility may be applied to the real rather than the nominal exchange rate to come up with an exchange rate regime classification. We will deal with these less conventional classification criteria first. As always in this book, the exchange rate is measured as the domestic currency price of one unit of the foreign currency, so that a higher value of the exchange rate, E, implies a stronger foreign currency and a weaker domestic currency and vice versa. Thus domestic currency devaluation (depreciation) is indicated by a higher value of E.

Theoretical classification: preliminary considerations

Dornbusch and Kuenzler (1993) put forward a theoretical scheme for classifying exchange rate regimes in terms of two criteria. The first criterion pertains to whether the foreign exchange market is unified (which means that all foreign exchange transactions are settled at the same exchange rate) or segmented (different exchange rates are used for different purposes). The second criterion is whether the supply of foreign exchange is rationed or freely available on demand, which pertains to the convertibility of the domestic currency. Hence, four arrangements are theoretically possible:

1. Rationed supply of foreign exchange in a unified market.
2. Rationed supply of foreign exchange in a segmented market.
3. Unrestricted supply of foreign exchange in a unified market.
4. Unrestricted supply of foreign exchange in a segmented market.

The case of unrestricted supply of foreign exchange in a unified market, which is also known as unrestricted convertibility, is the most common amongst developed countries where one exchange rate is applied to all transactions without any restrictions on the amount of foreign exchange involved. Under this arrangement, exporters do not have to surrender the foreign exchange they obtain by selling domestic goods to foreigners, whereas importers can buy foreign exchange freely in the market. Moreover, no distinction is made between the treatment of trade transactions and financial transactions because the same exchange rate is applicable to both sets of transactions.

The most common case amongst developing countries is that of rationed foreign exchange supply under a unified market. In this case the government draws up a list of specified transactions (an import list, an authorized transfer list and an authorized capital flow list) for which foreign exchange is supplied at a specific (preferential) rate. Exporters have to surrender their foreign exchange earnings (in exchange for the domestic currency) at the same rate. The restrictions on the availability of foreign exchange at the specified rate give rise to black market transactions. This kind of arrangement typically implies an overvalued domestic currency because foreign exchange is in short supply at the specific rate, hence rationing and requisitioning are required. One ramification of this arrangement is the inevitable misallocation of resources: goods that do not make it onto the import list cannot be obtained, and if the list is poorly drawn it may exclude essential inter-mediate inputs. When the black market and associated smuggling and faking of trade invoices become a major issue, one alternative is to move to multiple exchange rates for commercial transactions while maintain-ing rationing and requisitioning of foreign exchange. Case 4, a flexible rate for each separate market, is possible in principle but not in reality. This case does not exist because governments get into the practice of segmenting markets for the purpose of actively managing a disequilib-rium rate for some particular class of transactions.

Another way of classifying exchange rate regimes is based on whether rates are fixed or flexible in nominal or real terms. Thus, the following possibilities arise:

1. Fixed nominal exchange rates.
2. Fixed real exchange rates.
3. Flexible nominal and real exchange rates.

Recall the relationship between the nominal and real exchange rate, $R = E(P^*/P)$, where E is the nominal exchange rate measured as the domestic price of one unit of the foreign currency, whereas $P(P^*)$ is the domestic (foreign) price level. Case 1 arises by fixing the nominal exchange rate against one or more currencies (depending on whether the objective is to stabilize the bilateral or effective exchange rate). In this case the real exchange rate fluctuates according to the inflation differential, as shown in Figure 4.1(a). If the nominal exchange rate is fixed at $\bar{E}$, the real exchange rate rises with the price ratio, implying that the foreign currency appreciates in real terms when the foreign inflation rate is higher than the domestic inflation rate. In case 2, the real exchange rate is fixed by changing the nominal exchange rate period-ically to offset the effect of the inflation differential on the real exchange rate. This is shown in Figure 4.1(b). In case 3, the nominal rate is determined by market forces, with or without central bank inter-vention, in which case the real exchange rate fluctuates according to changes in the nominal exchange rate and prices. In Figure 4.1(c) both rates fluctuate randomly by assuming no systematic relationship between the nominal exchange rate and prices (that is, PPP does not hold). This will also be the case even if PPP holds but factors other than prices (such as interest rates) affect the nominal exchange rate.

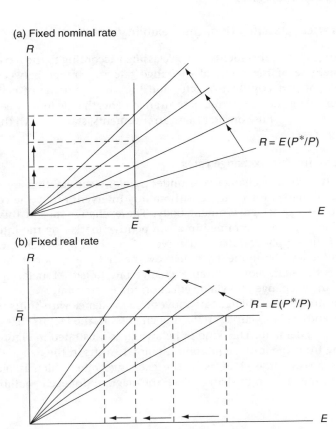

(a) Fixed nominal rate

(b) Fixed real rate

(c) Flexible nominal and real rates

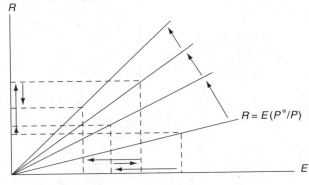

Figure 4.1 Fixed and flexible nominal and real exchange rates

Theoretical classification: the flexibility criterion

Exchange rate arrangements can be classified according to the flexibility or otherwise of the nominal exchange rate in a range between the extreme of perfectly flexible rates and the other extreme of perfectly fixed exchange rates. Intermediate arrangements that lie in-between can also be found. Let us consider these arrangements, starting with the two extreme cases.

Perfectly flexible exchange rates

Perfectly flexible exchange rates under pure or clean floating are determined by market forces alone without any intervention by the central bank or any other government body. The exchange rate in this case resembles a price determined in a competitive market by the intersection of the supply and demand curves. However, the exchange rate is still influenced by monetary policy except that policy is not directed towards the achievement of an exchange rate target. Monetary policy affects the exchange rate via its effect on the interest rate.

Over time, the exchange rate moves in accordance with shifts in the supply and demand curves, reflecting changes in the factors that affect supply and demand. This kind of behaviour is illustrated in Figure 4.2. Starting from the initial equilibrium point 1, shifts in the demand and supply curves cause changes in the exchange rate, which is plotted against time in the right-hand side of the diagram (for each equilibrium

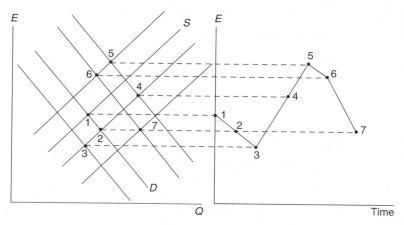

Figure 4.2 The behaviour of flexible exchange rates

point from 1 to 7, there is a corresponding equilibrium level of the exchange rate). The simplifying assumption implicit in Figure 4.2 is that during a particular episode shifts occur either in the demand or in the supply curve, but this is not necessarily the case as simultaneous shifts can also occur.

Perfectly fixed exchange rates

It is invariably the case that the fixed exchange rate is set below the equilibrium rate that is determined by the market. This means that the domestic currency will be overvalued, which results in a shortage of foreign exchange (excess demand that is equivalent to the deficit in the balance of payments). To maintain the fixed exchange rate, the monetary authorities must intervene in the foreign exchange market by selling an amount of foreign exchange that is equal to the excess demand for foreign exchange (otherwise, capital controls and rationing must be imposed). For this purpose the central bank uses its stock of international reserves.

The situation is illustrated in Figure 4.3. As the demand and supply curves shift, the exchange rate is maintained at $\bar{E}$, so what happens is that the excess demand for foreign exchange fluctuates as shown in the bottom part of the diagram. The excess demand is measured by the difference between the quantity demanded, Q_d, and the quantity supplied, Q_s. At any point in time, excess demand for foreign exchange represents the change in international reserves.

Fixed but adjustable exchange rates

Under a system of fixed but adjustable exchange rates, the fixed (or par or central) value of the exchange rate is adjusted whenever the need arises to correct a balance of payments disequilibrium. The adjustment could take the form of devaluation (reducing the par value of the domestic currency) or revaluation (increasing the par value of the domestic currency). Corden (2002) distinguishes between low-speculation fixed but adjustable exchange rates (low capital mobility) and high-speculation fixed but adjustable rates (when capital mobility is high and exchange controls are not in place).

The working of this system is illustrated in Figure 4.4 under the assumption that the central bank aims at maintaining excess demand for foreign exchange (the balance of payments deficit) close to a particular level (the level prevailing at the initial exchange rate). If the demand for foreign exchange rises, without a change in supply, excess demand will rise. To prevent excess demand from rising, the domestic

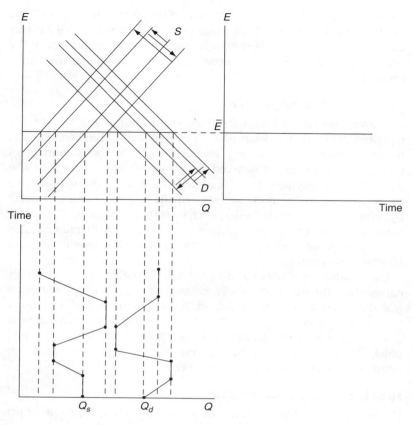

Figure 4.3   The foreign exchange market under fixed exchange rates

currency is devalued by raising the exchange rate from 1 to 2. This devaluation keeps the excess demand at approximately the same level, as we can see from the bottom part of the diagram. If demand rises further, devaluation will take place once more, taking the exchange rate up to level 3. If, on the other hand, the supply of foreign exchange increases, then revaluation will be needed to maintain excess demand at the same initial level. In this case, the exchange rate is taken from level 3 down to level 4.

Now compare the behaviour over time of a perfectly flexible exchange rate, as in Figure 4.2, with a fixed but adjustable exchange rate, as in Figure 4.4. The movements in flexible exchange rates are

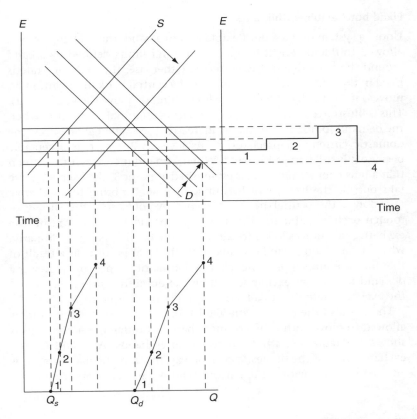

Figure 4.4 The foreign exchange market under fixed but adjustable exchange rates

small and continuous, resulting from changes in market forces (shifts in the supply and demand curves). Changes in fixed (but adjustable) exchange rates are large and discrete, resulting from deliberate policy actions (changing the par value of the domestic currency). While a change in a fixed exchange rate is called devaluation (downwards) and revaluation (upwards), the corresponding changes in a flexible exchange rate are called depreciation and appreciation respectively. It is often the case (particularly in the media, but also in academic work) that the words depreciation and devaluation are (mistakenly) used interchangeably as if they meant the same thing.

Fixed but flexible within a band

Under a system of fixed but flexible within a band, the exchange rate is allowed to fluctuate within upper and lower limits defined by a band around the par value of the currency. Otherwise, the exchange rate is fixed in the sense that it is not allowed, by central bank intervention, to move outside the band (below the lower limit or above the upper limit). This is illustrated in Figure 4.5, starting from an initial position 1. When the demand for foreign exchange increases, the exchange rate rises (the domestic currency depreciates) to its level at 2, which is acceptable because it is still within the band. When demand increases further, such that a new equilibrium level is established at point 3, the exchange rate falls outside the band, which is unacceptable. To bring the exchange rate down, the central bank intervenes by increasing the supply of foreign exchange (buying the domestic currency), and as a result the exchange rate moves lower to fall within the band at point 4. Similarly, when the exchange rate falls outside the band at point 6, as a result of the increase in supply, the central bank intervenes by increasing demand for foreign exchange (selling the domestic currency), so that the exchange rate rises to a level within the band at point 7.

There is also the case of multiple bands, where the exchange rate is allowed to move within two or more bands of different widths. This is shown in Figure 4.6, where there are three bands: A, B and C. The exchange rate of the domestic currency against a particular currency is allowed to move within the narrow band A, against another currency

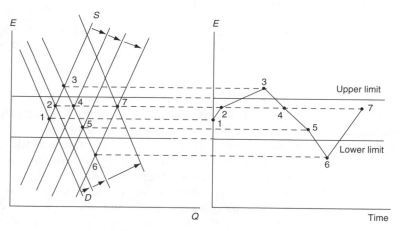

Figure 4.5   Fixed exchange rates and flexible within a band

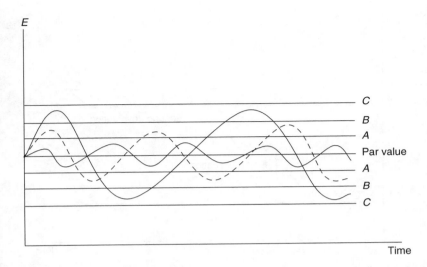

Figure 4.6   The case of multiple bands

within band B and against a third currency within the wide band C. This may be dictated by the desire to maintain more stable exchange rates against important trading partners and less stable rates against the currencies of other countries.

Svensson (1994) investigated the effect of the bands using the case of the Swedish krona. He strongly argued that the presence of bands gives the monetary authorities some monetary independence even if capital is highly mobile. He found the extent of monetary independence in the Swedish case to be significant. For example, increasing the Swedish krona bands from zero to ±2 per cent may result in reducing the standard deviation of the interest rate by about half a percentage point.

Fixed but adjustable and flexible within a band

A fixed exchange rate that is flexible within a band may also be adjustable, a case that is illustrated in Figure 4.7. Initially the exchange rate is rather stable, fluctuating within the initial band, 1. After a while the domestic currency depreciates so that the exchange rate breaches the upper limit of the band. When central bank intervention fails to take the exchange rate back to a level that falls within the band, the domestic currency is devalued, such that the exchange rate is allowed to fluctuate within band 2 around a new (higher) par value. The same thing happens

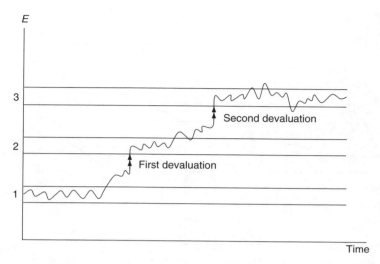

Figure 4.7 Fixed but adjustable exchange rates and flexible within a band (fixed band width)

again after a while, when central bank intervention fails and the currency is devalued for the second time. After the second devaluation the exchange rate fluctuates within band 3 around a new par value. As long as central bank intervention is capable of bringing the exchange rate within the band when it breaches the upper or lower limits of the band, there is no need for further devaluation. Figure 4.8 shows the case when the band is widened following each devaluation. It is noteworthy that as the band width increases the system becomes a *de facto* flexible exchange rate system, which is exactly what happened to the European Monetary System in 1993, when the band width was taken from ±2.5 to ±15 per cent.

Flexible exchange rates with market intervention

Managed floating (also called dirty floating), independent floating and target zones are exchange rate regimes that fall under the heading 'flexible rates with market intervention'. The main difference lies in the degree and frequency of market intervention, and hence the flexibility of the exchange rate. Exchange rate flexibility is lower under managed floating than under independent floating. But under both of these systems, intervention is mainly directed at combating speculative

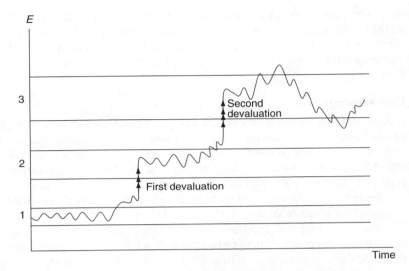

Figure 4.8 Fixed but adjustable exchange rates and flexible within a band (variable band width)

pressure and reducing exchange rate volatility (this is at least what is normally claimed, although there is the view that managed floating has the objective of influencing the market trend of the exchange rate). Indeed, the difference between managed floating and independent floating is often blurred. Some further reference to the distinction between managed floating and independent floating will be made when we discuss the IMF classification in Chapter 5.

A system of target zones differs from managed floating and independent floating in at least two respects: (i) establishing a range for the exchange rate for a future period of time, and (ii) observing closely the exchange rate in the conduct of monetary policy so as to keep it within the target range. But unlike the adjustable peg system, a target zone system does not imply a formal commitment to intervene in the foreign exchange market to keep the exchange rate within the target range. The target range is reviewed and changed if necessary.

There are various versions of target zones, depending on the following four characteristics: (i) the width of the target zone, (ii) the frequency of changes in the zone, (iii) the degree of publicity, and (iv) the degree of commitment to keeping the exchange rate within the zone. Thus, we may have a hard target zone that entails keeping the exchange rate within a narrow and publicly announced range via monetary policy, a soft target zone characterized by monetary policy that pays limited attention to the level of the exchange rate and a wide, frequently revised and undeclared zone. For more details on target zones, see Frenkel and Goldstein (1986).

Dual exchange rates

A dual exchange rate system in its basic form is a mixed (hybrid) system of fixed and flexible exchange rates. A commercial (fixed) rate is used for imports and exports (current account transactions), whereas a financial (flexible) rate is used for trading financial assets (capital account or financial account transactions). This system is resorted to when there is a desire to insulate commercial transactions from exchange rate fluctuations that result from speculative capital flows.

There are at least two problems with a system of dual exchange rates. First, the commercial rate may be fixed at such a low level as to make the domestic currency overvalued, thus adversely affecting the competitiveness of the domestic economy. This, however, is a problem with any system of fixed exchange rates, and it has no particular relevance to dual exchange rates as such. The second problem is that the system works properly only if the two foreign exchange markets can be segmented. When the difference between the two rates is high, transactions leak from the official market (where the fixed rate is used) to the free market (where the flexible rate is determined) via fraudulent means such as underinvoicing exports and overinvoicing imports. Dornbusch (1986) suggests that for the system to work, the two rates must be closely related and that if the financial rate changes for some fundamental reason, the commercial rate must be changed in the same direction. The effect of leakages on the viability of dual exchange rate systems has been examined by Guidotti (1988) and by Bhandari and Vegh (1990).

Figure 4.9 illustrates the case of dual exchange rates when the two rates are not related (that is, when the fixed rate is not changed to match changes in the flexible rate). As the financial rate rises (the domestic currency depreciates) because of an increase in the demand for foreign exchange to settle financial transactions, the commercial rate is unchanged. Hence, the premium of the financial rate over the commercial rate rises, making it increasingly attractive to buy at the commercial rate and sell at the financial rate (via fraudulent means, of course). In Figure 4.10, the commercial rate is changed to match changes in the financial rate. If this is done, the premium of the financial rate over the commercial rate is maintained (or at least it is prevented from rising

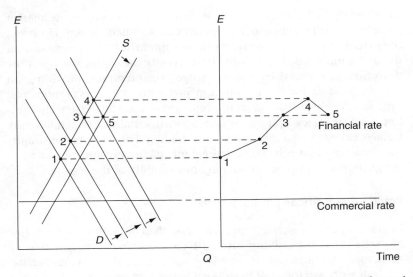

Figure 4.9 A dual exchange rate system when the commercial rate is not changed

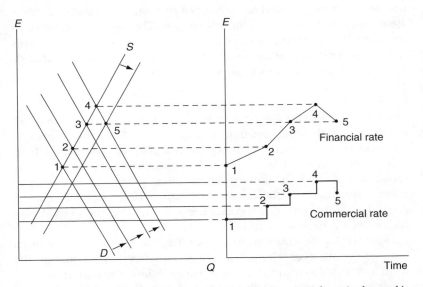

Figure 4.10 A dual exchange rate system when the commercial rate is changed in response to changes in the financial rate

significantly). Of course, as long as there is a premium, some market participants will attempt to make profit via fraudulent means. However, the extent of this illegal activity can be contained by keeping a cap on the premium. Frenkel and Razin (1986) specify the characteristics of the distortion introduced by the exchange rate premium, providing an explicit formula for the equilibrium premium, for its evolution over time and for the welfare cost induced by the distortion. They also outline a set of policy options consistent with sustaining a permanently viable dual exchange rate system and highlight the severe constraints that intertemporal solvency requirements of the private sector and of the government impose on the long-run viability of the regime.

Practical classification: hard pegs

In practice, exchange rate regimes are classified according to the degree of exchange rate flexibility into (i) fixed exchange rates, (ii) flexible exchange rates, and (iii) intermediate regimes. In the previous section we dealt with two forms of flexible exchange rate regimes (independent floating and managed floating). The so-called clean floating or perfectly flexible exchange rate hardly exists these days, and not even the free-market champions of the IMF advocate a system like this. Therefore, we will deal with the practical forms of fixed exchange rates and intermediate regimes in the remainder of this chapter. This section is devoted to one form of fixed exchange rates: hard pegs. The following section deals with the second form of fixed exchange rates: soft or conventional pegs. The last section deals with intermediate regimes.

Dollarization

The term 'dollarization' is generic, implying the use of the currency of one country as the legal tender of another country. Since the US dollar is the most commonly used currency for this purpose, we use the term 'dollarization' and not 'euroization' or 'poundization'. However, some economists and commentators take the term 'dollarization' literally to mean using the US dollar as its legal tender (for example, Roubini, 2001). Gulde *et al.* (2004) emphasize the point of using the word 'dollarization' in a generic sense.

Most developing and transition countries have a limited, unofficial form of dollarization whereby a foreign currency (predominantly the US dollar) is used as the medium of exchange. Informal dollarization arises as a response to economic instability and high inflation. However, full dollarization is an (exchange rate) arrangement under which a country abandons its own currency and adopts instead a more stable currency of another country as its legal tender. De Zamaroczy and Sa (2003) describe the Cambodian experience with dollarization by pointing out that it was neither sought nor encouraged by the monetary authorities. It rather arose from a combination of supply and demand factors (dollar inflows from overseas and lack of confidence in the domestic currency). In addition to the distinction between official (*de jure*) dollarization and partial (*de facto*) dollarization (which is effectively a bicurrency system), Gulde *et al.* (2004) distinguish between payments dollarization, financial dollarization and real dollarization. Payments dollarization involves the use of foreign currency for transaction purposes, whereas real dollarization boils down to the indexing (formally or *de facto*) of local prices and wages to the anchor currency. Financial dollarization implies that residents hold foreign currency assets and liabilities. It can be classified into domestic dollarization (involving the use of the anchor currency in claims of residents) and external dollarization (involving the use of the anchor currency in claims between residents and non-residents). Since we are concerned with exchange rate regimes, our emphasis is on official dollarization.

Berg and Borensztein (2000) summarize the pros and cons of dollarization as follows, starting with the pros:

- Dollarization enables adopting countries to avoid currency and balance of payments crises. With a 'fragile' domestic currency there is always the possibility of sharp depreciation or massive capital outflows triggered by fear of impending devaluation.
- Closer economic integration follows from low transaction costs and an assured stability of prices in terms of the chosen currency.
- Avoiding inflationary financing helps countries in their drive to strengthen their financial institutions and create better investment climate.

Moreover, Hausmann (1999) suggests that dollarization promotes a healthier financial system because it avoids currency mismatches and deepens the financial system, making it less prone to crises.

On the other hand, the cons are:

- Abandoning the domestic currency is like abandoning a symbol of nationhood. Hence, there will always be political pressure against dollarization.
- Dollarization leads to the loss of seigniorage, the revenue obtained by issuing the national currency. This will not be the case if the anchor

country is willing to share the seigniorage gains with the dollarizing country.

- It also leads to the loss of monetary and exchange rate policies.

Berg and Borensztein (2000) do not reach a clear-cut conclusion on the net benefits of dollarization, saying that the question on the balance of costs and benefits of full dollarization seems 'frustratingly two-handed'. In another article, Berg and Borensztein (2003) tackle the pros and cons of dollarization by comparing it with a currency board arrangement, arguing that the pros of dollarization include lower interest rates and the benefits obtained from stability and integration. Indeed, when the Argentine currency board came under pressure in 1999, the proponents of dollarization argued that it would eliminate the persistent spread between the interest rates on the dollar and peso, which by that time had reached three percentage points. Some economists have examined dedollarization (the reestablishment of a domestic currency). Caballero and Krishnamurthy (2002) suggest that dedollarization may require a major overhaul of the domestic financial sector. For example, development of the necessary institutions to support a successful domestically oriented monetary policy takes time, which supports Calvo and Mishkin's (2003) view on the importance of institutions.

Edwards (2003) is not that enthusiastic about dollarization, arguing that little is known about its costs and benefits. He criticizes the view that dollarization enables the dollarized country to avoid macroeconomic mismanagement, casting doubt on the presumed outcomes of lower interest rates, high investment and superior economic performance. Edwards (2002) refers to the 'myth of dollarization' because we know very little about how countries have performed under dollarization. Apart from Panama, which has been dollarized since 1904, there are twenty independent dollarized countries with a median population of 145,000 people and not much in terms of collected data (see also Edwards and Magendoza, 2002). However, Edwards (2004) was unable to find evidence supporting the hypothesis that countries with a higher degree of dollarization are more severely affected by current account reversals than countries with a lower degree of dollarization. Eichengreen (2003) expresses mixed feelings about this issue, arguing that whether dollarization is good or bad depends on whether it significantly speeds the pace of fiscal, financial and labour market reform in the dollarized country. The problem is that we do not have precise answers for these questions. Corbo (2003) concludes that for countries with a poor record of financial stability and where economic relations are mostly with the anchor country, dollarization can be very advantageous. Schuler (2003) argues against the perceived disadvantage of losing monetary sovereignty by casting doubt on its benefits.

Roubini (2001) has compiled a comprehensive list whereby it is possible to judge the readiness of a country to adopt dollarization. The list contains three groups of factors: (i) monetary, financial and fiscal factors; (ii) real trade and related factors; and (iii) other factors. These factors are summarized in Table 4.1.

Table 4.1 Factors determining the suitability of dollarization

Factor	Comment
Monetary, financial and fiscal factors	
Policy credibility	Countries that lack credibility benefit from dollarization
Inflation experience	Dollarization is most appropriate for countries with a history of monetary stability
Current exchange rate regime	Dollarization is suitable for a country that has already shown commitment to a stable currency
Reserve coverage of monetary base	A minimum is that foreign exchange reserves should cover at least the monetary base
Soundness of banking system	A competitive, well-supervised and well-regulated banking system is important
Extent of informal dollarization	The greater the degree of unofficial dollarization, the greater are the potential benefits of formal dollarization
Lender of last resort function	Channels are needed to perform this function in a dollarized economy
Seigniorage loss	For countries in which seigniorage accounts for a significant fraction of government revenue, such loss has serious fiscal consequences
Central bank solvency	The extent to which seigniorage loss affects the solvency of the central bank
State of public finance	The smaller the budget deficit and public debt, the smaller the risk that dollarization might fail
External debt/financing requirements	The stock of external debt and debt servicing affect the success of dollarization

Table 4.1 (Continued)

Factor	Comment
Real and trade-related factors	
Ability to pursue countercyclical policy	If a country is unable to use monetary policy to stabilize output, there is no need to worry about the effect of dollarization
Correlation of business cycles	Preferable for cycles to be highly correlated with those of the anchor country
Trade integration	Dollarization is suitable when the anchor country is a major trading partner
Vulnerability to terms of trade shocks	This factor plays an ambiguous role
Openness to trade	Greater openness to trade may strengthen the case for dollarization
Other factors	
Flexibility of labour markets	Flexibility is important to deal with shocks under dollarization
Degree of labour mobility	As above
Degree of capital mobility	Capital mobility can substitute for the lack of labour mobility
Income insurance schemes	These schemes cannot be at work in a dollarized economy
Political factors	Dollarization requires strong public support

Currency unions

A currency union is another hard-peg system (or what Corden (2002) calls an absolutely fixed regime). There are, however, two important differences between dollarization and a currency union. A dollarized country must accept the monetary policy of the anchor country, but in a currency union the country's representatives may be on the board of the central bank of the union, which means that they have some influence on the common monetary policy of the union. The second difference is that while a dollarized country loses seigniorage, a country in a currency union obtains some share of the seigniorage generated by issuing the common currency. Alesina and Barro (2002) attribute the tendency to join currency unions (as well as moving towards dollarization) to the proliferation of currencies and the renewed emphasis on price stability, which casts doubt on the validity of the 'one country one money' slogan.

There is some evidence supporting the proposition that currency unions (and hard pegs in general) do encourage openness to trade and integration with the other countries in the union (Rose, 2000; Rose and van Wincoop, 2001; Frankel and Rose, 2002; Glick and Rose, 2002). Trade openness can reduce the vulnerability of emerging markets to financial crises, whereas economic integration with an anchor country reduces the cost of loss of domestic monetary policy. In his study of the effects of the EMU, Faruqee (2004) attributes the ability of currency unions to boost trade among its members to three factors: (i) lower transaction costs, (ii) lower exchange rate uncertainty, and (iii) enhanced competition through greater transparency.

Tenreyro and Barro (2003) examined the economic effects of currency unions, coming up with three conclusions. The first is that sharing a common currency enhances trade, supporting the previous results. The second is that a common currency boosts price co-movements, a finding that is consistent with the observation that a large part of the variation in real exchange rates is caused by fluctuations in nominal exchange rates. Third, a common currency reduces the co-movements of shocks to real output.

If this is the case, why then is there heated debate about whether or not Britain should join the EMU? The proponents of joining the EMU envisage that the move would save business the costs and uncertainties of exchange rate movements, as well as generating lower interest rates and faster growth. However, Redwood (1997) argues against joining the EMU on political and economic grounds. He points out that the preparation for the EMU, which took the form of fixed exchange rates within the EMS, brought with it high interest rates, higher taxes, less growth and higher unemployment. He specifically argues that 'for most British business it would be all cost and no benefit'. But Faruqee (2004) concludes, on the basis of his empirical results, that the EMU has had a positive impact on intra-area trade and that gains in intra-area trade do not occur at the expense of extra-area trade. One has to be careful not to attribute all economic mishaps to the exchange rate regime in place at the time, which is exactly what Redwood preached. This is the hazard of trying to justify an ideologically driven view on economic grounds without rigorous empirical evidence obtained by controlling for the effect of other factors.

Currency boards

A currency board is a system of fixed exchange rates that was common in colonial territories during the first half of the twentieth century. It is a system whereby the currency board is obliged to supply, on demand and without limit, the foreign currency to which the domestic currency is pegged. The dismantling of colonial regimes led to the virtual disappearance of currency boards, but interest in this arrangement has revived in recent years as financial crises triggered thinking about means of stabilizing exchange rates and bringing order to economic conditions in general. Currency boards are believed by some economists to be one of these means.

Klyuev (2001) argues that the principal difference between a currency board and a simple (conventional) peg is the consequent difficulty of changing the regime, which is much greater under a currency board. Because of this property, currency broads are much more stable than other regimes. Corden (2002) argues that a 'proper' or 'pure' currency board operates not only on a commitment to a firmly fixed exchange rate but also as a strict regulation that effectively prohibits an independent monetary policy. Thus, neither budget deficits nor the rescue of commercial banks (the lender-of-last-resort function) can be financed by resorting to the printing press. Ho (2003) points out that currency boards are controversial for several interrelated reasons. The first is naturally that they severely limit monetary policy discretion (as well as the lender-of-last-resort function), which boils down to surrendering traditional central banking functions. The second issue is that the use of institutional constraints to achieve and maintain policy credibility is itself a controversial notion. Finally, and this is probably a trivial issue, currency boards are an invention of nineteenth-century British colonialism, which some people may find offensive.

In operational terms, a currency board can be characterized by the requirement that the entire monetary base is backed by holdings of the reserve currency. In a pure currency board system the monetary authority does not hold domestic assets, which makes it unable to sterilize its foreign exchange operations. In other words, the monetary authority has no discretion in the conduct of monetary policy, which is dictated by the actions of the authority that issues the reserve currency. A pure currency board also means that the central bank cannot extend loans to the government, the banking system or anyone else. However, if foreign exchange reserves exceed what is required to back the monetary base, then there is a limited scope for functioning as a lender of last retort. For more details on how currency boards work, see Balino and Enoch (1997) and Enoch and Gulde (1997).

There are certain criteria whereby it is possible to judge the suitability of a currency board for a particular country. These include purely domestic factors such as low inflation, a high level of reserves, high labour mobility and nominal flexibility. There are also some criteria for the choice of the reserve currency, which include such features as the symmetry of shocks in the home country and the country of the reserve currency, as well as the extent of trade links. Some preconditions are envisaged for the successful introduction of a currency board, including: (i) fiscal discipline, (ii) robust banking system, and (iii) flexible wages and prices in the absence of labour market distortions.

The first reintroduction of a currency board, which has proved to be successful, was in Hong Kong in 1983. In 1991, Argentina set up a similar arrangement, whereby the peso was linked to the US dollar at a parity exchange rate (one to one). In 1992, Estonia began to operate a currency board, followed by Lithuania in 1994. But the desirability or otherwise of currency boards is a highly controversial issue, as this arrangement has contrasting pros and cons. The pros are:

- Currency boards are an effective means of pegging the exchange rate when a hard peg is required.
- They can be very effective in countries suffering from hyperinflation or in countries in which financial stability has not yet been established (for example, East Timor and Iraq). This is because no unit of the domestic currency can be issued without placing a corresponding amount of a foreign currency in the reserves, valued at the fixed exchange rate.
- Currency boards help to curb wasteful government spending financed by printing money. While a deficit is allowed under a currency board, it cannot be financed by printing money.
- Currency boards are better for developing countries than the alternatives of soft pegs (for example, Thailand before the onset of the Asian crisis) and free floating. The argument that a currency board is better than soft pegs rests on the belief in the bipolar view advocating the choice of an extreme regime. The perceived superiority over free floating rests on the arguments presented in Chapter 2 on the case for flexible exchange rates in developing countries.

On the other hand, those to whom the idea of a currency board is not that appealing argue for their view on the following list of cons:

- Governments operating currency boards must accept restrictions on the way they conduct policy.

- Countries on this system must swallow their pride and abandon their monetary sovereignty, simply because they have to follow the (monetary) policy of the anchor country.
- Governments have to give up seigniorage, the implicit profit gained by printing national money.
- The fixed exchange rate can get excessively out of line with those of its trading partners, giving rise to a problem of misalignment. This argument is valid for all forms of fixed exchange rates.
- Currency boards are not immune to speculative attacks. Again, no fixed exchange rate regime is immune to speculative attacks.
- Currency boards (and other hard pegs) cannot accommodate the function of a money-printing lender of last resort. However, Calvo and Mishkin (2003) argue that 'the scope for a lender of last resort for emerging economies with floating rates is oversold'.

The experience of the countries that have adopted currency boards recently may provide some evidence in favour of or against this arrangement. While the experience of Hong Kong has been pleasant, we have not heard much of the experience of Estonia and Lithuania. On the other hand, it is widely believed that the Argentine financial crisis of 2001–02 was exacerbated by the exchange rate arrangement to the extent that the government decided to abandon it and resort to floating the peso in January 2002. But some economists, such as Dornbusch (2001), argue that the demise of Argentina would have happened with or without a currency board. The crisis, according to Dornbusch, was waiting to happen because of the legacy of high debt and earlier deficits, trade unions that have consistently thwarted reform, and obsolete industry that would not be competitive at any exchange rate. Irwin (2004) presents a theoretical model showing why a currency board does not necessarily provide a durable basis for a fully binding (and hence credible) commitment to fix the exchange rate. With the aid of his model, Irwin demonstrates how a currency board can become vulnerable to a crisis in which the policy-maker is forced to devalue.

Oppers (2000) argues that the most important drawback of a currency board is that it forces the choice of one particular reserve currency to which the domestic currency is pegged. The problem is that a single-currency peg may not be optimal, particularly if shocks are not highly correlated, and also because of trade diversification. To circumvent this problem, Oppers (2000) suggests the introduction of a dual currency board, which entails the use of an alternative reserve currency when the initial reserve currency appreciates above a certain level. This can be done by extending the promise of convertibility to a second reserve currency. The choice of the reserve currency to be received in exchange for the domestic currency would (in principle) be up to the payee, but the convertibility guarantee can be made explicitly subject to availability of the currency of choice in the reserves of the central bank. If it is not available, the payee is guaranteed convertibility to the other currency. In April 2001, the Argentine Minister of the Economy wanted to experiment with a dual currency board by pegging the peso to the US dollar and the euro on the grounds that the strength of the dollar had hurt the competitiveness of the Argentine economy. The repegging was scheduled to take place when the euro reached parity with the dollar. The board collapsed before that happened.

Practical classification: soft pegs

Soft or conventional pegs may be either single-currency pegs or multi-currency pegs. Recall from Chapter 1 that soft pegs may be classified as intermediate regimes, but this difference in classification does not affect the following exposition.

Single-currency pegs

Pegging to one currency amounts to fixing the bilateral exchange rate against another currency (the anchor currency). The bilateral exchange rates of the domestic currency against other countries will be as stable or volatile as those of the anchor currency against the same currencies. The fixed exchange rate may be allowed to move within a narrow band. Heller (1978) and Bird (1979), for example, have invoked optimum currency area considerations as relevant to the decision of a country to adopt a fixed link between the domestic currency and an external standard. Pegging to a single currency gives rise to a form of currency area in which the exchange rates of the currencies concerned float jointly against other foreign currencies.

A major benefit of single-currency pegging arises from the anti-inflationary discipline provided by this arrangement, assuming that the anchor country has a stable and low inflation rate. Several mechanisms promote this anti-inflationary discipline: (i) international commodity arbitrage, (ii) the link between the balance of payments and the domestic money supply, (iii) the macroeconomic policies that the government is forced to pursue to defend the exchange rate, and

(iv) the credible expectations generated by all of these mechanisms. The counter-argument is that a single-currency peg would equalize inflation rates with the peg country only if exchange rate movements between major currencies follow PPP. In the short run, when exchange rate movements are random (as a result of the influence of non-inflation factors), the domestic inflation rate would be dictated by average inflation rates in the country's trading partners and the movements in its effective exchange rate. However, this would probably not matter much: if we consider a typical country as having pronounced inflationary propensities but trading with countries having significantly lower inflation rates, a single-currency peg is a perfectly good anchor against inflation.

A single-currency peg does not look so good if we consider other aspects of the internal balance and external balance, and this depends on whether trade is concentrated or diversified. If trade is heavily concentrated with the anchor country then the case against single-currency pegging is basically the traditional case against fixed exchange rates. If the balance of payments adjustment requires a fall in the level or growth of money wages and prices and if such flexibility is not present (because of strong unions, for example) then the domestic currency could remain overvalued in real terms for a long period of time, resulting in negative effects on employment, output and the balance of payments. On the other hand, if trade is diversified and the anchor currency floats against major currencies, the country's nominal and real exchange rates also float but without any reference to its own needs. This is exactly what happened to the currencies that were pegged to the dollar in the early 1980s, when they appreciated excessively against other currencies.

As far as microeconomic efficiency is concerned, if trade is largely with the anchor country then the exchange rate stability that comes from a single-currency peg offers significant benefits. The reduction in the variability of the price level underpins the liquidity of domestic money. The stability of the value of the currency in which trade is invoiced and prices are quoted promotes trade and capital flows. Temporary shocks (such as a bad harvest) change the stock of foreign exchange reserves, not the exchange rate and the price level, implying reduction in the wasteful movements of resources. But these benefits are eroded if trade is diversified. In such a case, movements in the anchor currency, which alter the domestic currency's exchange rates against all other currencies, lead to foreign exchange risk and instability.

Crockett and Nsouli (1977) summarize the pros and cons of single-currency pegs in a world of floating as follows. The pros are:

- Exchange rate stability facilitates growth and capital flows between the home country and the anchor country.
- To the extent that the exchange rates of the anchor country against other currencies are stable, the exchange rate of the domestic currency against other currencies will also be stable.
- A country that pegs its currency to the currency of a major country with stable prices and sound policies gains confidence in its currency, which may boost foreign investment.
- Pegging to a single currency provides a clear criterion for intervention in the foreign exchange market.
- Defending a pegged exchange rate may promote willingness to impose unpopular domestic constraints.

On the other hand, the cons are:

- The need for international reserves may increase. This will be the case if the factors affecting the equilibrium exchange rates of the two countries against the rest of the world are not closely related.
- Fluctuations of the exchange rate against the rest of the world are exogenous and independent of government policy, and this may interfere with the internal policy objectives.
- If small regional countries peg to different currencies their cross-exchange rates will be highly volatile, which works against the promotion of intra-regional trade.

Multicurrency pegs

Unlike single-currency pegs, multicurrency pegs (or basket pegs) do not give rise to a form of currency area. Rather than reflecting acceptance of optimum currency area arguments in favour of a link to a single currency, the choice of a basket peg may be interpreted as a rejection of such arguments. Again, it is possible that the pegged exchange rate is allowed to move within a band, giving rise to what Frankel *et al.* (2001) call a 'band around a basket peg'.

It is arguable that the problems with single-currency pegs can be circumvented by resorting to multicurrency pegs. The objective of multicurrency pegging is to eliminate the effect of third-currency fluctuations by pegging the nominal effective exchange rate or, in other words, by pegging the domestic currency to a suitable average of foreign currencies (the so-called basket of currencies). It follows that the choice of weights needed to construct the basket is a matter of some importance, a subject on which there is a large body of theoretical and empirical literature. In general, however, the following points are valid. For a small economy wishing to stabilize the price of traded goods, bilateral trade shares of partner countries are the appropriate weights. For a large country that is concerned about the internal balance and external balance, the object of stabilization should be the trade balance, which requires the use of elasticity-based weights. In practice this is too complicated and it is difficult to do better than using bilateral trade weights.

Eichengreen (1999b) attributes the tendency to use multicurrency pegs to the removal of tariffs and other barriers, which has made trade more multilateral. He argues that pegging to a particular currency is dicey for countries that trade and borrow from a variety of different partners, as the recent experience of the Asian countries shows. However, he asserts that pegging to a basket can attenuate but not eliminate the problem. With the co-movements of major currencies changing over time, pegging to a fixed basket is likely to be problematical. Figure 4.11 shows that the pattern of the co-movements of the nominal exchange rates (against the US dollar) of the yen, pound and Canadian dollar has been changing over time.

Multicurrency pegging is effectively an attempt to mimic a fixed exchange rate in a world of floating rates. The question therefore is whether multicurrency pegging secures the benefits of a fixed exchange rate better than single-currency pegging. As regards the external balance and internal balance, a comparison between a multicurrency peg and a single-currency peg is generally favourable to the former. With a

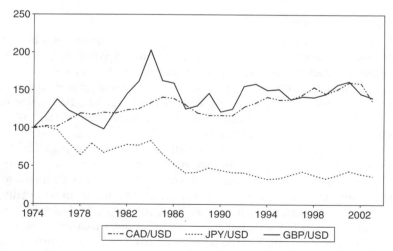

Figure 4.11   Nominal exchange rates against the US dollar (1974 = 100)

single-currency peg, third-currency fluctuations (unrelated to PPP) take on the character of macroeconomic shocks. A multicurrency peg goes some way to preventing unnecessary variations in the real effective exchange rate, output, the balance of trade and inflation that would ensue with a single-currency peg. As far as microeconomic efficiency is concerned, the comparison between single-currency and multicurrency pegging is somewhat more ambiguous. It is arguable that, although these regimes involve uncertainty, pegging to a single currency is less uncertain. This point is emphasized by Corden (2002, p. 77), who points out that a single-currency peg is more easily monitored, which makes it more effective as a nominal anchor.

It is arguable that pegging to a basket that reflects the import-weighted effective exchange rate is more suitable for developing countries. By weighting changes in the exchange rates of major industrial countries by their import shares, the effect on the average level of local prices of variations in exchange rates is offset. The problem for developing countries as a whole is that their cross-rates will not be stable if they peg to different baskets (which is likely to be the case). For this reason, the Special Drawing Rights (SDR) basket may be chosen to reduce cross-rate variation, which promotes intra-regional trade. Furthermore, pegging to the SDR is convenient from a practical perspective as it has an established value that is calculated and published daily. However, it has the disadvantage that it does not necessarily reflect movements in the 'true' effective exchange rate as compared with the import-weighed effective exchange rate. If the difference between the SDR basket and the import-weighted basket is not significant then pegging to the SDR could be beneficial. On the other hand, Crockett and Nsouli (1977) point out that although the SDR is inferior to the import-weighted basket in reducing fluctuations in import prices, it may be somewhat better in other respects. Since the SDR does a better job than the import-weighted basket in reflecting the world pattern of absorption of primary products, the former is better for stabilizing developing countries' export receipts in domestic currency terms. They also argue that since the dollar has a bigger weight in the SDR basket than its share of world trade, it may be considered as an appropriate reflection of the dollar's relative importance in financial transactions.

Practical classification: intermediate regimes

Given the disadvantages of fixed and flexible exchange rates, some countries may resort to intermediate regimes to combine the advantages of the two systems (this view is rejected by the proponents of the bipolar view). Intermediate regimes include: (i) adjustable pegs, and (ii) crawling pegs. It may be worthwhile to mention that what Corden (2002) calls 'in-between regimes' are not the same as the intermediate regimes. For example, he classifies currency boards as an 'in-between' regime because this regime falls (in terms of exchange rate flexibility) between the absolutely fixed rate regimes and fixed but adjustable rates. He also considers managed floating, target zones and crawling pegs as in-between regimes because they fall in-between pure floating and fixed but adjustable rates.

Adjustable pegs

Under adjustable pegs (fixed but adjustable exchange rates), the country undertakes an obligation to defend the peg, but reserves the right to alter the exchange rate to correct a fundamental disequilibrium. The rationale for using an adjustable peg is to secure the advantages of nominal exchange rate stability (avoidance of unnecessary exchange rate changes in response to temporary shocks and the provision of anti-inflationary discipline), while avoiding the disadvantages of a misaligned rate in the face of prolonged disequilibria. A question that immediately arises is how developing countries can operate such a system, given that it broke down in 1973 as far as industrial countries are concerned. The answer is that industrial countries found the system unworkable in the face of enormous increases in capital mobility, whereas most developing countries have controls over capital movements.

A distinction is made between single-currency adjustable pegs and multicurrency adjustable pegs. Collier and Joshi (1989) argue that the abandonment of the idea of permanent pegging strengthens the case for multicurrency adjustable pegs. From a macroeconomic perspective, multicurrency pegging scores over single-currency pegging. On the other hand the possible microeconomic superiority of single-currency over multicurrency pegging disappears if the peg is adjustable, since the exchange rate is no longer stable against the anchor currency.

The main problem with the adjustable peg arrangement is that it tends in practice to lead to delayed adjustment of the exchange rate, which is exactly what happened under the Bretton Woods system. This is because the government is tempted to manage the balance of payments for prolonged periods with a fixed nominal exchange rate combined with international borrowing and trade controls of increasing severity. This has adverse implications for the macroeconomic balance and microeconomic efficiency. Since the adjustable peg regime tends in practice to breed trade controls, this arrangement loses the anti-inflationary anchor of a genuinely fixed exchange rate. As for microeconomic efficiency, the reliance on permanent trade controls, which is a characteristic of adjustable peg regimes, is clearly highly inimical to efficiency.

Crawling pegs

One variation on fixed exchange rates that is common among high-inflation developing countries is the crawling peg, whereby the government announces a schedule of small, discrete devaluations. The underlying idea is to prevent inflation differentials from cumulating, making it necessary to have one big devaluation. Crawling pegs were first introduced in Brazil and Colombia in the 1960s.

A country adopting a crawling peg undertakes an obligation to defend the peg but either commits itself to moving the peg in small steps in accordance with a preannounced rule or reserves the right to change the peg in small steps that are discretionary in size and timing. This is called a discretionary crawling peg. Like the adjustable peg, a crawling peg involves a choice between pegging to a single currency and pegging to a basket of currencies. Again, the presumption is that pegging to a basket is superior.

Rule-based crawling (or passive crawling or PPP crawling) generally takes the form of adjusting the nominal exchange rate sufficiently to keep the real exchange rate constant (that is, by an amount sufficient to offset the difference between domestic and foreign inflation). This process is shown in Figure 4.12. If the domestic inflation rate is higher than the foreign inflation rate, then the price ratio (P^*/P) declines, which means that the real exchange rate should decline (the domestic currency appreciates in real terms). In order to avoid real appreciation (hence, the loss of competitiveness), the nominal exchange rate is raised (the domestic currency is devalued in nominal terms).

On the criterion of microeconomic efficiency, the PPP crawl is superior to a fixed exchange rate and adjustable peg since it stabilizes the profitability of trading in real terms. As for the internal balance and external balance, the advantage of PPP crawling is that corrective changes in the nominal exchange rate are carried out frequently and automatically, in which case real exchange rate misalignments arising out of differential rates of inflation are not allowed to build up. Furthermore, this arrangement allows a country to have a different inflation rate from its trading partners without being subject to adverse output effects. However, one has to bear in mind that there is

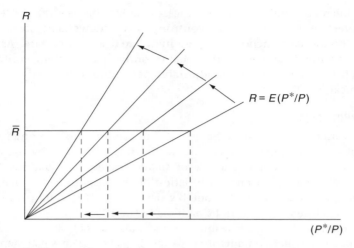

Figure 4.12 Keeping the real exchange rate constant via a crawling peg

no external anchor against inflation, which means that domestic monetary policy has to be used for controlling inflation. A further objection to a PPP crawl is that keeping the real exchange rate constant is inappropriate if there are permanent real shocks (in such a case the appropriate real exchange rate changes). For example, if there is an exogenous and permanent terms of trade deterioration, the currency would have to be devalued in real terms more than the simple PPP formula would suggest.

Because of these problems, a discretionary crawling peg (active crawling peg) may be used. But it is desirable that the discretion should be limited, since the presence of complete discretion often leads bureaucracies in the direction of inertia or bending to special interests. Therefore, it is better to use something like a modified PPP crawl, which operates on the following lines. Under this framework, there is a rule postulating that the nominal exchange rate should be altered with regularity to keep the real exchange rate constant and a proviso that the rule can be overridden if a clear case can be made for a larger or smaller exchange rate adjustment (i) to compensate for mistakes in the initial level of the real exchange rate, (ii) in response to real shocks, and (iii) as deliberate non-compensation for anti-inflationary purposes. Discretionary crawling pegs have been part of the exchange rate-based stabilization programmes of many Latin American countries. Experience with crawling pegs has been reasonably satisfactory with respect to maintaining competitiveness.

5
The Taxonomy of Exchange Rate Regimes: Official and Behavioural Classification Schemes

Introduction

This chapter deals with the official and behavioural classifications of exchange rate regimes. The official classification of the IMF is the most common practical classification. This classification scheme is based on what individual member countries tell the IMF about the exchange rate arrangements they have in place. In recent years, economists started to develop systems of behavioural classification of exchange rate arrangements based on the observed behaviour of exchange rates and related variables, such as international reserves. One motivation for these efforts is the desire to find out if the exchange rate regime is irrelevant for economic performance, an issue that will be discussed in Chapter 7 and also in Chapter 8. Distinction is, therefore, made between the announced (*de jure*) and the actually practised (*de facto*) arrangements. Several studies that have made this attempt will be discussed in this chapter.

Some related issues will be considered in this chapter. One of these issues is the bipolar view, the view that countries should adopt either completely fixed or completely flexible exchange rates in preference to any intermediate regime. Another problem pertaining to exchange rate regime choice is the exit problem of why countries find it difficult to move from fixed to flexible exchange rates. And there is also the verifiability problem of ascertaining which exchange rate regime is actually in place if the exchange rate is neither perfectly fixed nor perfectly flexible.

The IMF classification of exchange rate regimes

The IMF regularly publishes exchange rate arrangements reported by its member countries according to its own classification. These can be

Table 5.1 The IMF classification schemes, 1973–96

Period	Classification categories
1950–73	1. Par value or central rate exists 2. Fixed or flexible rate other than par value or central rate applicable to all or most transactions
1974–82	1. Exchange rate maintained within narrow margins against a single currency or a basket of currencies 2. Exchange rates not maintained within narrow margins
1983–96	1. Pegged to a single currency or a basket 2. Limited flexibility with respect to a single currency, cooperative arrangement (the EMS) 3. More flexible arrangements: adjusted according to a set of indicators, other managed floating 4. Independent floating

found in the annual publication *Annual Report on Exchange Arrangements and Exchange Restrictions* as well as the monthly publication *International Financial Statistics*. Table 5.1 shows the classification categories used by the IMF during the period 1950–96.

Starting in 1997 and until the end of 1998, the IMF classification comprised the following categories:

1. Fixed exchange rates, including those pegged to the US dollar, French franc, British pound, German mark, Russian rouble and other currencies, as well as those pegged to the SDR and other baskets.
2. Limited exchange rate flexibility, in which case the domestic currency is allowed to move within a very narrow range against another currency. Another arrangement that falls under this category is joint floating, which is also called limited flexibility with respect to a cooperative arrangement. This system comprised the currencies of the member countries of the EMS.
3. More flexible arrangements, including (i) adjusted according to a set of indicators, (ii) other managed floating, and (iii) independent floating. Adjustment according to indicators is the system of crawling peg, whereby the exchange rate is adjusted periodically according to one or more indicators, such as inflation. Managed floating involves heavy central bank intervention, whereas independent floating involves occasional intervention that is intended mainly to counter speculative pressure.

As of 1 January 1999, a new classification system was implemented. The new system is comprised of the following exchange rate regimes:

1. Fixed exchange rates, including (i) exchange rate arrangements without a separate legal tender, (ii) currency board arrangements, and (iii) other conventional fixed peg arrangements.
2. Limited exchange rate flexibility, which includes the system of pegged exchange rates with horizontal bands.
3. Managed floating, including (i) crawling pegs, (ii) exchange rates with crawling bands, and (iii) managed floating with no preannounced path for exchange rates.
4. Independent floating.

The following is a brief description of these exchange rate arrangements. Under arrangements with no separate legal tender, the currency of another country circulates as the sole legal tender. Alternatively, a country may belong to a monetary or currency union in which the same legal tender is shared by members of the union. This includes the European countries using the euro as well as members of other currency unions (for example, Grenada is part of the East Caribbean Currency Union). A currency board, which we dealt with in some detail in Chapter 4, is an arrangement that is based on an explicit legislative commitment to exchange the domestic currency for a specified foreign currency at a fixed exchange rate, combined with restrictions on the issuing authority to ensure the fulfilment of its legal obligation. Other conventional fixed peg arrangements include pegging to a single currency and pegging to a basket of currencies, such as the SDR. Under this arrangement, the country pegs its currency at a fixed exchange rate to a single currency or a basket of currencies, allowing the actual exchange rate to fluctuate in a narrow margin of less than ±1 per cent around a central rate (the rate determined by the arrangement). Examples are Bahrain (the US dollar) and Kuwait (undeclared basket until the end of 2002, after which the country switched to pegging to the US dollar). An arrangement of pegged exchange rates with horizontal bands is similar, except that the band within which the exchange rate is allowed to fluctuate is wider than ±1 per cent (an example is Egypt).

Under managed floating falls the arrangement of a crawling peg whereby the exchange rate is adjusted periodically at a fixed, preannounced small rate or in response to changes in some quantitative indicators (for example, inflation). An arrangement of crawling bands requires the exchange rate to be maintained within a certain band

around a central rate that is adjusted periodically at a fixed preannounced rate or in response to changes in some indicators (an example
is Romania). Under an arrangement of managed floating with no preannounced path, the exchange rate is determined by market forces but
the monetary authority intervenes actively in the foreign exchange
market without specifying a path for the exchange rate (examples are
Vietnam and Thailand).

Under independent floating the exchange rate is determined by market forces. Any intervention in the foreign exchange market aims at
curbing exchange rate volatility. Examples of the countries adopting
this arrangement are Australia, the USA and the UK. Nitithanprapas
and Willett (2002) argue that the least useful feature of the IMF classification is the distinction between independent floating and managed
floating. According to the IMF's Annual Report, the exchange rate under
independent floating is determined by market forces, such that any
foreign exchange intervention is aimed at moderating the rate of change
and preventing undue fluctuations in the exchange rate, rather than at
establishing a level for it. Under managed floating, attempts are made to
influence the movements of the exchange rate through active market
intervention. Nitithanprapas and Willett (2002) correctly argue that this
distinction is not useful for analytical purposes, suggesting instead a
distinction between 'lightly' and 'heavily' managed floating. Bofinger
and Wollmershauser (2001) distinguish among 'pure floating', 'managed floating' and 'independent floating' by constructing an index of
floating as the ratio of the sum of effective changes in reserves to the
sum of absolute changes in reserves. When the index is close to +1 or
−1, the underlying regime can be considered as managed floating
because these values can be interpreted to imply that the central bank
has tried to influence the trend of the exchange rate.

De facto versus *de jure* classification

The IMF classification of exchange rate regimes that is published regularly in the IMF's *Annual Report on Exchange Rate Arrangements and
Exchange Restrictions* is based on self-declaration by member countries
as to which category they belong to. Countries are required to notify
the IMF of their exchange rate arrangements within 30 days of becoming members and promptly after any regime change. Yet, actual experience may suggest that countries do not practise what they declare,
implying the presence of a gap between *de facto* and *de jure* exchange
rate arrangements.

The *de jure* classification is based on the announcements made by members of the IMF on the grounds that announcing a regime has important forward-looking credibility effects. The *de facto* classification (also called the behavioural classification) starts with the premise that for various reasons (including fear of floating and lack of credibility) countries do not do exactly what they say they do. This classification is based on the observed behaviour of exchange rates, international reserves and other variables. Nitithanprapas and Willett (2002) argue that the IMF classification suffers from two serious problems: (i) it does not distinguish between all of the major different categories of exchange rate regimes that are relevant for research, and (ii) it is based on national government statements that their exchange rate policies and their official descriptions often differ greatly from actual practices. They give the following examples:

- In 1996, the Philippines was identified as having a floating rate, but in practice the exchange rate against the dollar moved within a narrow range.
- As of 31 December 1997, Brazil is classified under pegged within horizontal bands, but in practice the system is a crawling peg.
- As of 31 December 1997, China is classified under pegged with horizontal bands, but in practice it is a conventional peg.
- As of April 1999, Pakistan is classified under managed floating but in practice it is a dollar peg.

Kawai (2003) argues that the reported arrangements do not always describe the actual practices of exchange rate policies, nor do they offer sufficient information as to which currency or basket of currencies is chosen as a target *de facto* exchange rate stabilization. For example, Eichengreen (1999b) points out that a number of countries that report their regime as one of limited or managed flexibility attempt in practice to hold their exchange rates within a relatively narrow range or to peg it formally. Levy-Yeyati and Sturzenegger (2000a) similarly argue that 'many alleged floaters intervene in the exchange market while several fixers devalue periodically to accommodate independent monetary policies'. They refer to the 'fear of floating' by putting forward the idea that countries claiming to float do not allow their nominal exchange rates to move freely. Calvo and Reinhart (2002) confirm the fear of floating by showing that emerging economies shy away from substantial exchange rate volatility by intervening actively in the foreign exchange market.

Levy-Yeyati and Sturzenegger (2000a) also argue that many countries that in theory have flexible rates intervene in the foreign exchange market so pervasively that in practice very little difference (in terms of observable performance) exists between them and countries that have explicit fixed exchange rate regimes. Conversely, they argue, periodic devaluations of pegs in inflation-prone countries are the result of the implementation of monetary policies that are inconsistent with fixed exchange rates, which makes the effective regime closely resemble a flexible arrangement. Frankel (1999) points out that 'most of the countries classified as having fixed exchange rates have in fact had realignments recently and that most of those listed as having floating exchange rates intervene in the foreign exchange market frequently'. Reinhart and Rogoff (2004) talk about 'the pegs that float' and 'the floats that peg'.

Alesina and Wagner (2003) consider the factors and institutional characteristics that make countries fearful of following through with actions what they announce in words, thus reneging on announce-ments of exchange rate regimes. Therefore, they identify the forces that lead countries to announce a peg and practise floating and vice versa. They find that countries (and periods) with relatively poor political institutions (more corruption, less protection of property rights and so on) are less able to stick to their announcements of fixing, ending up floating. This is probably indicative of the inability of the government to maintain macroeconomic stability, which is a precondition for hold-ing pegs. On the other hand, countries that announce floating then follow fixed rates tend to have relatively good institutions.

It is easier to present arguments for why certain countries may aban-don pegs than for why countries announce floating then peg. Calvo and Reinhart (2002) explain it in terms of the effect of nominal volatility on the risk premia paid on borrowing, as monetary and exchange rate volatility affect the credibility of the country. Another argument is that currency depreciation may be perceived by the market as an indicator of turbulence and monetary fragility. Alesina and Wagner (2003) put for-ward the idea that 'the fear of floating may be viewed as a signalling device to create confidence in the country'. They also provide answers to the question 'why announce a float then peg rather than simply announce a peg and stick to it'. Interestingly, they provide measures of 'cheating' or the extent of broken promises as the difference between the IMF's *de jure* classification and the *de facto* classification. Finally, Bubula and Otker-Robe (2002) explain the divergence between what countries announce and what they do in practice in terms of concern about the political cost of undertaking visible devaluation under a formally announced peg. They also mention the fear of floating and the desire to limit the potential impact of depreciation on inflation and balance sheets when there is a high degree of dollarization or large foreign currency exposure in the domestic economy.

A few studies have reconsidered the IMF classification either by extending it into a more informative and meaningful classification (for example, Ghosh *et al.*, 1997; Bubula and Otker-Robe, 2002) or by reclassifying countries according to purely statistical criteria. Frankel (2003) argues that although the IMF's current classification system does not follow countries' self-description as slavishly as it did before 1999, it is 'useful to keep in mind that it is nevertheless an official or *de jure* classification'. Bubula and Otker-Robe (2002) construct a monthly database (covering the period 1990–2001) of *de facto* exchange rate regimes of all IMF members using the IMF's 1999 classification scheme. The database also provides refinements on some regime categories, distinguishing backward-looking crawls (when the crawl aims at accommodating past inflation differentials) from forward-looking ones (when the exchange rate is adjusted at a preannounced rate) and tightly managed floats (when intervention takes the form of very tight monitoring that results in a stable exchange rate) from other managed floating regimes (when the exchange rate is influenced in a more ad hoc fashion). This classification is based primarily on information obtained through bilateral discussions with member countries and from contacts with the IMF desk economists. Rogoff *et al.* (2004) identify two points of strength in the Bubula and Otker-Robe classification: (i) the use of quantitative and qualitative information, and (ii) the coverage (with updating) of all IMF member countries. On the other hand, they refer (as a point of weakness) to the requirement of subjective judgement, which may differ across countries and over time.

Kawai (2003) argues that to understand what exchange rate arrangements are actually in place, one must examine statistically the behaviour of observed exchange rates. One way to do this is to use regression analysis following Frankel and Wei (1993, 1994, 1995) and Kawai and Akiyama (1998, 2000) to identify which major currency or currency basket is chosen as an anchor for a particular country's exchange rate stabilization and how closely such a relationship can be observed. Kawai (2003) classifies the observed exchange rate arrangements of developing economies according to exchange rate volatility into three broad categories: (i) pegged, (ii) intermediate, and (iii) flexible. Volatility is measured in relation to the monthly percentage changes in exchange rate. Hence, a volatility of less than 0.75 per cent indicates a pegged exchange rate, a volatility of 0.75–1.5 indicates an intermediate arrangement, whereas volatility of more than 1.5 indicates a flexible exchange rate.

Based on data covering the period January 1990–December 1999, 56 countries were found to have pegged exchange rates (classified as pegged to the US dollar, to other single currencies and to baskets). Forty-one countries were classified as intermediates (classified officially as pegged to the US dollar, to other single currencies and to baskets of currencies). And 61 countries were found to have flexible exchange rates (officially classified as pegged to the US dollar, other single currencies and baskets). The results show that while an increasing number of developing countries have shifted away from fixed towards more flexible exchange rate arrangements on a reported basis, almost all countries in reality attempted to stabilize their exchange rates against one currency or a currency basket even in the 1990s, although the degree of exchange rate stabilization varied considerably across countries. Many countries regard the US dollar as their anchor currency despite the absence of a formal US dollar-pegged regime. Also, many countries use currency baskets as their anchor without officially announcing it.

Levy-Yeyati and Sturzenegger (2000a) applied cluster analysis to data from all IMF-reporting countries over the period 1974–99 to classify regimes according to the behaviour of their exchange rates and international reserves. They obtained results indicating that: (i) there is no support for the hypothesis that intermediate regimes have been disappearing, (ii) pure floats are associated with only relatively minor exchange rate volatility, (iii) the recent increase in the number of *de jure* floats reflects a more than proportional increase in the number of *de facto* dirty floats, and (iv) an increasing number of *de facto* pegs shy away from an explicit commitment to a fixed regime. They proposed a new *de facto* classification based on the behaviour of three classification variables: nominal exchange rate volatility, $\sigma(E)$, volatility of changes in the nominal exchange rate, $\sigma(\Delta E)$, and volatility of international reserves, $\sigma(R)$. The rationale for choosing these variables is straightforward: fixed exchange rate regimes are associated with high volatility of international reserves coupled with little volatility in the nominal exchange rate, whereas flexible regimes are characterized by substantial volatility in nominal rates with relatively stable reserves. Once the number of groups are determined, cluster analysis is used to sort out the cases according to the characteristics of the three variables. For example, the cluster with high volatility of reserves and low volatility in the nominal exchange rate identifies the group of fixers, whereas the

Table 5.2 The Levy-Yeyati and Sturzenegger classification criteria

	$\sigma(E)$	$\sigma(\Delta E)$	$\sigma(R)$
LYS (2000a)			
Inconclusive	Low	Low	Low
Flexible	High	High	Low
Dirty float	High	High	High
Crawling peg	High	Low	High
Fixed	Low	Low	High
LYS (2001)			
Flexible	High	High	Low
Intermediate	Medium/high	Medium/high	Medium/high
Fixed	Low	Low	High
Inconclusive	Low	Low	Low

cluster with low volatility of international reserves and substantial vola-tility in the nominal exchange rate corresponds to countries with flex-ible arrangements. Table 5.2 shows the classification criteria used in Levy-Yeyati and Sturzenegger (2000a) as well as the slightly modified criteria in Levy-Yeyati and Sturzenegger (2001).

Nitithanprapas and Willett (2002) identify some loopholes in the classification scheme of Levy-Yeyati and Sturzenegger. To start with, they argue that the wide-band crawling peg cannot be distinguished from dirty floating. In addition, their classification does not address the problem that the rate of crawl may change over time. There is also the problem that the classification is not suitable for the study of currency crises, because they classify regimes for countries during a calendar year, which creates a problem when the regime is changed within a year. Rogoff *et al.* (2004) identify the strengths of the Levy-Yeyati and Sturzenegger classification. These are (i) the use of information on the volatility of reserves, and (ii) it is a systematic approach that needs no judgement. On the other hand, they identify the following weaknesses: (i) exchange rate stability or reserve changes may occur for reasons other than inter-vention, (ii) data on reserves may not cover derivatives, (iii) many observations are not classified, and (iv) other countries affect classifica-tion because of the use of cluster analysis.

Reinhart and Rogoff (2004) look at the *de facto–de jure* distinction in terms of the market-determined rates (in parallel markets) rather than the official rates. They argue against the use of reserves as in the Levy-Yeyati and Sturzenegger classification because it gives rise to many cases of 'one classification variable not available'. For example, the

Levy-Yeyati and Sturzenegger algorithm could not provide a classification for the UK until 1987. They find that when market-determined rates are used instead of the official rates it becomes obvious that *de facto* floating was not uncommon during the Bretton Woods era of supposedly pegged exchange rates. By focusing on market-determined rates, they find little difference in exchange rate behaviour between the two periods. The importance of this distinction is the fact that in 1950, 45 per cent of the countries in the sample they examined had thriving illegal parallel markets. Based on this premise, Reinhart and Rogoff (2004) used what they call a 'natural classification algorithm' to come up with their *de facto* classification. If there is no parallel or black market, then they check for an official preannounced arrangement. If there is one, they examine summary statistics to verify the announced regime. If the regime is verified it is classified accordingly, and if not a *de facto* statistical classification is used. If there is no preannounced path for the exchange rate, or the announced regime cannot be verified, the regime is classified on the basis of actual exchange rate behaviour. What is new in this classification scheme is that there is a separate category for countries with an annual inflation rate of over 40 per cent (called 'free falling'). If the country is in hyperinflation (over 50 per cent per month) this is a hyperfloat. Rogoff *et al.* (2004) identify the strengths of the Reinhart–Rogoff classification as (i) the use of free market information, (ii) the separation of 'freely falling' episodes, (iii) the use of long time series, and (iv) it is a systematic approach that needs no judgement. But like the Levy-Yeyati and Sturzenegger classification, it suffers from the weaknesses of (i) attributing exchange rate stability to intervention only, and (ii) failure to classify all countries for all years.

A less well-known *de facto* classification has been proposed by Shambaugh (2004), which is intermediate between the Reinhart–Rogoff and Levy-Yeyati and Sturzenegger classifications. Like the Reinhart–Rogoff classification, it is based solely on the behaviour of the exchange rate, but like the Levy-Yeyati and Sturzenegger classification, it is based on official exchange rates. This classification focuses on whether the exchange rate stays within a band. A country with a one-time realignment but percentage changes of zero in 11 out of 12 months is considered as having a fixed exchange rate. Table 5.3 reconciles the classification schemes.

Nitithanprapas and Willett (2002) have suggested yet another behavioural classification scheme, arguing that other schemes failed to give sufficient attention to the 'microanayltic foundation of the measures'. In particular, they highlight three problems, the first of which is that it

Table 5.3 Reconciliation of classification schemes

Classification	1	2	3	4
IMF	Pegged to a single currency, composite of currencies	Flexibility limited	Managed floating	Independent floating
Reinhart and Rogoff	No separate legal tender up to *de facto* peg	Preannounced crawling peg up to *de facto* crawling band of $\leq \pm 2\%$	*De facto* crawling band of $\leq \pm 5\%$ up to managed floating	Freely floating or freely falling
Levy-Yeyati and Sturzenegger	Fixed	Crawling peg	Dirty float	Flexible
Shambaugh	Zero per cent change in the exchange rate, realignment but zero change in 11 out of 12 months	Stays within 1% bands	Stays within 2% bands	No peg

is inappropriate to use standard deviations or variances when the time series are trended (which is what would happen under crawling pegs) or discrete breaks (which is what happens under adjustable pegs). The second problem is that the concept of the 'propensity to intervene' in the face of market pressure is clearly defined only in the case of intervention that 'leans against the wind', which makes the variance ratio an improper indicator. The third issue is the extent to which exchange rate policy is mutually determined with monetary policy (the degree to which market intervention is sterilized). Furthermore, they suggest that a more appropriate measure of exchange rate flexibility is currency market pressure measured with reference to changes in reserves as opposed to changes in the exchange rate, which is what they call the 'propensity to intervene'. They also argue that changes in reserves are an imperfect proxy for official intervention in the foreign exchange market. They classify exchange rate regimes into the following categories: (i) hard fixes, (ii) narrow-band sticky pegs, (iii) crawling pegs/ bands, (iv) heavily managed floating, and (v) lightly managed floating. The empirical results reveal that, in some cases, this classification produces substantially different results from other schemes.

Ghosh *et al.* (1997) assert that neither the *de jure* classification nor the *de facto* classification is entirely satisfactory. They argue that while the *de facto* classification has the obvious advantage of being based on observable behaviour, it does not allow a distinction between stable exchange rates resulting from an absence of shocks and stability that results from policy actions offsetting shocks. Therefore, they argue, the *de facto* classification 'fails to capture what is perhaps the very essence of an exchange rate regime, the commitment of the central bank to intervene in, and subordinate its monetary policy to, the foreign exchange market'. By contrast, the *de jure* classification captures this formal commitment, but it 'fails to control for actual policies inconsistent with the commitment'. In the case of pegged exchange rates, this leads to either a collapse or frequent changes of parity, transforming a *de jure* peg into a *de facto* float. They suggest instead using a combination of the two approaches: using the IMF's *de jure* classification as the primary classification together with a secondary classification whereby pegged regimes are divided into 'frequent' and 'infrequent' adjusters. The frequent adjusters are those changing the par value or the weights of the basket more than once per year.

Ghosh *et al.* (2002, p. 39) again show their lack of enthusiasm for *de facto* classifications, arguing that the exchange rate regime might be best defined by the stated intentions of the central bank (which every IMF member country is required to report and publish every year), *resulting* in the *de jure* classification. This classification, they argue, emphasizes the importance of public pronouncements as a signal for private sector expectations. This argument is similar to that used to justify the validity of estimating and testing econometric models using data suffering from measurement errors on the grounds that economic behaviour is based on observed data. If two countries have identical monetary histories, the announced exchange rate regime matters because 'it conveys information about future policy intentions, thus influencing expectations and outcomes'.

Then they go on to demonstrate that *de facto* classifications have their own drawbacks. Unlike the *de jure* classification, which conveys information about future policy intentions, observed behaviour pertains to the past. Moreover, *de facto* classifications encounter a lot of problems, which make it rather difficult to infer the underlying regime from the observed behaviour of exchange rates and related variables. One of the problems that have been mentioned is the difficulty of interpreting changes in reserves. Ghosh *et al.* (2002) come up with what they call a 'consensus classification' by using 'the intersection of the *de jure* classification and their own *de facto* classification'. They compute a continuous behavioural *de facto* measure then convert it into a discrete three-way classification into pegged, intermediate and floating regimes using the relative frequency distribution of regimes in the *de jure* classification. They define the *de facto* measure as

$$z = \sqrt{\bar{\dot{E}}^2 + \sigma^2(\dot{E})} \tag{5.1}$$

where $\bar{\dot{E}}$ is the mean of the monthly percentage change in the nominal exchange rate and $\sigma^2(\dot{E})$ is its variance.

Rogoff *et al.* (2004) describe the Ghosh *et al.* (2002) classification as 'fine taxonomy, proclaiming the use of quantitative and qualitative information as a point of strength'. On the other hand, they identify the following aspects of weakness: (i) reliance to a large extent on stated policy intentions, which may deviate significantly from what is actually practised; (ii) the requirement of subjective judgement, which may differ across countries and over time; and (iii) failure to cover all countries for all time periods.

The bipolar view and the hollowing out hypothesis

The bipolar view (also called the bipolar solution and the corner solution) is the view that it is better for countries to adopt one of the extreme systems of totally fixed or perfectly flexible exchange rates and shy away from intermediate arrangements. The tendency of countries to do this is called the hollowing out hypothesis, the hypothesis of the missing middle, the hypothesis of the excluded middle, the hypothesis of the vanishing intermediate regime and the hypothesis of the unstable middle. Eichengreen (1994) is the initiator of the hollowing-out hypothesis, postulating that intermediate regimes are inherently vulnerable to capital flows, which makes them bound to disappear in a world of integrated capital markets. According to Levy-Yeyati and Sturzenegger (2000a), the hypothesis is confirmed by the collapse of pegs in South East Asia and Latin America, the swift move to monetary integration in Europe following the EMS crisis of 1992, and the adoption of the dollar as legal tender in some countries like Ecuador. Hernandez and Montiel (2001) argue that the Asian crisis of 1997–98 has played a key role in generating the perception of a 'vanishing middle ground for exchange rate regimes in developing countries'.

The rationale for the tendency to adopt one of the two extremes is rather different from the traditional textbook arguments. The new argument is that this tendency is a response to the volatility of capital flows and the threat of self-fulfilling speculative attacks. Frankel *et al.* (2001) argue that one reason why intermediate regimes have fallen out of favour is that they are not transparent and that it is difficult to verify them. They also argue that intermediate exchange rate regimes are 'no longer feasible' and that 'they are going the way of the dinosaurs'. They make the interesting observation that the bipolar view has gone 'from birth to conventional wisdom in a remarkably short period of time'.

As stated earlier, the original reference to the hypothesis of the 'vanishing intermediate regime' is believed to be Eichengreen (1994), who made it in reference to European countries following the EMS crisis of 1992 and the (consequent) band widening of 1993. Obstfeld and Rogoff (1995) argue that even a wide-band system would pose difficulties and that there is little 'comfortable middle ground between floating rates and the adoption by countries of a common currency'. Eventually, European countries leaped from wide bands to a currency union in 1998–99. After the Asian crisis of 1997–98 the hypothesis of the vanishing intermediate regime was applied to emerging economies. Summers (1999a) argued in the aftermath of the crisis that 'in a world of freely flowing capital there is shrinking scope for countries to occupy the middle ground of fixed but adjustable pegs'. Subsequently, the IMF decided that countries that get in trouble by following an intermediate regime will in the future not be bailed out. *The Economist* (1999, pp. 15–16) summarized the status quo by saying that 'most academics now believe that only radical solutions will work: either currencies must float freely or they must be tightly tied through a currency board or, even better, currency union'. In a nutshell, Frankel *et al.* (2001, p. 355) argue that countries facing rapidly disappearing foreign exchange reserves 'had little alternative but to abandon their pegs and baskets and bands and crawls and move to a float, unless they were prepared to go to the opposite corner'.

The bipolar view seems to have been accepted by a large number of economists despite the fact there is no agreement on the theoretical foundation of the hypothesis. There are three possible explanations: the impossible trinity, the dangers of unhedged dollar liabilities and the political difficulty of exiting. While these explanations have elements of truth, none of them can stand alone as a theoretical rationale for the superiority of the corner solution over intermediate regimes.

The principle of the impossible trinity (or trilemma), which originated in the work of Mundell (1963) and Fleming (1962), postulates that a country must give up one of three objectives, which cannot be maintained simultaneously: (i) exchange rate stability, (ii) monetary independence, and (iii) financial market integration (capital mobility).

Given that financial markets are becoming increasingly integrated, a choice must be made between exchange rate stability and monetary independence. Summers (1999b) describes the trilemma by saying that 'capital mobility, an independent monetary policy, and the maintenance of a fixed exchange rate objective are mutually incompatible', which means that 'as capital market integration increases countries will be forced increasingly to move to pure floating or more purely fixed exchange rate regimes'. Bordo (2003) gives a very interesting historical account of the impossible trinity. Under the gold standard, fixed exchange rates were maintained with capital mobility because monetary policy was not geared to full employment.The gold standard collapsed in the interwar period because the target of full employment became important. The Bretton Woods era encompassed fixed exchange rates and monetary independence because extensive capital controls were in place. And recently, the same factor led to the bipolar view that with high capital mobility a choice is made between hard pegs and floating (developed countries are currently either floating or part of the EMU). Frankel *et al.* (2001) dispute this line of reasoning by arguing that it is possible to give up half of each and to pursue a peg that is abandoned whenever there is a shock that is large enough to use up half its reserves.

The second explanation is that when a government establishes an exchange rate target, its banks wrongly believe that this system would not break down, becoming tempted to incur huge dollar liabilities (which is what happened during the Asian crisis). When currency devaluation takes place, domestic firms find themselves unable to service their debts, inflicting devastating damage on the economy when they go bankrupt as a result. Eichengreen (1999b) points out that if the exchange rate moves regularly, firms will have an incentive to hedge their positions, thus advocating a move towards flexible exchange rates. Frankel *et al.* (2001) undermine this line of reasoning on several grounds, including the possibility that 'a country would be better off by gratuitously introducing extra noise into the exchange rate'. A third explanation is that governments that adopt fixed exchange rates react to a major reversal of capital inflows rather sluggishly, waiting too long before abandoning the fixed exchange rate (the exit problem). The problem is that exiting from fixed exchange rates can be difficult politically.

The bipolar view does not go without real challenge. Reinhart and Reinhart (2003) argue that the hypothesis of the excluded middle is a fallacy that is contrary to theory and evidence. Reinhart (2000) and Calvo and Reinhart (2002) have documented the record of what countries do rather than what they report and found that the excluded middle is indeed a fallacy. This is because exchange rate regimes in developing countries exhibit limited flexibility to the extent that they become either 'very dirty floats' or 'quite soft pegs'. The tendency to resort to such systems is a reflection of unwillingness on the part of the authorities to trust the foreign exchange market. For Calvo and Reinhart, this is evidence of the fear of floating. Frankel (2003) talks about 'the rise and fall of the bipolar view', arguing strongly for the lack of theoretical justification. And while Bubula and Otker-Robe (2002) provide informal evidence indicating that the proportion of countries adopting intermediate regimes has been shrinking in favour of greater flexibility or greater fixity, analysis based on Markov chains of regime transition provides mostly evidence against the bipolar view.

Opposition to the bipolar view is not insignificant. For example, Irwin (2004) contends that the failure of the Argentine currency board in January 2002, more than a decade after its inception, suggests that one element of the corner solution is questionable. Frankel (1999) points out that although there are understandable reasons for believing in the bipolar view, the generalization is in danger of being overdone. He also argues that most of the countries classified as having fixed exchange rates have had realignments and that most of those listed as having floating rates intervene in the foreign exchange market frequently. Support for the middle ground is also found in Goldstein (2002) and Williamson (1999, 2000a, 2000b, 2002). Williamson argues for inter-mediate regimes on two grounds: (i) corner solutions too can be subject to market pressure, as illustrated by speculative attacks on the currency boards of Hong Kong and Argentina; and (ii) some types of intermediate regimes (for example, bands, baskets and crawls) could help prevent misalignment, providing greater flexibility to cope with shocks, whereas some corner regimes could generate misalignments that could damage sustainability. More recently, Rogoff *et al.* (2004) argued in a lengthy study that 'the bipolar view is neither an accurate description of the past nor a likely scenario for the next decade'.

Edwards (2001) believes that support for the bipolar view in the case of developing countries is largely based on the shortcomings of intermediate regimes, not the historical merits of the two extremes, with which developing countries have had little experience. He also argues that while the bipolar view has become increasingly popular in the academic circles in the USA and Europe, it is resisted in other parts of the world, particularly in Asia. For example, the Asian Policy Forum (2000, p. 4) has argued that 'the two extreme exchange rate regimes ... are not appropriate for Asian economies' and that 'an inter-mediate exchange rate system that could mitigate the negative effects of the two regimes would be more appropriate for most Asian economies'.

An attempt has been made by Masson (2001) to test the hollowing out hypothesis that eventually all regimes do converge to fixed or float-ing. By using a Markov chain model of exchange rate transition, he tested two versions of the hypothesis: (i) hard pegs are an absorbing state (lack of exit from the regime), and (ii) fixes and floats form a closed set with no transition to intermediate regimes. The results provide some support for the first version of the hypothesis, indicating that inter-mediate regimes will 'continue to constitute a sizeable proportion of actual exchange rate regimes'. On the other hand, Bubula and Otker-Robe (2003) claim some supporting evidence for the bipolar view by finding that intermediate regimes (which they define as soft pegs and tightly managed floating regimes) are more crisis-prone than both hard pegs and other floating regimes.

The exit problem

The exit problem pertains to the transition from pegged to adjustable exchange rates. According to Eichengreen (1999a), the historical experi-ence of a number of countries shows that exit has occurred under unfavourable conditions and speculative pressure, producing adverse results (for example, the EMS crisis of September 1992). These episodes are also associated with negative economic outcomes and loss of credi-bility by the authorities. Policy-makers have an incentive to cling to the peg in the hope that the storm will pass, which suggests that countries should take advantage of periods when capital is not flowing out to introduce greater exchange rate flexibility. Ideally, this would occur when there is no pressure for either appreciation or depreciation.

Eichengreen (1999a) suggests the following step-by-step procedure to move smoothly:

1. Establishing an alternative nominal anchor, once the pegged exchange rate is no longer the reference point for monetary policy. This may mean adopting an inflation or money supply target.
2. Maintaining confidence once the exchange rate has been removed as an anchor for monetary policy, which may require strengthening fiscal policy and institutions.
3. It is desirable, where possible, to move gradually. Banks and firms have to adapt themselves to the new environment (for example,

exchange rate stability encourages them to acquire large unhedged foreign exchange positions).
4. It will be desirable to continue managing the exchange rate, at least to an extent. Exiting from fixed to flexible exchange rates does not necessarily mean exiting to a free float.
5. It is desirable to strengthen the condition of the banking system before exiting if this can be done without waiting too long.

The IMF has also published a lengthy study on exit strategies, setting the conditions for a successful abandonment of fixed exchange rate regimes (International Monetary Fund, 1998). The study reached the following conclusions:

- Most emerging countries would benefit from greater exchange rate flexibility.
- The probability of a successful exit strategy is higher if the pegged rate is abandoned at a time when capital flows are abundant.
- Countries should strengthen their fiscal and monetary policies before exiting the pegged exchange rate system.

The study also recommended exiting from a position of strength rather than weakness, suggesting that the probability of a successful exit will be higher if the currency appreciates under the new floating regime. This is important for maintaining credibility, which could otherwise be dented under the alternative circumstances of devaluation in the midst of a crisis, which has been invariably the case. Edwards (2001) points out that an appropriate exit strategy amounts to estimating the time when the marginal benefit of maintaining a fixed exchange rate regime becomes equal to the marginal cost of the policy.

Duttagupta and Otker-Robe (2003) conducted some empirical analysis on the determinants of exit from pegged exchange rate regimes over the period 1985–2002, defining exits as involving 'shifts to more or less flexible regimes, or adjustment within the existing regime'. For example, Mexico, Thailand and Brazil exited fixed exchange rate regimes and adopted floating in 1994, 1997 and 1999 respectively. The same had happened to Britain and Italy when they left the EMS in 1992. Adjustment within the regime may take the form of widening a band, which is what happened to the EMS in 1993. Duttagupta and Otker-Robe (2003) distinguished episodes characterized by 'exchange market pressure' from orderly exits. Exits to more flexible regimes are associated with both emerging markets and other developing countries, and an increase in trade openness and government borrowing from banks. They also concluded that economic and financial conditions and regime duration play important roles in determining the future course of exchange rate regimes.

The verifiability problem

Verification is the ability to ascertain that observable exchange rate behaviour is consistent with the preannounced policy. If the announced exchange rate regime is a simple peg, verifiability is easy: it requires no more than checking that the exchange rate today is the same as the exchange rate yesterday. If the announced regime is a pure float, this can also be checked easily: by finding out whether the central bank has intervened in the foreign exchange market as indicated by changes in reserves. It is easier to verify fixed than floating arrangements. However, the verification of a system like a basket band requires months of data to find out if the central bank is indeed implementing the announced policy. It is rather difficult to verify systems like a band around a basket peg or an adjustable peg when the central bank has an explicit or implicit rule of abandoning the peg when an exogenous shock of a particular size occurs and when a particular percentage of foreign exchange reserves have been exhausted.

Hernandez and Montiel (2001) made an attempt to identify how exchange rate regimes changed in Asian countries from the pre-crisis to the post-crisis period. The crisis presumably forced Asian countries to abandon their *de facto* fixed exchange rates and resort to floating. However, it is arguable that these countries tend to use practices that are similar to those of the pre-crisis period by attempting to stabilize their exchange rates against the dollar without any strong commitment mechanism. The evidence Hernandez and Montiel found indicates that the crisis countries are 'floating more than before, though less than real floaters do'. The only exception to this conclusion is Malaysia, which adopted a hard peg and imposed capital controls in the aftermath of the crisis.

Frankel *et al.* (2001) conducted Monte Carlo experiments to confirm the proposition that more complex regimes take a larger amount of data to be verified. A number of factors determine verifiability: the band width, the number of currencies in a basket peg, the rate of crawl, the sample period, and periodic adjustment of central parity. They obtained results confirming the intuition that the amount of information necessary to verify the exchange rate regime increases with the complexity of the regime.

Verification is invariably based on statistical testing. A general model that encompasses various pegged exchange rates can be written as

$$E_{0,t} = \alpha + \beta t + \sum_{i=1}^{n} w_i E_{i,t} + \varepsilon_t \tag{5.2}$$

where $E_{0,t}$ is the exchange rate of the underlying currency against a numeraire, t is time, β is the rate of crawl, and $E_{i,t}$ is the exchange rate of currency i against the numeraire. The stochastic error term reflects the error made by the central bank in setting the exchange rate. For a simple peg, $n = 1$ and $\beta = 0$; for a basket peg, $n > 1$ and $\beta = 0$; for a crawling peg $n = 1$ and $\beta > 0$; and for a crawling basket $n > 1$ and $\beta > 0$.

Exchange rate regime verification does not have to be based on a formal model such as that represented by equation (5.2). It can also be based on some volatility criteria. For example, Hernandez and Montiel (2001) suggest that a fixed bilateral exchange rate would exhibit variation of no more than 2.25 per cent, whereas a clean float would exhibit no intervention in the foreign exchange market, as indicated by changes in reserves. Naturally, one has to correct for exogenous changes in reserves resulting from interest earnings and valuation changes. More specifically, Hernandez and Montiel suggest the use of the following criteria for verification: (i) exchange rate volatility, (ii) foreign exchange reserves, (iii) interest rate volatility, and (iv) severity of shocks.

Some attempts have been made to measure the *de facto* exchange rate flexibility quantitatively (for example, Weymark, 1997 and Poirson, 2001). A popular measure involves the ratio of the average absolute value of the monthly change in reserves normalized by the monetary base in the previous month. A 12-month average is used to eliminate the effect of short-term fluctuations in either reserves or exchange rates, because these do not reflect long-run exchange rate policies. Hence:

$$F = \frac{\sum_{k=0}^{11} |E_{t-k} - E_{t-k-1}|/E_{t-k-1}}{\sum_{k=0}^{11} |R_{t-k} - R_{t-k-1}|/B_{t-k-1}} \tag{5.3}$$

where E is the exchange rate, R is international reserves and B is the monetary base. Another measure of exchange rate flexibility, which has been developed by Calvo and Reinhart (2002), is calculated as

$$F = \frac{\sigma^2(\Delta E)}{\sigma^2(i) + \sigma^2(B)} \tag{5.4}$$

where $\sigma^2(\Delta E)$ is the variance of the change in the exchange rate, $\sigma^2(i)$ is the variance of interest rate and $\sigma^2(B)$ is the variance of the monetary base. And we have already come across the measure of flexibility suggested by Ghosh *et al.* (2002).

6
The History of Exchange Rate Arrangements

Introduction

In Chapters 4 and 5 we examined exchange rate arrangements from theoretical and practical perspectives. Most of these exchange rate arrangements have been experimented with in various shapes and forms in the past 150 years or so as the world went through various international monetary systems. The international monetary system refers to the framework of rules, regulations and conventions that govern the financial relations between countries. The importance of the international monetary system is implied by Adam Smith's (1776) description of it as the 'Great Wheel' because 'when it does not turn well it adversely affects the welfare of nations'.

The international monetary system has two components: (i) a public component consisting of a series of governmental agreements as well as the functions of international public institutions (such as the IMF); and (ii) a private component, which is represented by the banking system and finance industry. In this chapter (and this book) we are concerned with the public component, since it encompasses exchange rate arrangements. The connection between the international monetary system and the exchange rate arrangement is straightforward: one of the criteria used to classify international monetary systems is the degree of exchange rate flexibility, which is also the criterion used earlier to classify exchange rate arrangements. But international monetary systems are also classified on the basis of the nature of international reserves. Thus, we may have a pure commodity standard, where the reserve asset is a commodity such as gold and silver; a pure fiat standard, where reserves consist entirely of fiat currencies (inconvertible into gold); and mixed standards, where reserves consist of commodities and fiat currencies.

Perhaps the best way to illustrate the connection between exchange rate arrangements and international monetary systems is to compare the gold standard and the present system. Under the gold standard there was one exchange rate arrangement: fixed exchange rates. Under the present system, countries can choose any exchange rate arrangement between the two extremes of hard pegs and independent floating, provided that they inform the IMF. Thus, we could have an international monetary system with a single exchange rate arrangement and one that encompasses several arrangements. One has to remember, however, that even under systems that supposedly have one arrangement, other arrangements may coexist with it. For example, not every single country had a fixed exchange rate under the gold standard, and not every single country had a fixed but adjustable exchange rate under the Bretton Woods system. Under these two systems some countries experimented with free floating, managed floating and crawling pegs.

This chapter examines the international monetary systems and exchange rate arrangements that have been used in practice since 1870, which is (more or less) the year that marks the beginning of the classical gold standard. Apart from this system, we will examine, in a chronological order, the interwar period, the Bretton Woods system and the present system (the post-Bretton Woods system) that has been in operation since the early 1970s. We will also contemplate the future.

The classical gold standard

The gold standard is often remembered with nostalgia because the international economy prospered when this system was in operation, while the period that followed its collapse was a dark phase in the economic history of the world. The gold standard did not encompass the entire world but only a core of major countries led by Britain and including France, the Netherlands, Germany and the USA as well as a number of smaller West European countries. There is widespread disagreement on the years that mark the period in which the gold standard was in operation on what can be described as a 'global scale'. The gold standard came to an end abruptly, almost overnight as Cassel (1936) put it, at the beginning of the First World War in August 1914, when the warring countries abolished the convertibility of their currencies into gold and into each other. While the timing of its end is indisputable, the problem is to identify the year that marks the beginning of the system.

Britain went on the gold standard in 1821, when the Bank of England was legally required to redeem its notes and coins in gold and when the prohibition of the melting of coins and the export of gold was repealed (Bordo (2003) actually argues that Britain had been on the gold standard since 1717). In doing so, Britain formally met the conditions of being on the gold standard. By the mid-1870s, France had abandoned bimetallism in favour of gold. In 1870, Germany was still on the silver standard, but war reparations in the form of gold payments from France enabled it to adopt the gold standard. And in 1879, the USA returned to the gold standard after the suspension of gold convertibility during the Civil War. In general, 1870 is regarded as the year in which the gold standard became operational on a global scale. While Ghosh *et al.* (2002, p. 6) argue that 'no single date marks the emergence of the gold standard', they also point out that 'the widespread shift from bimetallic standards to gold in the 1870s and 1880s provides a convenient starting point'. Grubel (1977) puts the beginning of the 'universal gold standard era' at 1880, although Russia, Austria, Hungary, India and Japan did not meet the gold standard requirements until after 1895, and for this reason some observers put the beginning of the system as late as 1900. But Grubel also argues that the exact beginning of the gold standard era is not really important because its effective life represents at the maximum a very short span in the history of the world.

The classical gold standard is based on the following pillars:

- Member countries adhere to gold convertibility of their currencies, a commitment that can be viewed as a mechanism to the pursuit of sound monetary and fiscal policies (Bordo and Kydland, 1996).
- The monetary authority in each country fixes the price of gold in terms of the domestic currency, standing ready to buy or sell any amount of gold at that price.
- This establishes a fixed exchange rate between any two currencies called the 'mint parity'.
- The actual exchange rate can vary above and below the mint parity only between certain limits called the 'gold points', which are determined by the cost of shipping gold between the two countries.

The automatic adjustment in the balance of payments is based on the 'price–specie flow mechanism', where the word 'specie' means precious metal. This mechanism hinges on two assumptions: (i) the money supply consisting of gold or paper money backed by gold, and (ii) the quantity theory of money. Grubel (1977) points out that 'the theoretical blueprint of the basic classical gold standard is based on the assumptions about the real world that are normally made in the teaching of classical economic theory and general equilibrium analysis'. These assumptions are: (i) the economy operates under conditions of perfect competition, (ii) prices and wages are perfectly flexible, (iii) there is always full employment of resources, (iv) money is held for transaction purposes only, and (v) the institutional arrangements determining the transaction demand for money change slowly. Moreover, it is convenient to assume that the money supply consists of gold only, which is also acceptable in the settlement of debt among countries. If these basic assumptions are valid the quantity theory of money holds.

Determination of the mint parity and the gold points

Suppose that the price of an ounce of gold is a units of the domestic currency and b units of the foreign currency. The mint parity, measured as the price of one unit of the foreign currency, is

$$E^M = \frac{a}{b} \tag{6.1}$$

Suppose that the cost of shipping gold between the two countries is a fraction, e, of the value of the gold shipped. From the perspective of the home country, the gold export point, which is the upper limit on the exchange rate, is given by

$$E^U = \frac{a}{b} + e\left(\frac{a}{b}\right) = (1+e)\left(\frac{a}{b}\right) \tag{6.2}$$

The gold export point implies that no resident in the home country would pay more than $(1+e)(a/b)$ units of the domestic currency for one unit of the foreign currency. This is because it is possible to buy a/b units worth of gold of the domestic currency, ship it to the foreign country and sell it for one unit of the foreign currency. Likewise, the gold import point, which is the lower limit on the exchange rate, is given by

$$E^L = \frac{a}{b} - e\left(\frac{a}{b}\right) = (1-e)\left(\frac{a}{b}\right) \tag{6.3}$$

The gold import point implies that no resident of the home country is willing to accept less than $(1-e)(a/b)$ units of the domestic currency for one unit of the foreign currency.

The gold export and import points have some implications for the shape of the supply of and demand for foreign exchange curves. The supply curve becomes infinitely elastic (or horizontal) at the gold export point, whereas the demand curve becomes infinitely elastic at the gold import point. In-between they have the normal upward-sloping and downward-sloping shapes. This is illustrated in Figure 6.1, which shows that the equilibrium

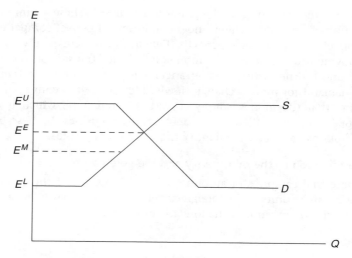

Figure 6.1 Supply and demand curves under the gold standard

exchange rate E^E is above the mint parity rate, E^M. The exchange rate can move between the gold import and export points (E^L and E^U) but not outside this range. The gold points can be viewed as a modern target zone as suggested by Krugman (1991), which allows the monetary authorities some flexibility to conduct expansionary monetary policy by lowering interest rates to compensate for declining output.

The price–specie flow mechanism (PSFM)

The PSFM works as illustrated in Figure 6.2. The process may be described as follows:

- A deficit country loses gold. As soon as the domestic currency dips below the mint parity, people sell it to the central bank for gold and ship the gold overseas, selling it in exchange for the foreign currency. Similarly, a surplus country accumulates gold.
- The movement of gold out of the deficit country causes monetary contraction. This is bound to happen if the central bank keeps a minimum reserve ratio of gold. Similarly, the movement of gold into the surplus country causes monetary expansion.
- Given the quantity theory of money, deficit countries experience deflation whereas surplus countries experience inflation, and this leads to a correction in the balance of payments.

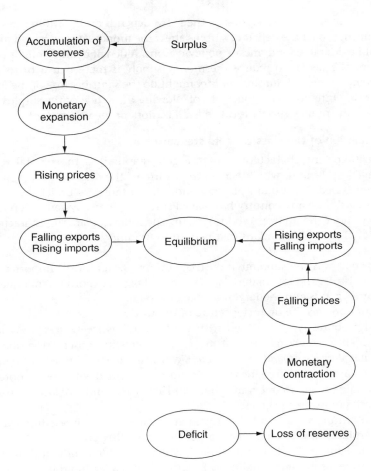

Figure 6.2 The price–specie flow mechanism

It is arguable that the PSFM works not only via changes in relative prices between countries, but also via changes in relative prices (of traded and non-traded goods) within each country. In a deficit country, the prices of non-traded goods decline but the prices of traded goods do not. This is because the latter are determined by the world supply and demand, not by the domestic money supply. Thus, resources will be redistributed in such a way as to increase the production of traded goods and consequently exports.

Moreover, the effectiveness of the PSFM depends on the willingness of countries to let the deficit or surplus affect the money supply, which may not be desirable for domestic policy reasons. A deficit country might not allow the deficit to reduce the money supply if there is fear of rising unemployment. A surplus country might do the same because of the fear of rising inflation. The policy of not allowing the deficit or the surplus to affect the money supply is called 'sterilization' or 'neutralization'.

Evaluation of the classical gold standard

An important characteristic of the gold standard is the pivotal role played by Britain, which was at the centre of the system. In fact, it is often stated that Britain played a more important role under the gold standard than any country has played since under any system, even the USA under the Bretton Woods system. The following are the characteristics of the gold standard that pertain to Britain:

- Britain was the supreme industrial country, a significant importer of foodstuffs and raw materials, the world's biggest exporter of manufactured goods and the largest source of capital.
- London was the financial centre of the world.
- The pound was identified with gold, as it was freely accepted and widely used. Yeager (1976) makes an interesting observation about Jules Verne's *Around the World in Eighty Days*: when Fogg was embarking on his adventure, he took with him a bag filled with pound notes.
- Britain pursued a free trade policy and acted as a lender of last resort in times of exchange crisis.
- Britain played a stabilizing role, particularly the readiness to recycle surpluses into foreign loans rather than hoarding gold.
- The Bank of England functioned as the 'invisible conductor' of the system, as monetary policy in Britain took a leadership role.

The outcome of this environment was (or appeared to be) rather positive. During the gold standard era, world trade and investment flourished, promoting international specialization and global welfare. The balance of payments adjustment mechanism (PSFM) seemed to be working smoothly. And because of such a positive atmosphere, conflicts among countries were extremely rare. So, was the gold standard a success? In retrospect the answer is 'maybe, maybe not'. It is arguable that the apparent success of the gold standard was due to the fact that it existed during a rather tranquil period, which means that it was not really put to the test (for example, against the oil shocks of the 1970s).

Grubel (1977) argues that the short period of the gold standard is held in high esteem because of the system's 'alleged' record of performance in contributing to human welfare. The last half of the nineteenth century witnessed remarkable growth in per capita real income and a movement towards personal and political freedom. But Grubel casts doubt on the contribution of the gold standard to the growth of welfare, attributing the observed increases in overall well-being to the move towards democracy and the acceleration of industrial development that was taking place for other reasons. The gold standard was, therefore, no more than a 'passive agent'. In casting doubt on the macroeconomic effects of the gold standard, some economists and observers refer to the rapid growth witnessed in the post-Second World War period under an alternative system. Moreover, Ghosh *et al.* (2002) note that 'not everything was golden' because both real and financial volatility was present while booms and busts plagued the peripheral countries, which suffered frequent shifts in their terms of trade.

There are two myths about the 'golden age' of the gold standard. The first is that the PSFM worked smoothly and maintained external equilibrium. Historical data show that during the period 1870–1914 prices in major trading countries moved in a parallel fashion, rather than in a divergent fashion as required by the PSFM. Figure 6.3 shows that prices in the USA and Britain moved in the same direction, although the USA was a deficit country while Britain was a surplus country. A problem would also arise if prices were sticky downwards. It can be argued, however, that if prices are flexible upwards, and if prices in surplus countries rise faster than those in deficit countries, the PSFM would still work, but it would be weaker than if prices could actually fall. It was also noticed that small gold flows and relative price changes restored equilibrium. A missing link was the income adjustment mechanism.

The second myth is the proposition that the monetary authorities of various countries followed the 'rules of the game' by allowing gold flows to exert their full influence on the money supply and price level. This was not the case, however, because they sterilized balance of payments imbalances. If so, then a question arises as to what maintained and restored the balance of payments equilibrium. It seems that interest rate changes did the trick. In Britain, changes in the bank rate were the tool whereby equilibrium was restored. Other countries did not have any major degree of monetary independence (they simply followed the Bank of England).

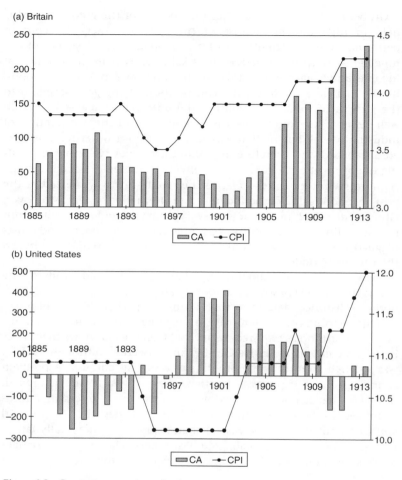

Figure 6.3   Current accounts and prices

Rethinking the gold standard

Taussig (1927) examined statistics of price and gold movements and found
that prices in the major trading countries moved in the same direction,
rather than in a divergent fashion as required by the PSFM. He also found
that small gold flows and relative price changes seemed to restore payments equilibrium. Moosa (2001a) also examined US and British prices
over the period 1885–1913 and found that they were positively correlated.

In general, the whole idea that the gold standard represents an automatic self-equilibrating adjustment mechanism has been questioned.

As a result of the work of Taussig, some theoretical modifications have been introduced to the model of the gold standard. First, the model was adapted to account explicitly for private short-term capital movements. The second modification provided an explanation for the small actual gold movements discovered by Taussig, which is essentially a logical rival to the explanation involving capital movements. In this strand of analysis the classical model of the economy is made more realistic by the explicit recognition of the downward rigidity of real wages and prices. The third adaptation is to discard the one-to-one correspondence between gold lost in balance of payments deficits and reduction in the money supply. This would be the case when there are gold substitutes serving as money, giving rise to what Grubel (1977) calls the difference between a 'gold specie standard' and a 'gold bullion standard'.

One of the pillars of the gold standard that have been questioned is the quantity theory of money, which describes the relationship between money and prices. Two of the underlying assumptions of the quantity theory make it questionable, the first of which is the assumption of full employment. If this is not the case, then an increase in the money supply will cause prices generally to rise much less than under full employment, because the physical volume of output may keep pace with nominal spending. Therefore, the PSFM is unlikely to work if there is unemployment. The second assumption is that costs and prices are flexible (that is, they are responsive to a decrease in money expenditure). If they are sticky, a decrease in nominal spending causes a contraction in the volume of output and employment rather than a decline in costs and prices. Several factors contribute to price and wage inflexibility. Labour is ordinarily resistant to wage cuts and if it is organized in strong unions the power to resist wage cuts is strengthened. Some costs (such as wages under collective bargaining) are contractually fixed for given periods. Any type of monopolistic element tends to reduce cost and price flexibility.

Irrespective of the pluses and minuses of the gold standard, the system collapsed with the outbreak of the First World War as the warring countries suspended the convertibility of their currencies into gold and prohibited gold exports. That was the end of the classical gold standard.

The interwar period

In the period between the end of the First World War and 1926, a system of flexible exchange rates was adopted. During that period many countries experienced hyperinflation: the German hyperinflation of 1919–23 was the most notorious case. There was a desire to go back to the gold standard, but there was an obvious shortage of gold at the prewar levels of the fixed exchange rates. In 1922, the Genoa Conference recommended worldwide adoption of a gold exchange standard, whereby the pound would be convertible into gold while other currencies would be convertible into the pound. In 1925, Britain reestablished the convertibility of the pound into gold. Soon after, other countries restored convertibility at the prewar parities. The gold exchange standard was born.

The gold exchange standard was never based on an explicit agreement among nations, but it rather represents the outcome of a historical evolution. One has to remember that even during the heyday of the gold standard some central banks held national currencies as international reserves. In 1885, the central banks of Denmark, Norway and Sweden were authorized to hold balances with each other and to count these balances as reserves on which to issue notes. In 1849, Russia began to hold some of its reserves in Berlin and other places. According to Nurkse (1944), fifteen European central banks held about 12 per cent of their total reserves in the form of foreign exchange in 1913. The Genoa Conference met to consider the problem caused by the general rise in prices and the retention of the old price of gold, together with the fall in production by one-third. The existing stock of gold became a smaller fraction of world output and trade than it had been before the war. The Conference recommended the gold exchange standard to economize on the use of gold. While official agreement on the implementation of the recommendations was never reached, the basic idea had considerable influence. Most major countries subsequently adopted legislation permitting their central banks to hold gold and foreign assets exchangeable for gold, some without limits on the fraction of reserves to be held as gold. In 1927 and 1928, foreign exchange was about 42 per cent of the total reserves of 25 major countries. But by 1932 that percentage of gold had fallen to 8 per cent.

Things were fine until France (and other countries) decided not to accept any more pounds and to convert foreign exchange holdings into gold at a time when the Great Depression had given rise to serious balance of payments difficulties for Britain. According to Grubel (1977), the urge to convert foreign exchange holdings into gold was motivated by two factors. The first was the desire of some countries to obtain national prestige by serving as world bankers. For a country to serve as a world banker, its currency must be freely convertible into gold, which required the availability of a substantial gold stock. The second factor was that competitive devaluations against gold had the effect of endowing the metal with greater capital value gains than was available on currencies, while reducing the desirability to use currencies as reserves. Ellsworth and Leith (1975) refer to the international financial crisis of 1931, caused by financial panic. It began in Austria where a revaluation of the assets of the Credit Ansalt, the largest commercial bank in Vienna, showed that they had depreciated to the point where the bank was technically insolvent. This revelation led immediately to a withdrawal of foreign short-term credits. A standstill agreement with creditors, followed by restrictions on withdrawals, stopped the run on Austria but did nothing to stem the anxiety that lay behind it. Because of these crises and the lack of agreement, the demise of the system came about. Grubel (1977) argues that 'if agreement on these matters had existed the gold exchange standard might well have worked'.

Beginning with Britain in 1931, one country after another left the gold exchange standard. The immediate reason was the breakdown of confidence following the world economic crisis, but more fundamentally, the reason was the rejection of the internal consequences of the gold standard adjustment mechanism. Price and income deflation is an effective method of eliminating a balance of payments deficit but in the presence of price and wage inflexibility, unemployment is bound to rise. And unless there is a slack in the economy the adjustment mechanism tends to cause inflation in surplus countries. Few countries were willing to pay the price of internal economic and monetary instability for the sake of external equilibrium.

Conflict between domestic equilibrium at full employment, reasonably stable prices and balance of payments equilibrium is most prone to occur in a system of stable exchange rates and freedom of trade and payments. Under such a system the internal and external economies are closely bound together, such that developments in one country directly affect the others. Let us take the example of a country with recession and unemployment but which has a balance of payments equilibrium. To get rid of unemployment, expansionary monetary and fiscal policies must be used. As income and employment respond, the demand for imports will rise, leading to a balance of payments deficit. Some partial compensation may be forthcoming through the foreign repercussions but this cannot be counted upon to prevent a deficit from arising. Thus, a balance of payments deficit is the cost of achieving internal equilibrium at full employment. If a country has large gold reserves it may be able and willing to allow the deficit to continue, but if this is not the case then an expansionary domestic policy is inconsistent with the commitment to the rules of the gold standard. In short, the gold standard imposes constraints on domestic policies that can be expected, at least on certain occasions, to clash head-on with important goals.

So, why did the interwar experiment fail? First because the 'golden age' of the gold standard was actually a myth. Second, the world economy had experienced significant changes because of the war and the Great Depression, including the following: (i) the prewar parities were inappropriate because of widely divergent inflation rates, (ii) prices and wages became rigid (particularly downwards), (iii) countries tended to sterilize balance of payment imbalances on a greater scale because of concern about domestic economic instability, and (iv) London was no longer the single dominant financial centre. Bordo (1993) attributes the short life of the gold exchange standard to flaws in its design, whereas Eichengreen (1992) attributes its demise to a decline in credibility, reflecting the fact that, consequent upon the growth of democracy, monetary authorities had the domestic goal of full employment to satisfy as well as the need to maintain gold convertibility.

Obstfeld *et al.* (2004a) explain what happened in the interwar period in terms of the trilemma: the inconsistency of fixed exchange rates, capital mobility and autonomous monetary policy. They argue that during the interwar period 'the trilemma forcefully made its presence felt for the first time in the great debate over the political economy of macroeconomics'. Furthermore, Eichengreen (1996) and Obstfeld and Taylor (1998, 2004) point out that it was during the interwar period that the ingredients of the trilemma came into collision.

The Bretton Woods system

The Bretton Woods system was born in 1944 in Bretton Woods (New Hampshire) and endorsed by the delegates of 44 countries. The creation of this system was accompanied by the birth of international institutions, including the International Bank for Reconstruction and Development (presently known as the World Bank) and the International Monetary Fund (IMF). The IMF was entrusted with the supervision of the new international monetary system as well as the function of granting loans to deal with balance of payments difficulties, whereas the World Bank specialized in granting loans for the reconstruction of Europe and for development purposes.

Negotiators at Bretton Woods sought an exchange rate system that would combine the advantages of both fixed and flexible exchange rates. The choice was a system of fixed but adjustable exchange rates, the adjustable peg. Therefore, the dollar was pegged to gold at the fixed parity of $35/ounce, and the USA was prepared to buy and sell unlimited amounts of the metal at this price. Other countries were required to declare the par values or parities of their currencies in terms of gold or dollars, and to defend the declared parity rate in the foreign exchange market by buying and selling the dollar. Hence, the dollar became the key and intervention currency. Exchange rates could only vary within the support or intervention points, initially fixed at ±1 per cent. The IMF was given the responsibility of supervising the system and making sure that member countries adhered to the agreement.

Since the system required an adequate supply of monetary reserves, a parallel system of IMF quotas and subscriptions was developed whereby each member country was assigned a quota equal to the subscription. This quota was paid 25 per cent in gold or a currency that is convertible into gold. Borrowing rights were limited to five tranches, where a tranche is equal to 25 per cent of the quota. The first tranche (the gold tranche or the reserve tranche) is unconditional, whereas the other four (credit tranches) require the approval of the IMF. It turned out to be the case that the IMF's pool of international liquidity was totally inadequate. As a result, the USA became the main source of international liquidity growth through its balance of payments deficit. The Bretton Woods system also catered for currency convertibility and multilateral trade. All currencies were to be freely convertible into one another at the official exchange rates. However, because of the consequences of the war, it was agreed that the abolition of controls would be gradual. European currencies did not return to convertibility until 1958.

The problems of the Bretton Woods system

The Bretton Woods system suffered from a number of problems that led to its eventual collapse. The first of these problems pertains to the adjustment mechanism. Multilateral trade and currency convertibility need a real adjustment mechanism, which the system lacked. Governments had to demonstrate the existence of a fundamental disequilibrium in the balance of payments before they could adjust their par values. The adjustable-peg system lacked the stability, certainty and automaticity of the gold standard, and the flexibility of free floating. The second problem is that speculation can be very destabilizing because of the possibility of parity changes. Speculation is destabilizing when traders buy a currency when it is strong, thinking that it will strengthen further, and sell it when it is weak, thinking that it is going to weaken further. Hence, it is a self-fulfilling prophecy, producing actions that can only accentuate exchange rate movements. The reason why speculation tends to be destabilizing under such a system is the one-way option offered to speculators. When a currency is under pressure (perhaps because the country concerned is running out of reserves) it can only be devalued, motivating speculators to sell it.

An important loophole in the system was the defects in the liquidity creation mechanism. In the early 1960s, the prospect of a global liquidity shortage caused widespread concern in official circles as attention focused on proposals for new reserve creation mechanisms. This problem has led to the emergence of the so-called 'Triffin Dilemma' or the 'Triffin Paradox' (Triffin, 1960). To avoid a liquidity shortage, the USA must run a balance of payments deficit, and this would undermine confidence in the dollar. To avoid speculation against the dollar the deficit must shrink, which would create a liquidity shortage. So, it was a vicious circle. One solution to this problem was suggested in 1968, which was the creation of Special Drawing Rights (SDRs) as an international currency. The liquidity shortage receded during the period 1970–72 as international reserves grew rapidly, partly resulting from the allocation of SDRs, but primarily reflecting the expansion of private capital markets and the accumulation of borrowed reserves.

The liquidity problem, in a nutshell, pertains to the provision of an appropriate amount of internationally liquid assets. Sufficient international reserves are indispensable for the operation of a system with fixed or stable exchange rates and a commitment to international payments free of controls. In the absence of an adequate quantity of international reserves to finance temporary balance of payments deficits, there is a general tendency for deficit countries to impose trade and payments restrictions. Alternatively, the task of reducing deficits may force the countries concerned to restrict aggregate demand and employment. In either case, the shortage of liquidity restrains international trade and investment and may result in a general deflationary bias in the world economy.

Let us now elaborate on the adjustment problem and the related confidence problem. From a long-run point of view, the crucial weakness of the Bretton Woods system was the absence of an efficient balance of payments adjustment mechanism (that is, the process whereby disequilibrium is eliminated). Adjustment takes place through: (i) changes in relative national income or price levels, (ii) movements in exchange rates, and (iii) the imposition of direct controls on foreign transactions. The Bretton Woods system outlawed (with some exceptions) the imposition of direct controls. Another principle underlying the system was that exchange rates should be held stable unless a fundamental disequilibrium warrants exchange rate adjustment (a fundamental disequilibrium is the opposite of a temporary, reversible disequilibrium). But then there was the operational difficulty of recognition, because exchange rate adjustment can only be used to correct a fundamental disequilibrium. Several episodes of exchange rate adjustment took place (major European currencies in 1949, France in 1957 and 1958, Germany and the Netherlands in 1961, the UK in 1967, France and Germany in 1969). Yet, the general tendency was to resist exchange rate adjustment until forced by the pressure of the balance of payments position.

Resisting exchange rate adjustment can be attributed to several factors. Devaluation is opposed because it could be perceived as a sign of policy failure, leading to a loss of national prestige. Revaluation is also resisted by the economy's export industries. In the face of a persistent tendency towards balance of payments disequilibrium, the failure to adjust the exchange rate implies either the operation of other adjustment mechanisms or the cumulative worsening of the disequilibrium. The problem is that alternative adjustment mechanisms are not frequently acceptable. Adjustment through price and income changes may be inconsistent with the domestic goals of full employment and price stability. Adjustment through quantitative controls distorts the allocation of resources and reduces economic efficiency. Consequently, the tendency was to adopt a 'wait and see' attitude, hoping that somehow the disequilibrium would vanish eventually.

Using exchange rate adjustment as a last resort to correct balance of payments disequilibrium has several unfortunate aspects. By the time it is used, maladjustments will have accumulated and the disequilibrium deepened, requiring a larger adjustment than would have been required earlier. Moreover, undue delay in correcting disequilibrium can easily cause an aggravation of the problem arising from speculative capital flows. Thus, the longer a deficit continues the more probable becomes currency depreciation, and the longer a surplus continues the more probable becomes currency appreciation. Hence, the risk of capital loss from transferring funds from deficit to surplus countries is virtually zero while the prospect for capital gain is great.

The additional pressure on the foreign exchange market from speculative capital flows compounds the problem of determining the equilibrium level of the exchange rate at which the currency should be repegged (after adjustment). There is no reliable method of determining equilibrium rates, and the deeper the disequilibrium is the more difficult the problem becomes. Because of the difficulty of predetermining equilibrium exchange rates the risk is great that in repegging a currency the level chosen will be either overvalued or undervalued. Corden (2002, p. 14) describes the adjustment problem by arguing that the Bretton Woods system did not turn out to be the way it was intended, pointing out that reluctance to adjust the exchange rates made the system closer to a fixed exchange rate system.

Now, we turn to the related confidence problem. This problem manifests itself in large-scale speculative capital movements, usually induced by the expectation of an imminent sharp exchange rate movement. Expectation of this sort is commonly based on the failure of balance of payments adjustment in the face of persisting disequilibrium, which means that the confidence problem is largely a by-product of the adjustment problem. While speculative capital movements can occur under all international monetary systems and exchange rate arrangements, the Bretton Woods system was particularly vulnerable because of delays in adjustment. Delays lead to the need for an eventual sharp change in exchange rates and eliminate any risk involved in transferring short-term funds from deficit countries to surplus countries.

Several confidence crises were experienced during the 1960s. By 1967, the continuing deficit of the British balance of payments accompanied by dwindling official reserves suggested that the pound would be devalued shortly. The withdrawal of foreign capital from the UK resulted in the inevitable devaluation of the pound from $2.80 to $2.40. In 1968–69, the large German surplus indicated that the mark would soon be revalued. Short-term capital flows moved from France to Germany, leading to the imposition of stringent exchange controls by the French authorities. The inevitable end came with the revaluation of the mark and devaluation of the French franc.

The collapse of the Bretton Woods system

The Bretton Woods era can be divided into two periods: (i) the period of the dollar shortage, 1944–58; and (ii) the period of the dollar glut, 1958–71. The second period was characterized by a significant deficit in the US balance of payments at a time when the surplus countries (Germany and Japan) were resisting revaluation of their currencies. In 1962, France began to exchange dollars for gold despite the objection of the USA. Not only were the French doubtful about the future value of the dollar, but they also objected to the prominent role of the USA in the Bretton Woods system. The French action led other countries to worry about whether sufficient gold would remain for them after the French had finished selling dollars. Under pressure, the USA felt severely constrained, being unable to change its exchange rate.

The status of the dollar as an international reserve currency rested fundamentally on the strength of the US economy and its leading position in the world economy. The symbol of the dollar's status was its convertibility into gold upon demand of official foreign holders (central banks and governments). However, the ability of the USA to maintain convertibility into gold was undermined by a continuing balance of payments deficit, accompanied by an ever-increasing accumulation of dollars in the possession of foreign official agencies. Uneasiness about the future of the dollar grew as the balance of payments position of the USA deteriorated after the mid-1960s. The deterioration manifested itself in a reversal of the surplus into deficit, while it became evident that the dollar was overvalued. Expectations that the dollar would be devalued reached a climax in early 1971, and massive short-term capital flows from the USA ensued. By mid-August 1971, the dollar crisis had reached a stage requiring immediate action. On 15 August 1971, the convertibility of the dollar was suspended (rather, abolished), which effectively marked the end (or the beginning of the end) of the Bretton Woods system. A new pattern of exchange rates was negotiated in the Smithsonian Institution in December 1971. The currencies of Japan and Germany were devalued by 17 per cent and 14 per cent respectively, and exchange rates were allowed to fluctuate within a wider band of ±2.5 per cent. This agreement, however, did not solve any of the problems of the Bretton Woods system.

The first break in the pattern of exchange rates agreed upon in the Smithsonian Agreement affected the pound in mid-1972, when Britain decided to cease support of the exchange rate, allowing it to respond to market forces. As a result, the value of the pound dropped by 10 per cent below the level specified by the Smithsonian Agreement. In 1972, it became evident that the deficit in the US balance of payments was not being corrected by the devaluation of the dollar. By early 1973, another crisis was brewing, as the dollar was devalued by 10 per cent in February (and even that did not work). At the same time, Japan and Italy rescinded their previous policies of maintaining stable exchange rates, joining Britain in allowing their currencies to float. Finally, when foreign exchange markets opened on 19 March 1973, all of the world major currencies were floating. That was the burial of the Bretton Woods system.

The post-Bretton Woods system

The Jamaica Accord of 1987 allowed countries the freedom of choice of the exchange rate arrangement they deemed appropriate for their economies, encouraging them not to resort to competitive devaluation. There was also an agreement to pursue domestic economic policies conducive to stability. Finally, the official price of gold was abolished and replaced with a market-determined price. Currently, major industrial countries adopt a system of floating exchange rates, whereas major European countries (with the exception of Britain) are members of the European Monetary Union.

The current system has not solved the problems of the Bretton Woods system and has failed in three major areas. The first of these is exchange rate misalignment, since misalignment has been the rule rather than the exception, as we saw in Chapter 1. The second area is that the system failed to deliver what was expected from it, policy autonomy, in the sense that it has failed to cut the policy links between countries. The consequence of these links is that economic policy in one country, particularly if it is a major country, leads to effects that are transmitted abroad. This happens mainly because prices move more slowly than nominal exchange rates after a policy change. But then there is the argument that the present system has not delivered the policy autonomy because it is not a system of clean floating. Finally, there is the problem of protectionism. Because of financial deregulation, international capital flows have dominated trade flows in determining exchange rates. The resultant currency misalignments have distorted international competitive positions, leading to strong pressure for protectionism. It seems, after all, that countries have not maintained one of the rules of the game as prescribed by the Jamaica Accord.

In the 1980s and 1990s some major events took place: the Plaza Accord, the Louvre Accord, the EMS crisis, the creation of the EMU and the onset of financial crises. The first of these events is the signing of the Plaza Accord in September 1985 to bring the dollar down. The remarkable appreciation of the dollar in the first half of the 1980s adversely affected the competitive position of the US economy. For example, this development led the giant company, Caterpillar, to lose its share of the market for earth-moving equipment to its competitor, Kamatsu of Japan. Similarly, Eastman Kodak's pre-tax earnings were reduced by $3.5 billion, and its share of foreign markets fell substantially in the period 1980–85. Corporate executives felt that depreciation of the dollar was necessary to restore the competitiveness of their products, and they started to lobby the first Reagan administration to do just that.

At that time, the Treasury Secretary was Donald Regan, an investment banker who firmly believed in the power of the market. He held the view that the market knew better than policy-makers the appropriate levels of exchange rates. Driven by this belief, he opposed active intervention in the market (although the Federal Reserve System participated occasionally with other central banks in concerted intervention, this participation was not full-hearted). In one way, Regan was right not to bother about intervention because it was ineffective, but it seems that the lobbying was effective. In the second Reagan administration, starting in January 1985, James Baker, a lawyer who did not have ideological views against intervention, replaced Donald Regan as Treasury Secretary. In September of the same year, Baker and his counterparts from Japan, Germany, France and the UK signed the Plaza Accord in New York, committing them to concerted central bank intervention to bring the dollar down. The consequent action produced this end result, helped by the fact that the dollar had been depreciating for the previous six months. By early 1987, the dollar had depreciated to reach its 1980 levels, at least against the yen and the German mark. In February 1987, the major seven industrial countries (G7) signed the Louvre Accord, whereby they agreed to cooperate in order to achieve greater stability in the foreign exchange markets.

The EMS and the EMU

Early history and features of the EMS

The agreement to establish the EMS as a 'zone of monetary stability in Europe' was reached in the European Council meeting held in Bremen, Germany, on 6–7 July 1978. The system started functioning on 13 March 1979, while its predecessor, the Snake in the Tunnel, ceased to exist. All members of the European Economic Community (EEC) (nine at that time) agreed to participate in all aspects of the EMS, except the UK, which chose not to join the exchange rate mechanism (ERM).

The core of the EMS is a system of fixed but adjustable exchange rates whereby each currency has a central rate expressed in terms of the European currency unit (ECU). This created a grid of bilateral central rates around a band of ±2.25 per cent, except for the Italian lira (6 per cent). If the exchange rates moved above or below these limits, central bank intervention was obligatory. As a warning device, the grid was supplemented by 'divergence indicators' that measure the divergence of the actual rate against the ECU from the central rate as a percentage of the maximum allowable by the band. Intervention was triggered when the divergence indicator reached a threshold level of 75 per cent.

The second feature of the EMS pertains to the role the ECU played in the system. The ECU performed the following functions: (i) the numeraire for the exchange rate mechanism, (ii) the denominator for intervention and credit operations, (iii) a reference point for the divergence indicator, (iv) a means of settlement, and (v) a reserve asset. Like its predecessor, the European Unit of Account (EUA), the ECU was defined by fixed amounts of the nine currencies of the 1979 EEC member countries. However, a provision was made for periodic reexamination and revision of its components to take account of changes in member countries' economic situations and exchange rates, as well as new member currencies. Table 6.1 shows the composition of the ECU in 1979 and 1993.

Another feature of the EMS pertains to intervention and credit operations. For the financing of intervention in EMS currencies, there were mutual credit lines between the participating central banks, the so-called 'very short-term financing facility'. Other schemes included a 'short-term monetary support' and 'medium-term financial assistance'. At the start of the EMS, the central banks of countries participating in the ERM received an initial supply of ECUs against contributions of 20 per cent of their total gold holdings and gross US dollar reserves to the European Monetary Cooperation Fund (EMCF).

Table 6.1 The composition of the ECU (per cent)

Currency	1979	1993
Belgian/Luxembourg franc	9.40	8.34
British pound	13.80	11.47
Danish kroner	3.00	2.51
French franc	19.70	19.84
German mark	32.80	32.61
Greek drachma	–	0.54
Italian lira	9.70	8.25
Irish punt	1.10	1.04
Netherlands guilder	10.40	10.22
Portuguese escudo	–	0.71
Spanish peseta	–	4.47
Total	100.00	100.00

Developments and the collapse of the EMS

During its early life, the EMS experienced some turbulence that typically produced exchange rate realignment (that is, changes in the central rates of the currencies, involving some devaluations and revaluations). The first realignment took place on 24 September 1979, when the mark was revalued while the Danish kroner was devalued. The first realignment that involved all of the currencies took place on 21 March 1983, when the French franc, Italian lira and Irish punt were devalued while other currencies were revalued. During the period between the inauguration of the system and 11 January 1987, there were eleven realignments. However, tranquility prevailed during the period between January 1987 and September 1992, as the system went through one realignment only on 5 January 1990.

During this period, the pound joined the ERM at a central rate of 2.95 against the mark. The trouble started in September 1992, which was the beginning of the end of the EMS as a fixed but adjustable exchange rate system. Trouble coincided with the removal of capital controls in member countries in the spirit of the 1992 programme to unify financial markets within the European Community. Other relevant factors are the following: (i) the fact that the pound became an ERM currency at an artificially high central rate, (ii) German reunification, and (iii) the recession of 1992. The chain of events was as follows. German reunification put upward pressure on German interest rates, as the demand for funds rose to finance reunification with East Germany. As a result, the German mark started to appreciate against other currencies, at a time when other countries could not defend their currencies by raising interest rates since their economies were sliding into recession. For the UK the situation was even more difficult, as the task of defending what was thought to be an overvalued pound was extremely demanding.

When the crunch came in September 1992, the Bank of England tried to keep the pound within the band prescribed by the ERM, using market intervention and interest rates for this purpose. This action was ineffective in the face of massive speculative pressure on the pound, providing a classic example of the ineffectiveness of intervention and its inability to reverse a solid market trend. The Italian lira suffered a similar fate. The end result was that these currencies had to leave the ERM, simply because the exchange rates could not be maintained within the prescribed limits. Three realignments took place on 12 September, 16 September and 12 November. This series of realignments took the exchange rate between the French franc and the

German mark to 3.3539 on 22 November 1992 (it was 2.3095 on 13 March 1979).

This was not the end of the story, however. Speculative attacks against member currencies (particularly the Irish punt) continued in 1993. On 1 August 1993 it was decided that the band around central rates should be increased to ±15 per cent, in effect terminating the EMS as a system of fixed but adjustable exchange rates. The EMS ceased to exist in 1999 when the EMU was put in place.

Contribution of the EMS to economic stability

There is some evidence (albeit mixed) on the effect of the EMS on economic performance in EMS countries. The evidence may be summarized in the following points (Giavazzi *et al.*, 1988):

- The empirical assessment of the impact of the ERM on exchange rate variability has generally pointed to a reduction in the volatility of intra-ERM nominal and real exchange rates. Moreover, this reduction has not been achieved at the expense of more volatile interest rates (for example, Taylor and Artis, 1988). The available evidence also indicates that misalignment has been reduced by the very act of realignment, perhaps because realignments were based on purchasing power parity (that is, currencies of countries with higher inflation rates were devalued and vice versa).
- Available evidence also points to significant progress in the coordination of monetary policies among member countries.
- Convergence of economic indicators was achieved, most obviously with respect to inflation. However, Moosa and Bhatti (1996) present some evidence showing that EMS membership was not a necessary condition for the convergence of real interest rates *vis-à-vis* Germany.
- It seems to be the case that the EMS operated asymmetrically. In particular, the formulation of monetary policy was dominated by Germany.

The European Monetary Union

In December 1991, members of the European Community signed the Maastricht Treaty that specified a timetable for the move towards the EMU. The plan has its origin in the Delors Report of 1989 on the accomplishment of the transition to full monetary union. This report envisaged three stages: (i) removing the remaining exchange controls (completed by the end of 1992), (ii) establishing a European system of central banks and hardening the ERM, and (iii) full implementation of the monetary union when exchange rates become increasingly fixed and the European Central Bank takes charge of running the Union's monetary policy.

In January 1999, the common European currency, the euro, was introduced for trading but not in a hard form. Then in January 2002, the euro notes and coins were introduced, replacing twelve national currencies. For three years after its introduction in 1999, the euro lost ground against the US dollar, but this trend has been reversed, and the euro has regained all of its losses. The question of whether countries such as the UK and Sweden will join the common currency is still debated. In fact, the very issue of the costs and benefits of the EMU is still controversial. This is a topic that we will return to in Chapters 7 and 8.

In order to prepare for the EMU, the Maastricht Treaty called for the implementation of a process of convergence. The following convergence criteria were set: (i) the inflation rate should be no more than 1.5 per cent above the average for the countries with the three lowest rates, (ii) long-term interest rates should be no more than 2 per cent above the average for the countries with the three lowest rates, (iii) the fiscal deficit should be no more than 60 per cent of GDP, and (iv) government debt should be no more than 60 per cent of GDP.

The future of the international monetary system

Obviously, the present international monetary system has its loopholes and weaknesses. The future of the system is a hot topic, both in professional and academic circles, but there seems to be no consensus view on the issue and where to go from here. A number of courses of action have been suggested as the way to go in the future.

Several factors have contributed to the revival of interest in the gold standard since the 1980s: (i) dissatisfaction with the instability accompanying floating, (ii) a greater acceptability of the monetarist theories of inflation, (iii) political attitudes supporting balanced budgets and the operation of market forces, and (iv) the election in 1980 of Ronald Reagan, who in preelection speeches supported the idea of going back to the gold standard. In particular, it is believed that the gold standard provides some sort of discipline against excessive monetary expansion and, therefore, inflation. However, it is unlikely that the gold standard will solve the current problems of the international monetary system. In today's multi-financial-centre world, short-term capital flows are likely to move erratically in a destabilizing fashion from one centre to another, hindering the balance of payments adjustment mechanism. We have also seen that the classical gold standard did not really work as envisaged in theory, for reasons including non-conformity to the rules of the game.

The advent of currency crises in the 1990s has led economists and policy-makers to seek new designs for the 'international financial architecture'. In 1999, a group of twenty-nine economists (for example, Paul Krugman), former central bankers (for example, Paul Volcker) and currency traders (for example, George Soros) produced a report sponsored by the US Council on Foreign Relations. The reports contained the following propositions:

- Improving incentives for sound policy by linking IMF loans to crisis-prevention efforts.
- Encouraging the imposition of holding period taxes on short-term capital flows in countries characterized by financial fragility.
- Encouraging private sector burden-sharing by introducing collective-action clauses in sovereign bond contracts. This means making the private sector partly responsible for the consequences of sovereign bond issues.
- Discouraging fixed but adjustable exchange rates in favour of either managed floating or currency boards. This seems to be a reflection of a mild version of the bipolar view.
- Directing the IMF to lend less freely and to distinguish between country crises and systemic crises.
- Removing overlapping from the responsibilities of the IMF and the World Bank. The IMF should concentrate on macroeconomic issues, leaving the Bank to deal with the structural aspects of development.

There are obviously problems in implementing these propositions, not least their adequacy for solving the world's financial problems and for preventing financial crises. Moreover, these views are not universally acceptable, with some advocating the abolition of the IMF after its failure not only to predict but also to deal with the Asian financial crisis.

Another course of action has been suggested; a global currency, which is an extension of the idea of dollarization. The idea has its pros and cons. On the one hand, there is the convenience of a single currency, but on the other hand there is the loss of the exchange rate as a policy instrument that can be used if, for example, there is an abrupt fall in the demand for exports. In setting the costs against the benefits, the crucial factors are openness to trade and free movement of factors of production. A small open economy has more to gain from the convenience provided by a single currency.

Overall, there is no clear vision as to where to go from here. There is obviously no magic solution to the problems encountered by the international monetary system, simply because of the complexity of the issues under consideration. Every now and then we hear an ideologically driven view presented as an instant cure for the world's financial problems (one such example is dollarization). However, it is typically the case that ideologically driven views cannot handle the complexity of the issues on the ground or the specific characteristics of each situation. Problems have to be dealt with on a case-by-case basis, simply because of the hazards associated with the 'one size fits all' proposition.

7
Macroeconomic Performance and Exchange Rate Regimes

Introduction

In this chapter we examine the issue of whether macroeconomic performance is affected by the underlying exchange rate regime. It is arguable that the way in which monetary and fiscal policies affect inflation and growth depend on the exchange rate regime. Macroeconomic performance under various exchange rate regimes depends on macroeconomic policy as well as external effects. A study conducted by the International Monetary Fund (1984) lists four criteria for evaluating an exchange rate regime with respect to its effect on the economy. These criteria are the following:

- Contribution (or otherwise) of the regime to macroeconomic policy in pursuit of domestic economic objectives pertaining to inflation, growth and employment.
- The effectiveness of the regime in promoting balance of payments adjustment.
- The effect of the regime on the volume and efficiency of world trade.
- The robustness and adaptability of the regime to significant changes in the global economic environment.

The first criterion obviously pertains to macroeconomic performance, which is the subject matter of this chapter. The criterion reflects the view that the exchange rate regime is no more than a 'facilitating mechanism' for fundamental macroeconomic objectives. This is why the IMF's study does not consider the extent of exchange rate variability as a criterion for exchange rate regimes, restricting its importance only to the extent that it impinges upon the achievement of macroeconomic objectives. The study further considers the channels whereby the exchange rate regime might help or hinder macroeconomic policy, by asking the following questions:

- Does the system provide the discipline necessary for the imposition of responsible macroeconomic policies?
- Does exchange rate variability, coupled with downward price stickiness, produce an upward ratchet effect on the inflation rate?
- Does the regime exacerbate inflation differentials by drawing weaker countries into a 'vicious circle' of inflation and depreciation and stronger ones into a 'virtuous circle' of price stability and currency appreciation?
- Does the regime affect unemployment rates via the adverse effects on the efficiency of the price mechanism or by generating long-term disequilibria in the foreign exchange market?
- Does the nature of the regime influence the effectiveness of macroeconomic policy under conditions of high capital mobility?
- How well does the regime function as a shock absorber for different kinds of disturbances?

Therefore, it seems logical to start the chapter with a consideration of the effectiveness of monetary and fiscal policy under fixed and flexible exchange rates. We will also examine issues that are related to the points listed above, such as policy coordination and the effect of shocks, which we discussed in Chapter 3. Having done that, we move on to a consideration of how various macroeconomic variables behave under different regimes, using both theory and empirical evidence. We will in particular concentrate on inflation and growth.

The macroeconomic model used in this chapter is the conventional *IS–LM–BP* model, which describes simultaneous equilibrium in the real sector (*IS* curve), the monetary sector (*LM* curve) and the balance of payments (*BP* curve). Figure 7.1 shows that equilibrium occurs at a level of income Y_0 and a level of interest rate i_0. We have to remember the following:

- The *IS* curve slopes downwards because as the level of income rises, a lower level of interest rates is required to maintain balance in the goods market.
- The *LM* curve slopes upwards because as income rises, a higher level of interest rate is required to maintain equilibrium in the money market.

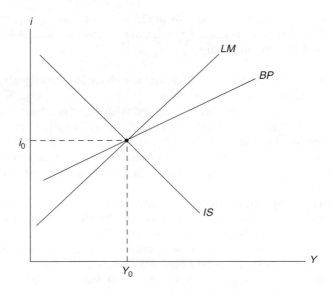

Figure 7.1 Simultaneous equilibrium in the real sector, monetary sector and the balance of payments

- The *BP* curve slopes upwards because as income rises, a higher level of interest is required to maintain equilibrium in the balance of payments.
- The *LM* curve is shown to be steeper than the *BP* curve in Figure 7.1 as a reflection of the assumption that the interest elasticity of the demand for money is lower than the interest elasticity of capital flows.

Automatic adjustment under fixed exchange rates

Consider an increase in foreign demand for domestic goods, leading to an increase in exports. In Figure 7.2, this is represented by a shift in the *BP* curve to the right because any level of interest rate is now associated with a higher level of income without affecting the balance of payments equilibrium. At the same time, the increase in exports leads to a shift in the *IS* curve, reflecting the expansionary effect on income. Both interest rate and income rise, while a balance of payments surplus emerges. Given the surplus that appears in the balance of payments, the central bank must intervene to prevent the domestic currency from appreciating. To do that it must buy the surplus foreign exchange supply against the domestic currency, which results in a domestic monetary

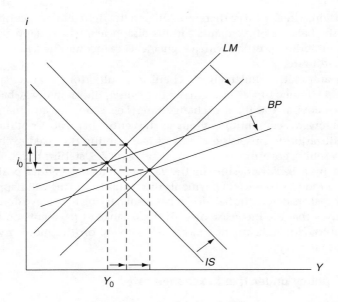

Figure 7.2 Automatic adjustment under fixed exchange rates

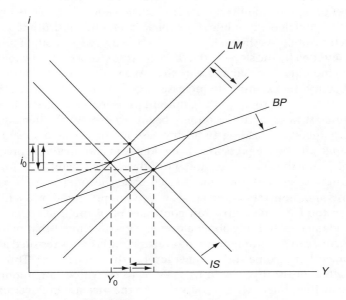

Figure 7.3 The effect of sterilization (selling government securities)

expansion. The *LM* curve therefore shifts to the right, and this continues until the balance of payments surplus disappears, which happens at a new equilibrium position with a higher level of income and a lower level of interest rate.

The automatic adjustment mechanism results from changes in the domestic money supply brought about by disequilibrium in the balance of payments at the fixed exchange rate. The economy automatically moves towards equilibrium as long as the central bank does not indulge in sterilization to offset the effects of maintaining the fixed exchange rate by selling government securities. In Figure 7.3, sterilization is represented by a backward shift in the *LM* curve to its original position, which produces balance of payments disequilibrium. This will happen if policy-makers ignore the balance of payments, trying to achieve domestic objectives that are inconsistent with the balance of payments position. This automatic adjustment process relies solely on the monetary and income effects.

Fiscal policy under fixed exchange rates

The effect of expansionary fiscal policy under fixed exchange rates and various degrees of capital mobility is illustrated in Figure 7.4. Four degrees of capital mobility are considered: (a) capital is perfectly immobile, (b) capital is immobile, (c) capital is mobile, and (d) capital is perfectly mobile. As shown in Figure 7.4, the degree of capital mobility is represented by the slope of the *BP* curve (the steeper it is, the lower is capital mobility). Consider case (a) first. As a result of the expansionary fiscal policy (for example, an increase in government spending), the *IS* curve shifts to the right, putting upward pressure on domestic income and interest rates. As the economy begins to expand the demand for imports increases, leading to an increase in the demand for foreign exchange and hence pressure on the domestic currency to depreciate. To maintain the fixed exchange rate, the central bank sells foreign exchange to support the domestic currency, leading to the loss of reserves and monetary contraction, which is represented by a leftward shift in the *LM* curve. This shift continues until the interest rate has risen adequately to bring about a decrease in investment that matches the increase in government expenditure. Equilibrium is restored at the initial level of income and a higher level of the interest rate. Thus, the only effect of fiscal policy in this case is to crowd out an amount of domestic investment that is equivalent to the increase in government spending, which occurs as a result of the increase in interest rate.

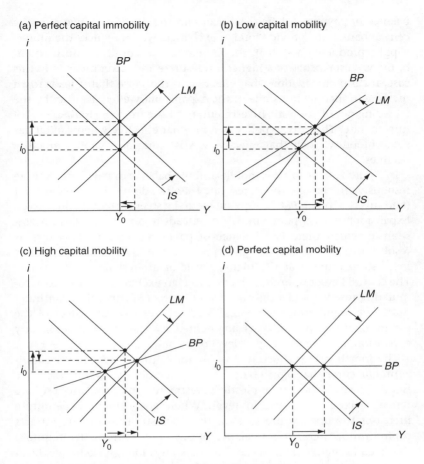

Figure 7.4 The effect of fiscal policy under fixed exchange rates

Income and employment do not change. Hence, fiscal policy is completely ineffective under fixed exchange rates and perfect capital immobility.

Figure 7.4(b) illustrates the situation when capital mobility is low, in the sense that capital flows are not highly responsive to changes in interest rates, which is represented by a *BP* curve that is steeper than the *LM* curve. Expansionary fiscal policy is represented by a rightward shift in the IS curve and a new equilibrium position at a higher level of income and interest rate. But at this point of equilibrium there is a balance of payments deficit. To maintain the fixed exchange rate, the central bank must provide foreign exchange, which reduces the money supply, producing a shift in the *LM* curve that continues until equilibrium is reestablished at a higher interest rate and lower income. In this case, fiscal policy is somewhat effective in the sense that it leads to an increase in income but some of the expansionary effect is offset by the crowding out of domestic investment, resulting from the higher level of interest rate. Thus, fiscal policy is somewhat effective when capital has some mobility, such that effectiveness is reduced as capital mobility declines.

In Figure 7.4(c) capital is mobile and the balance of payments is more responsive to changes in interest rate than the domestic money market (and this is why the *LM* curve is shown to be steeper than the *BP* curve). Expansionary fiscal policy in this case leads to a new equilibrium position at which there is a balance of payments surplus. This surplus results because the increase in capital inflows more than offsets the increase in imports at the higher levels of interest rate and income. The central bank responds by buying foreign exchange, leading to accumulating reserves and a rightward shift in the *LM* curve that continues until final equilibrium is reestablished. In this case the effect of the expansionary fiscal policy is augmented by the effect of monetary expansion, leading to a higher level of income.

The fourth case is illustrated in Figure 7.4(d), which shows a horizontal *BP* curve that signifies perfect capital mobility. In this case there is no crowding out of domestic investment since the interest rate remains fixed at the world level. When government expenditure increases the upward pressure on the domestic interest rate attracts capital inflows, creating a balance of payments surplus. To maintain the fixed exchange rate, the central bank buys foreign exchange, leading to monetary expansion. The *LM* curve shifts to the right until equilibrium is reestablished. Expansionary fiscal policy in this case is highly effective in the sense that no crowding out of domestic investment takes place.

The analysis of the effectiveness of fiscal policy under fixed exchange rates suggests that fiscal policy is effective except when capital is completely immobile. The higher the mobility of capital the greater the effectiveness of fiscal policy under fixed exchange rates, in the sense that it leads to income expansion with less-than-offsetting crowding out of domestic investment. It must be added that the analysis is symmetric in the sense that the same conclusion holds for contractionary fiscal policy.

Monetary policy under fixed exchange rates

The effectiveness of monetary policy under fixed exchange rates and various degrees of capital mobility is illustrated in Figure 7.5. Expansionary monetary policy (represented by increasing the money supply) causes a shift to the right in the *LM* curve. In all cases a balance of payments deficit arises, causing loss of reserves as the central banks sells foreign exchange. This in turn leads to monetary contraction, with the *LM* curve shifting back to its original position where equilibrium is

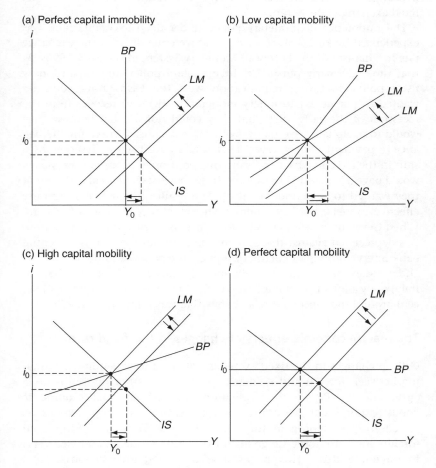

Figure 7.5 The effect of monetary policy under fixed exchange rates

reestablished at the initial level of income. Thus, monetary policy is completely ineffective under fixed exchange rates, in the sense that it does not affect the level of income, regardless of the degree of capital mobility. However, we have to bear in mind that the shift of the *LM* curve back to its original position can be delayed by sterilization, which takes the form of open market purchases of government securities. This postponement cannot be sustained indefinitely, because foreign exchange reserves may decline below a target level. Thus, discretionary monetary policy cannot be used to pursue economic targets under fixed exchange rates. Alternatively, of course, the country may abandon the fixed exchange rate system.

The impotence of monetary policy under fixed exchange rates was experienced by European countries that were members of the exchange rate mechanism of the European Monetary System in the early 1990s. At that time, Germany pursued tight monetary policy and expansionary fiscal policy following reunification with the East. Other countries wanted to pursue expansionary monetary policies to recover from the recession of the early 1990s but they could not do that because they would lose capital to Germany, with adverse consequences for the balance of payments and reserves. That would have been represented by a shift in the *LM* curve back to its original position. Of course, fiscal policy would have been useful but most of those countries had fiscal deficits that they wanted to keep under control. As a result of their inability to use effective monetary policy, unemployment rates remained rather high. When Germany resisted pressure to reduce its interest rates, EMS currencies depreciated against the German mark, resulting in massive central bank intervention, particularly to support the pound and the lira. In the end, fixed exchange rates were abandoned either completely (the UK and Italy) or by allowing exchange rates to fluctuate within a margin of 15 per cent around the central rates, a change that was introduced in 1993.

The macroeconomic effects of changes in the fixed rate

Official changes in the fixed exchange rate lead to expenditure switching between foreign and domestic goods, hence affecting both the *IS* curve and the *BP* curve. Devaluation, for example, makes domestic goods (exports) cheaper and foreign goods (imports) more expensive. Expenditure switching in this case takes the form of shifting from foreign goods to domestic goods for domestic residents and vice versa for foreign residents. This effect will be considered under various degrees of capital mobility as before.

Consider first the case of perfectly immobile capital, which is illustrated in Figure 7.6(a). Devaluation of the domestic currency causes a rightward shift in the *IS* and *BP* curves, taking the economy to a new equilibrium point where there is a surplus in the balance of payments. The central bank buys the foreign exchange necessary to keep the exchange rate at the new level. This leads to a rightward shift in the *LM* curve, until equilibrium is reestablished at a higher level of income. Thus, devaluation is effective in influencing income under perfect capital immobility.

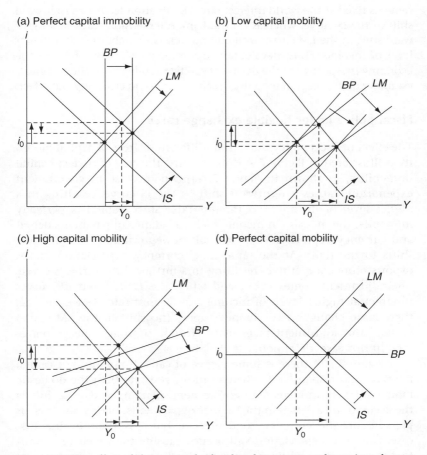

Figure 7.6 The effect of changes in the fixed exchange rate under various degrees of capital mobility

The case of imperfect capital mobility is shown in Figure 7.6(b) and Figure 7.6(c). Devaluation leads to shifts in both the *IS* and *BP* curves, leading to higher levels of income and interest rates as well as a surplus in the balance of payments. The central bank intervenes to maintain the new level of the exchange rate by buying foreign exchange, which leads to monetary expansion and a rightward shift in the *LM* curve. The process continues until equilibrium is reestablished. In both of these cases, devaluation leads to an expansionary effect on income.

The case of perfect capital mobility is illustrated in Figure 7.6(d). In this case devaluation does not alter the position of the *BP* curve, which remains fixed at the world interest rate. Devaluation leads to a rightward shift in the *IS* curve, whereas central bank intervention leads to a rightward shift in the *LM* curve until equilibrium is reestablished at a higher level of income. Thus, devaluation has an expansionary effect on the economy irrespective of the degree of capital mobility. The effect is greatest under perfect capital mobility because there is no crowding-out effect.

Fiscal policy under flexible exchange rates

The effect of fiscal policy under four different degrees of capital mobility is illustrated in Figure 7.7. Consider first the case of perfect capital immobility, as shown in Figure 7.7(a). An increase in government expenditure causes a rightward shift in the IS curve, resulting in a higher level of income and interest rate. Since capital is perfectly immobile, the increase in income forces a balance of payments deficit and currency depreciation. As a result of depreciation, the *BP* curve shifts to the right. At the same time, currency depreciation makes exports more competitive, resulting in a further shift in the *IS* curve. The adjustment comes to an end when the *IS*, *LM* and *BP* curves intersect at higher levels of income and interest rate. As we can see, there is no change in the money supply (no shift in the LM curve) because the adjustment takes place entirely thorough the exchange rate. In this case, fiscal policy is effective.

In Figure 7.7(b) there is some degree of capital mobility but capital flows are less responsive to changes in interest rate than the domestic money market. An increase in government spending leads to a shift in the *IS* curve and a deficit in the balance of payments. In this case there is pressure on the currency to depreciate but less than in the first case. However, depreciation still occurs, causing the *BP* curve to shift to the right. An additional shift in the *IS* curve occurs because of increased competitiveness of exports. Again, a new equilibrium position

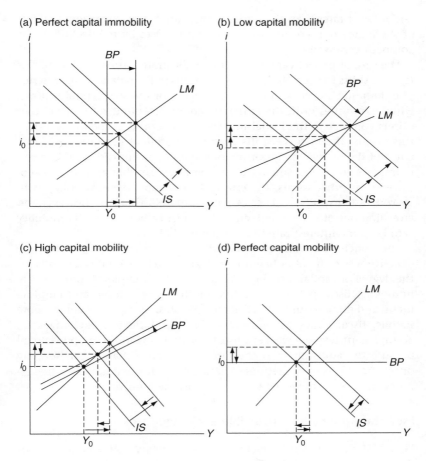

Figure 7.7 The effect of fiscal policy under flexible exchange rates

is established at a higher level of income but the increase in income is less than in the first case.

In Figure 7.7(c) capital is shown to be highly mobile. An increase in government spending leads to a surplus in the balance of payments because net capital inflows more than offset the current account deficit. Unlike the previous two cases, this case produces domestic currency appreciation, which means that the *BP* curve moves to the left. Currency appreciation also reduces competitiveness, causing the *IS* curve to shift to the left. Final equilibrium is established at higher levels of income and interest rates than the initial levels. Part of the expansionary effect of the increase in government spending is offset by the decline in the competitiveness of exports.

The case of perfect capital mobility is illustrated in Figure 7.7(d). The *IS* curve shifts to the right, creating a surplus in the balance of payments. The domestic currency appreciates because of massive capital inflows, which continues until the current account deteriorates to a level that offsets completely the initial increase in government spending. When this occurs, the IS curve shifts back to its original position. Thus, the effect of the increase in government spending in this case is an increase in imports and a decrease in exports, without any change in the level of income. In other words, the effect of expansionary fiscal policy is to 'crowd out' exports and 'crowd in' imports. There is, however, no crowding out of investment since the effect of perfect capital mobility is to keep the interest rate fixed at the world level.

The conclusion that we can derive from this analysis is that the effectiveness of fiscal policy under flexible exchange rates depends on the degree of capital mobility. When capital is completely or relatively immobile, fiscal policy is effective in changing income and employment, and more so under fixed exchange rates. As capital becomes more mobile, fiscal policy becomes less effective. A flexible exchange rate arrangement severely weakens fiscal policy in a world of mobile capital because the adjustment in the foreign exchange market can severely offset the effects of discretionary fiscal policy. It does, however, free up monetary policy, as we are going to see in the following section.

Monetary policy under flexible exchange rates

Figure 7.8 illustrates the effectiveness of monetary policy under various degrees of capital mobility. An expansionary monetary policy leads to a shift to the right in the *LM* curve, leading to a rise in the income level irrespective of the degree of capital mobility. The increase in the money supply leads to currency depreciation, hence an increase in net exports. Because of depreciation, both the *BP* curve and the *IS* curve shift to the right so that income ends up at a higher level. The greater is capital mobility, the more effective is monetary policy. It is also true that the more mobile capital is, the greater the degree to which expansionary monetary policy depends on the adjustment in the foreign trade sector to bring about the increase in income and employment.

When capital is perfectly immobile, as in Figure 7.8(a), the balance of payments deficit is caused by the increase in imports resulting from a

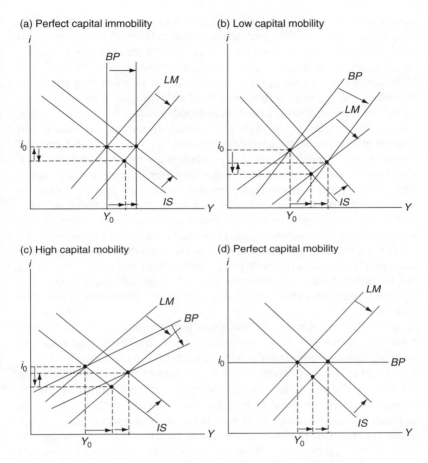

Figure 7.8 The effect of monetary policy under flexible exchange rates

higher level of income. Since capital flows are completely insensitive to changes in interest rates there is no change in capital flows as a result of the monetary policy action. Therefore, the currency depreciates only to the extent that it offsets the income effect on imports. As the currency depreciates, the *BP* curve shifts to the right and the increase in exports causes a shift in the *IS* curve as well. Eventually the economy comes back to equilibrium at a higher level of income. When capital is mobile as in Figure 7.8(b) and Figure 7.8(c), both capital movements and the increase in income put downward pressure on the domestic currency. In Figure 7.8(d) capital is perfectly mobile, in which case monetary expansion leads to very large capital outflow and currency depreciation. This depreciation leads to a large expansion of net exports that exactly offsets capital outflow, which in turn stimulates domestic income.

While the theory sounds nice, reality is not so nice. Proponents of flexible exchange rates believe that flexibility would enhance monetary policy because (i) flexible rates would enable countries to regain control over the money supply, and (ii) they would strengthen the output and employment effects of expansionary monetary policy via the positive effect of the induced currency depreciation on the trade balance. But this has not really materialized. Take the control of the money supply first, which presumably results from the absence of any obligation to intervene in the foreign exchange market to maintain the fixed rate. With no change in reserves resulting from intervention, the foreign component of the monetary base ceases to be a source of changes in the money supply. The problem here is that the authorities must regard the exchange rate exclusively as a policy instrument, not as a target. Thus, while countries have greater control over the money supply under flexible exchange rates than under fixed rates, the difference is not that significant.

As for the effectiveness of monetary policy under flexible exchange rates, this rests (as in the previous analysis) on the theoretical results of Fleming (1962) and Mundell (1968). A study by the International Monetary Fund (1984) has exposed four weaknesses of the Mundell–Fleming analysis: (i) the assumption that exchange rate changes translate quickly into changes in competitiveness, (ii) the assumption that changes in competitiveness yield rapid improvements in the depreciating country's trade balance, (iii) the assumption about the size of the exchange rate change induced by domestic monetary expansion when domestic and foreign assets are close substitutes, and (iv) the limitation of the model that exchange rate expectation is not incorporated into the choice between domestic and foreign assets. The study concludes that 'the case for monetary policy under floating rates was oversold'.

Policy coordination under flexible exchange rates

We have seen from the previous analysis that monetary policy is consistently effective under flexible exchange rates, and that it is stronger the more mobile capital is. Fiscal policy, on the other hand, is less effective under flexible exchange rates when capital is mobile. This is because the expenditure-switching effect can work against fiscal policy whereas it is complementary with monetary policy. Therefore, it may be useful to use both monetary and fiscal policy to achieve domestic targets. In this section it is demonstrated that the only way to achieve predefined income and interest rate targets without affecting the exchange rate (hence changing relative prices and the structure of the economy) is by using both monetary and fiscal policies. This is shown in Figure 7.9.

Figure 7.9(a) shows that monetary policy alone cannot take the economy from (Y_0, i_0) to (Y^*, i^*). The expansionary monetary policy that shifts the *LM* curve to the right also leads to currency depreciation (a rightward shift in the *BP* curve) and an expansion of net exports (hence a shift in the *IS* curve). At the final equilibrium position, income is below the target level whereas the interest rate is even below the initial level. In Figure 7.9(b) it is shown that fiscal policy alone cannot achieve the target levels of income and interest rate. The *IS* curve shifts to the right, but the expansionary fiscal policy also creates a balance of payments surplus and currency appreciation. As a result, the *IS* curve shifts back to the left and equilibrium is reestablished at a level of income that is below the target level and a level of interest rate that is higher than the target level. In Figure 7.9(c) it is shown that both target levels are achieved by using both monetary and fiscal policies.

The effect of exogenous shocks

In this section we consider the effects of four kinds of shocks, starting with a foreign price shock, as shown in Figure 7.10. If there is a sudden increase in the foreign price level, there will be an expansionary effect on the economy and the *IS* curve will shift to the right as net exports are stimulated. In addition, there will be a rightward shift in the *BP* curve because the expenditure-switching effect of the increase in foreign prices means that a higher level of domestic income is consistent with balance of payments equilibrium for each level of the interest rate. The resulting rise in the interest rate puts upward pressure on the currency and as a result both the *BP* and the *IS* curves shift back to their original positions. Thus, under flexible exchange rates the economy is insulated from foreign price shocks, which (as we have seen) is an argument in favour of flexible exchange rates.

The second shock we consider is a domestic price shock, whose effect is shown in Figure 7.11. This shock affects equilibrium in the real sector, the monetary sector and the balance of payments as the three curves shift in response to the shock. An increase in the domestic price level

184

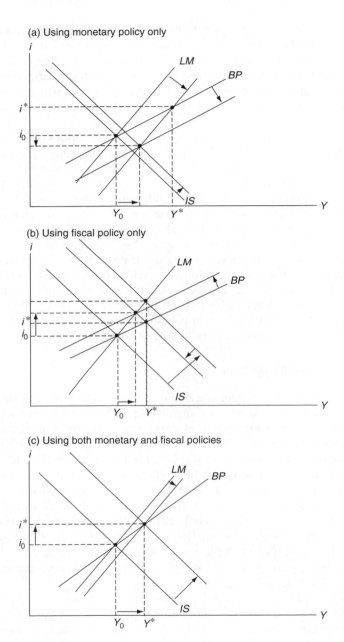

Figure 7.9 Achieving targets under flexible exchange rates

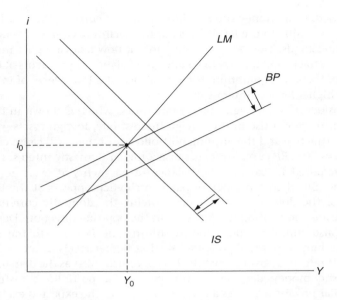

Figure 7.10 The effect of a foreign price shock under flexible exchange rates

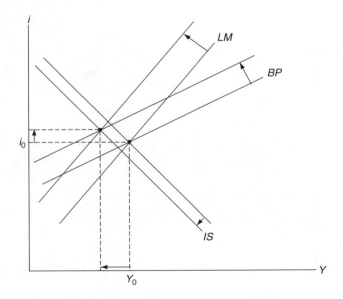

Figure 7.11 The effect of a domestic price shock under flexible exchange rates

reduces the real money supply, shifting the *LM* curve to the left. The *IS* curve also shifts to the left because of the declining competitiveness of domestic goods. The *BP* curve shifts since it now takes a higher interest rate to attract capital flows to balance the balance of payments at every level of income. Equilibrium is reestablished at a lower level of income and a higher level of interest rate.

Consider now a foreign interest rate shock, which is shown in Figure 7.12. If there is a rise in the foreign interest rate, foreign assets will be more attractive and the ensuing portfolio adjustment will cause capital outflows. The *BP* curve shifts because a higher domestic interest rate is now required to balance the balance of payments at every level of income. But then a balance of payments deficit appears at the initial level of the domestic interest rate, forcing the domestic currency to depreciate and shifting the *BP* curve in the opposite direction. Depreciation also stimulates net exports, shifting the *IS* curve to the right. Equilibrium is eventually reestablished at higher levels of income and interest rate. It is possible that the *LM* curve also shifts as the demand for domestic money declines in the process of portfolio adjustment. A similar process occurs as a result of a shock to the expected exchange

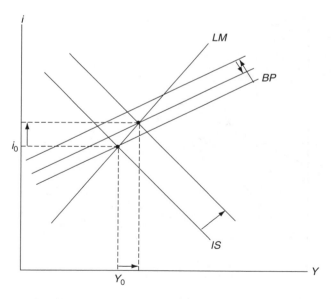

Figure 7.12   The effect of a foreign interest shock under flexible exchange rates

rate, which (via UIP) brings about capital outflows if the foreign currency is expected to appreciate more than before.

Macroeconomic performance under fixed and flexible exchange rates

There does not seem to be a consensus view on the relationship between macroeconomic performance and the underlying exchange rate regime. We have already come across the argument that fixed exchange rates are more conducive to growth (because they eliminate harmful exchange rate volatility) and the contrasting argument that flexible exchange rates boost growth (because they have a favourable effect on the efficacy of monetary policy). Another argument that we discussed in Chapter 2 is that fixed exchange rates provide the stability and credibility that lower inflation, whereas flexible exchange rates are inflationary by their very nature. Thus, the question remains largely empirical.

A typical argument for the connection between fixed exchange rates and inflation is the disciplinary effect they have on monetary policy as well as indirectly through inflationary expectations. This is based on the concept of the nominal anchor, whereby pegging to the currency of a country with low inflation is viewed as a precommitment mechanism to anchor inflationary expectations. But just as the main advantage of flexible exchange rates is to allow the authorities some discretion and flexibility to use monetary policy to deal with shocks, flexibility also allows too much discretion to monetary policy, and so it may not provide a sufficient nominal anchor (for example, Calvo and Mendoza, 2000; Calvo, 2001). This is probably why it makes sense to argue that the association between inflation and the exchange rate regime is not that clear. Furthermore, Calvo and Mishkin (2003) argue that a central bank can only work to reduce inflation if it is supported by the public and the political process.

On the other hand, it is generally believed that flexible exchange rates are inflationary because they (i) weaken the discipline to fight inflation, (ii) interact with downward price inflexibility to ratchet up both country and global price levels, and (iii) trap weaker countries in a vicious circle of inflation and currency depreciation, thereby exacerbating intercountry inflation differentials. These are respectively called the 'discipline hypothesis', the 'ratchet hypothesis' and the 'vicious circle hypothesis'. For a discussion of these hypotheses, see International Monetary Fund (1984).

As far as growth is concerned, Levy-Yeyati and Sturzenegger (2001) argue that the literature has not considered the exchange rate regime as an important determinant of growth. In fact, growth theory (which suggests a very large number of determinants of growth) does not consider the exchange rate regime to be an important factor. This is probably because we tend to associate nominal effects only with the choice of nominal variables. Razin and Rubinstein (2004) argue that output growth is affected by the direct and indirect effects of balance of payments policies geared towards exchange rate regimes and capital account openness. A direct channel works through the trade and financial sector similar to the optimum currency area arguments. An indirect channel works through the probability of a 'sudden-stop crisis'.

Several arguments have been put forward to explain the link between growth and a fixed exchange rate regime:

- By reducing relative price volatility, a fixed exchange rate regime is expected to foster growth through its positive effect on investment and trade.
- Lower price uncertainty should lead to lower real interest rates, which again boosts growth.
- The lack of exchange rate adjustment under fixed exchange rates, coupled with short-run price rigidity, may lead to price distortions and high unemployment as a result of external shocks. The need to defend a fixed exchange rate in the face of negative external shocks entails a significant cost in terms of real interest rates, as well as increased uncertainty as to the sustainability of the regime. Calvo (1999) has suggested that the external shocks faced by a country are not independent of the exchange rate regime. But while the lack of adjustment argument and the frequent external shocks arguments associated with fixed exchange rates may produce higher output volatility, the effect on long-term economic growth is not straightforward.

Caramazza and Aziz (1998) argue that neither fixed rates nor flexible rates rank above the other in terms of the implications for macroeconomic performance. Before the 1990s, inflation appeared consistently lower and less volatile in countries with fixed exchange rates but the difference has narrowed significantly since the 1990s. They also argue that output growth does not seem to differ across exchange rate regimes. They explain the higher median growth rate in countries with flexible exchange rates to the inclusion of rapidly growing Asian countries in this category. Finally, they argue that misalignment and currency crises are equally likely under fixed and flexible exchange rates. But a study published in the IMF's *World Economic Outlook* (October 1997) shows that inflation in countries with fixed exchange rates has been consistently lower and less volatile than in countries with flexible rates. However, the study shows no clear relationship between exchange rate regimes and growth over the period 1975–96.

Bordo (2003) examines the historical macroeconomic performance of fourteen countries collectively over the period 1880–1995, concentrating on three key variables: exchange rate volatility (measured by the absolute rate of change of the log exchange rate), consumer price index (CPI) inflation and per capita income growth. The period encompasses the classical gold standard (1880–1914); the First World War, the interwar period and the Second World War (1914–45); the Bretton Woods period (1946–71); and the present system. The Bretton Woods period is divided into the preconvertible period (1946–59) and the convertible period (1969–71). He concluded the following:

- In the classical gold standard and the convertible Bretton Woods system, exchange rates were extremely stable. The wars, the interwar period and the early Bretton Woods period were the most unstable, with moderate volatility in the current regime.
- For inflation, it was lowest during the gold standard and the convertible Bretton Woods system and highest during the wars. The 1970s and early 1980s were characterized by relatively high peacetime inflation. Since the mid-1980s, inflation has declined to levels reminiscent of the two convertible regimes. Bordo and Schwartz (1999) argue that this evidence suggests the importance of adherence to credible nominal anchors (gold pre-1914, gold and the dollar in the Bretton Woods system and inflation targeting and other domestic nominal anchors since the early 1980s).
- With the exception of the exceedingly high growth after the Second World War, which in large part reflects Europe's recovery, there does not seem to be much of a connection over the long run between the exchange rate regime and growth.

Other empirical studies have been conducted by Baxter and Stockman (1989) and by Flood and Rose (1995) who reached the conclusion of the absence of significant differences in business cycles across exchange arrangements. Mundell (1995) examined the growth performance of industrial countries in the pre- and post-Bretton Woods system. He found that the earlier period of fixed exchange rates witnessed faster growth. Ghosh *et al.* (1997) used data covering the period 1960–90 and found inflation to be both lower and more stable under fixed exchange rates. However, they failed to find any systematic evidence to support the link between the exchange rate regime and economic growth. These results have been challenged by Rolnick and Weber (1997) who found that output growth was higher under fiat standards than under commodity standards (for example, the gold standard). A similar conclusion is reached by Levy-Yeyati and Sturzenegger (2000b) who investigated the link using data covering the period 1974–99 and found fixed exchange rates to be associated with (i) lower per capita growth rate, and (ii) higher output volatility.

Ghosh *et al.* (2002) found, by conducting an informal examination of their data sample using the *de jure* classification, that (i) observations for pegged regimes cluster at low inflation rates but the distribution of intermediate and floating regimes is more even; and (ii) there is no clear pattern for the relationship between growth and exchange rate regimes, except that the distribution of growth rates under pegged regimes is dispersed, with a larger proportion at the top and bottom ends. By using formal econometric models applied in conjunction with the *de jure* classification and what they call the consensus classification, they concluded that: (i) inflation is lower under fixed exchange rates, reflecting both lower monetary growth (the discipline effect) and greater confidence in the currency (the credibility effect); (ii) the evidence on the connection between growth and the exchange rate regime is not robust, with the differences in growth rates attributed to country-specific factors. However, there is evidence showing that countries with fixed exchange rates experience greater output volatility.

Let us consider the historical evidence by examining growth and inflation in the UK under various exchange rate regimes over a period extending back to 1885. Figure 7.13 shows the behaviour of the dollar/pound exchange rate, real GDP (in 1980 prices) and the general price level measured by the CPI. Figure 7.14 shows the behaviour of the percentage change of the three variables, hence relating growth and inflation to exchange rate variability. Little association can be gleaned from the graphs, but more can be seen from Table 7.1, which reports exchange rate variability, growth rates and inflation rates over three historical periods: 1885–1913, 1949–72 and 1973–2003, which represent the classical gold standard, the Bretton Woods system and the present system respectively. As we can see, exchange rate variability was lowest under the gold standard and highest under the present system. As far as growth is concerned, it was highest under the Bretton Woods system, but this can hardly be attributed to the exchange rate regime. This period includes the fast-growth decades immediately after the Second

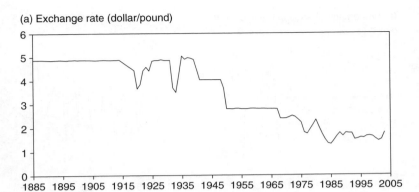

(a) Exchange rate (dollar/pound)

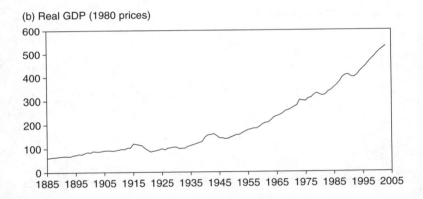

(b) Real GDP (1980 prices)

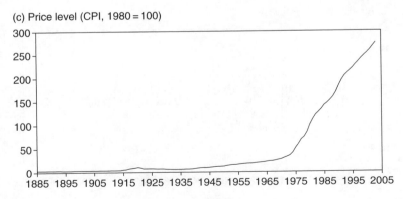

(c) Price level (CPI, 1980 = 100)

Figure 7.13 Exchange rate, output and price level in the UK

(a) Percentage change in the exchange rate

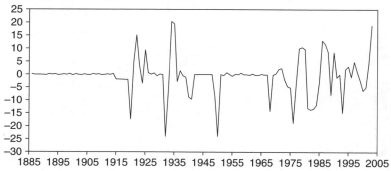

(b) Annual GDP growth rate (%)

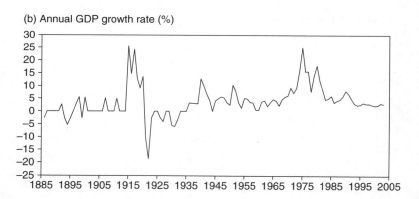

(c) Annual inflation rate (%)

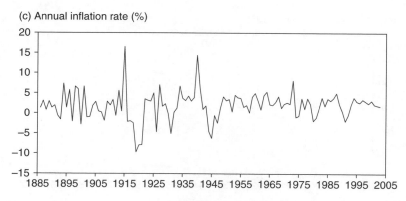

Figure 7.14 Exchange rate variability, growth and inflation in the UK

Table 7.1 Growth, inflation and exchange rate variability (the UK, 1885–2003)

Period	Percentage change in the dollar/ pound rate	Growth rate	Inflation rate
1885–1913			
Mean	0.00	1.9	0.4
Standard deviation	0.15	2.9	2.6
1949–72			
Mean	−1.8	2.9	4.3
Standard deviation	5.8	1.4	2.5
1973–2003			
Mean	−1.0	2.2	7.0
Standard deviation	8.8	2.2	6.1

World War. It is interesting to know that output growth was more erratic under the gold standard. However, there seems to be some link between exchange rate variability and inflation, as inflation was lower under the gold standard than during the other two periods.

One way to examine the relationship between exchange rate regimes and inflation is to find out what happened in hyperinflationary

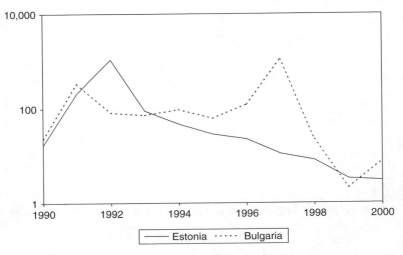

Figure 7.15 Inflation in Estonia and Bulgaria (logarithmic scale)

economies following the adoption of a currency board. Figure 7.15 displays inflation rates in Estonia and Bulgaria, which adopted currency boards in 1992 and 1997 respectively. In both cases, inflation dropped drastically following the introduction of the currency board. The immediate effect was astounding. In the year following the introduction of the board, the inflation rate dropped from 1,069 to 40 per cent in Estonia and from 1,082 to 22.3 per cent in Bulgaria. Although Ho (2003) casts doubt on the ability to distinguish between the contribution of the currency board and that of other factors, it is clear in this case that it was indeed the effect of the currency board. This contribution is not that clear in the case of Hong Kong, which adopted a currency board in 1983, as shown in Figure 7.16. The inflation rate rose after the adoption of the board but this could be a reflection of inflation in the anchor country (the USA).

Some economists regard the lack of evidence on the relationship between the exchange rate regime and macroeconomic performance as a puzzle, which they tried to resolve (for example, Dedola and Leduc, 2001). Calvo and Mishkin (2003) argue that no exchange rate regime can prevent macroeconomic turbulence, concluding that the choice of exchange rate regime is likely to be of secondary importance to the

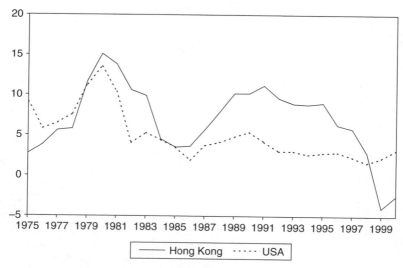

Figure 7.16   Inflation in Hong Kong and the USA

development of sound fiscal, financial and monetary institutions to produce macroeconomic success. But most economists working in this area believe that there is indeed a relationship that is obscured by the IMF's *de jure* classification, which does not reflect what countries actually do. Reinhart and Rogoff (2004) argue that the lack of supporting evidence can be attributed to the use of the *de jure* exchange rate classification, which they describe as being 'misleading'. Frankel (2003) argues that the empirical evidence on the economic performance of different regimes depends entirely on the classification scheme.

Nitithanprapas and Willett (2002) examine the contribution of the exchange rate regime to the Asian crisis by taking into account differences in the classification schemes. They point out that many of the crisis countries were not practising the classic narrow and adjustable peg of the Bretton Woods system (Thailand being the exception), highly flexible rates, or announced crawling bands. Countries such as Indonesia and Korea officially stated their regimes as managed floating but in practice followed some sort of unannounced crawling bands. Depending on whether one classifies these as more fixed or more flexible regimes, one can find that pegged rates did or did not contribute significantly to the Asian crisis.

Levy-Yeyati and Sturzenegger (2001) investigated the effect of exchange rate regime on macroeconomic performance using the *de facto* classification of Levy-Yeyati and Sturzenegger (2000a) that groups exchange rate regimes according to the actual behaviour of the main relevant variables as opposed to the official classification of the IMF. In particular they examined the inflation–growth trade-off using data on 154 countries covering the post-Bretton Woods period. They also distinguished between long and short pegs (those in place for five or more years and those in place for less than five years). One argument for this distinction is the desire to find out if the impact on macroeconomic variables is a product of the underlying regime rather the result of the short-run effect of a regime switch. The results are summarized in Figure 7.17, but more detailed findings can be stated briefly as follows:

- For industrial countries no significant link emerges between exchange rate regimes and economic performance.
- For non-industrial countries there is a robust relationship between fixed exchange rate regimes and lower inflation rates but only in the case of long pegs. The link between inflation and the exchange rate regime seems to work through the effect of the regime on monetary

growth as well as the effect of expectations. They also emphasize the importance of 'deeds' rather than 'words' for inflation.
• Real interest rates seem to be lower under fixed exchange rate regimes but only according to the *de jure* classification.

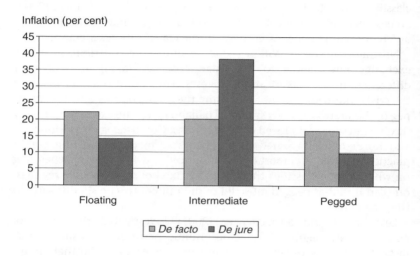

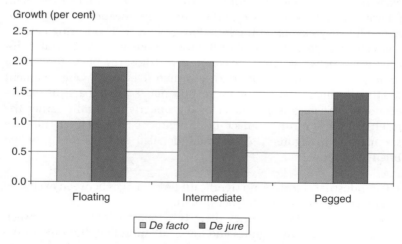

Figure 7.17 Macroeconomic performance under different regimes (Levy-Yeyati and Sturzenegger)

- For non-industrial countries, fixed exchange rates (both short and long pegs) are significantly and negatively related to growth.
- The inflation–growth trade-off implicit in the choice between fixed and flexible exchange rates is valid for long pegs only. On the other hand, short pegs underperformed flexible exchange rates as economies adopting the former grew more slowly without providing inflation gains.

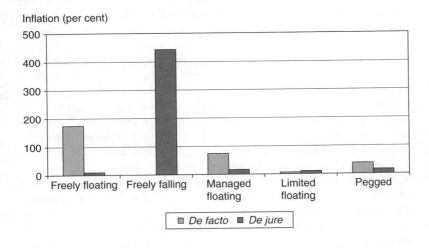

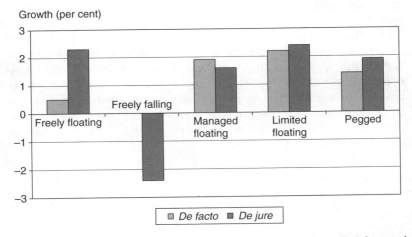

Figure 7.18 Macroeconomic performance under different regimes (Reinhart and Rogoff)

- Hard pegs result in superior inflation results but they do not eliminate the inflation–growth trade-off. Countries under hard pegs grew more slowly than under flexible rates.
- *De facto* pegs that shy away from legally committing to a fixed exchange rate benefit from better growth performance, which provides justification for the 'fear of pegging'.

Reinhart and Rogoff (2004) compare annual inflation under the official classification and under a modified classification that treats dual rates separately. They document significant differences in the inflation averages across the two classification schemes, as can be seen from Figure 7.18. Rogoff *et al.* (2004) present results comparing inflation, growth and growth volatility across regimes, taking into account exchange rate regime classification as well as the distinction between countries according to the level of development. They found that, on average, pegged and intermediate regimes have been associated with significantly lower inflation rates than floating regimes. However, they qualified this result by saying that this finding reflects an inflation benefit that accrues primarily to developing economies and not to emerging markets over advanced economies. As far as growth is concerned, their full sample reveals no association between exchange rate flexibility and growth using both the *de jure* and *de facto* classifications. Conversely, they found free floating to be more conducive to growth in advanced economies. They go as far as arguing that 'exchange rate rigidity is monotonically associated with slower growth'.

So, what is the verdict? The results are obviously a mixed bag, giving no clear-cut conclusion. Taking into account the distinction between *de facto* and *de jure* classifications and between developed and developing economies does not change the 'mixed bag' description of the results significantly. The results are not so universal as to make us comfortable about attributing differences in the growth and inflation patterns to differences in exchange rate regimes. This issue will be examined further in Chapter 8.

8
Modelling Exchange Rate Regime Choice

Empirical models of exchange rate regime choice

Empirical regime choice models are used to explain how the underlying exchange rate regime is related to the economic, financial and political characteristics of the country in question. In these models, the dependent variable can be either discrete, taking values representing the exchange rate regime (for example, zero for fixed and one for flexible) or it could be continuous, taking the form of a measure of exchange rate flexibility (like what we came across in Chapter 3). These values can be based on *de jure* or *de facto* classifications and they can be more disaggregated (for example, fixed, intermediate and floating, or even more classification categories). The explanatory variables, on the other hand, are numerous, but they can be classified under the headings: (i) optimum currency area (OCA) factors, (ii) other economic and monetary factors, (iii) fear of floating factors, and (iv) political economy factors. Some of these variables can be classified under more than one of these headings. Table 8.1, which is by no means exhaustive, lists the potential determinants of exchange rate regime choice (explanatory variables) classified under the four headings.

Efforts to estimate empirical models of exchange rate regime choice go back to the 1970s, soon after the availability of data following the breakdown of the Bretton Woods system. One of the earliest studies was Heller (1978) who used data from the mid-1970s. Other studies followed, including Dreyer (1978), Holden *et al.* (1979), Melvin (1985), Bosco (1987), Savvides (1990), Cuddington and Otto (1990, 1991), Honkapohja and Pikkarainen (1994), Rizzo (1998), Collins (1996), Edwards (1996, 1999), Berger *et al.* (2000), Poirson (2001), Juhn and Mauro (2002) and Papaioannou (2003). Some other models have dealt with the

Table 8.1   Explanatory variables in empirical models

OCA factors	Other factors	Fear of floating factors	Political economy factors
Openness	Growth	Foreign currency debt	Political instability
Economic development	Inflation	Degree of dollarization	Central bank credibility
Size of economy	Terms of trade volatility	Degree of exchange rate pass-through	Central bank independence
Inflation differential	Variability of export growth	Elasticity of supply of external funds	Majority of party in office
Capital mobility	Real exchange rate variability	Lack of credibility	Number of parties in coalition
Labour mobility	Growth of domestic credit		The presence of coalition government
Geographical trade concentration	Shocks		
International financial integration	Per capita GDP		
Diversification of production and exports	Reserves		

question of changes in exchange rate regimes, including Klein and Marion (1997), Masson (2001) and Duttagupta and Otker-Robe (2003).

Several methods have been used to estimate and test the empirical models of exchange rate regime choice, including discriminant analysis, probit models, OLS on a continuous dependent variable, multinomial logit, two-stage probit, and ordered/non-ordered logit. The results of these studies are mixed, being highly sensitive to the country coverage, sample period, estimation method and exchange rate regime classification. For example, no robust results have been obtained for the importance of openness, the most frequently used variable. Some studies found openness to be associated with fixed exchange rates, others found it to be associated with flexible exchange rates, and a third group of studies found out that it was unrelated to any of the regimes. Juhn and Mauro

(2002) refer to what they call 'skeptical papers' on the topic (including Honkapohja and Pikkarainen, 1994) in the sense that they found out that country characteristics (such as openness, development, geographical diversification of trade and fluctuations in the terms of trade) have hardly any power in explaining exchange rate regime choice. Although they introduce what they call 'innovations', they find no robust empirical regularities. The innovations are introduced to address the potential endogeneity of openness to exchange rate regime choice by using country characteristics and restricting cross-country regressions to those countries that have not changed their exchange rate regimes for a number of years.

Empirical models of exchange rate regime choice typically take the form of a functional relationship between a dependent variable representing regime choice and a large number of explanatory variables chosen from those displayed in Table 8.1. Starting with earlier studies, Heller (1978) applied discriminant analysis to a cross-sectional sample of 85 countries without distinguishing between developed and developing economies. Thus, he was trying to determine the characteristics that can be used to classify countries into fixers and floaters. He obtained the following discriminant function:

$$D = -1.608 + 0.015SIZ - 1.980DOP + 0.180DIF$$
$$+ 0.015DFI - 0.020DGC \tag{8.1}$$

where SIZ is the size of the economy, DOP is the degree of openness, DIF is the inflation differential, DFI is the degree of financial integration and DGC is the degree of geographical concentration of trade. On the other hand, Dreyer (1978) applied probit analysis to a sample of 88 developing countries, such that the dependent variable, Z, covers more than two exchange rate regimes. He obtained the following estimated equation (t statistics in parentheses):

$$Z = -1.38 - 0.06SIZ + 0.96DOP + 1.42DGC + 2.07DSC \tag{8.2}$$
$$(-7.79) \quad (-1.03) \quad (1.64) \quad (1.71) \quad (1.93)$$

Bosco (1987) used a pool of cross-section time series data covering 92 developing countries and three years (1978–80) to estimate an empirical model that has some theoretical foundations. The starting point of this model is that a country tends to choose an exchange rate regime to minimize the internal costs of shocks, taking into account feasibility considerations (whether or not a flexible exchange rate system is feasible for the underlying country). These costs can be regarded as a function of the degree of exchange rate flexibility as well as country characteristics. Therefore, a social loss function can be written as

$$C = f(DGC, DSC, DIF, X) \tag{8.3}$$

where X is the degree of exchange rate flexibility. If R^f is a set of feasible exchange rate regimes, then $R(DOP, DFI, SIZ, X)$ is equal to $\{X: (DOP, DFI, SIZ)\}$, the latter being the set of feasible degrees of flexibility given the values of DOP, DFI and SIZ. Hence, an optimization problem can be formulated as follows: minimize the cost function $C = f(DGC, DSC, DIF, X)$ subject to the constraint that X is in $R(DOP, DFI, SIZ, X)$. If this optimization problem has a unique solution, the optimal degree of flexibility will be given by

$$X^* = h(DGC, DSC, DIF, DOP, DFI, SIZ) \tag{8.4}$$

By applying binomial logit analysis to the whole sample, he obtained the estimated equation (standard errors in parentheses):

$$X^* = -0.96 - 2.62DOP + 0.78DFI + 0.64DIF + 0.19SIZ$$
$$\quad\ (0.77)\quad (1.45)\qquad (0.39)\qquad (0.16)\qquad (0.05)$$
$$-0.28DSC - 3.51DGC \tag{8.5}$$
$$\ (0.68)\qquad (1.64)$$

More recent studies tend to employ a larger number of explanatory variables and various definitions and measurements for the dependent variable. Significant differences exist with respect to the measurement of these variables. As an example, consider the model used by Papaionnou (2003), who examined the determinants of exchange rate regime choice in Central American countries. He used three different explanatory variables, depending on whether the objective is to test the pegging regimes against all others, floating versus all others or pegging versus crawling peg arrangements. The first of these variables, for example, takes the value of 1 if a country has a fixed exchange rate and 0 otherwise. The explanatory variables are classified into (i) optimum currency area variables, (ii) capital account openness variables, (iii) historical and institutional variables, and (iv) macroeconomic variables. The definition and measurement of these variables are shown in Table 8.2.

Little difference can be found in the variables used by Juhn and Mauro (2002). For the dependent variable they used five different classifications/years: (i) the IMF classification for the end of 2000, (ii) the IMF classification for the end of 1990 revised on the basis of the IMF staff's

Table 8.2 A description of the variables used by Papaioannou (2003)

Variable	Description
OCA variables	
Trade openness	Average of total imports and exports as a percentage of GDP
Trade with the largest partner	Exports to the largest trading partner as a percentage share of total exports
Economic size	Logarithm of GDP in US dollars at PPP rate
Per capita GDP	Total GDP in US dollars at PPP rate divided by population
Change in terms of trade	Annual change in actual terms of trade
GDP growth rate	Simple growth rate of domestic real GDP
US GDP growth rate	Simple growth rate of US real GDP
Volatility of real GDP	Five-year standard deviation of real GDP growth rate in domestic currency/US dollar terms
Volatility of inflation	Five-year standard deviation of the inflation rate measured as the percentage change in the CPI
Exchange rate volatility	Annual standard deviation of the percentage change of the bilateral nominal exchange rate against the dollar
Capital account openness variables	
Openness to capital flows	Absolute value of inward and outward flows of financial assets and liabilities
Historical/institutional variables	
Political instability	The average of government stability, political violence and internal conflicts (scale 1–12)
Macroeconomic variables	
External debt	Total external debt owed to non-residents denominated in US dollars
Inflation	Logarithm of one plus the percentage change in CPI
International reserves	The percentage share of international reserves in nominal imports

views on *de facto* regimes, (iii) the IMF *de jure* classification for the end of 1990, (iv) the Levy-Yeyati and Sturzenegger (2000a) classification for 1999, and (v) the Levy-Yeyati and Sturzenegger classification for 1990. They also used two instrumental variables to control for the endogeneity of openness to the exchange rate regime: (i) land area, and

Table 8.3 A description of the variables used by Juhn and Mauro (2002)

Variable	Description
OCA variables	
Trade openness	Ratio of imports plus exports to GDP
Trade with the largest partner	Exports to the largest trading partner as a percentage share of total exports
Economic size	Logarithm of GNP in US dollars at PPP
Per capita GNP	Total GNP in US dollars at PPP divided by population
Variability of terms of trade	Standard deviation of the terms of trade
Fuel exporters	Dummy variable taking the value of one if the country is a major fuel exporter and zero otherwise
Capital account openness variables	
Capital controls	The sum of four dummy variables that take the value of 1 if the country has (i) multiple exchange rates and (ii) current account restrictions, (iii) capital account restrictions, and (iv) export proceeds surrender requirements (0–4 scale).
Openness to capital flows	Absolute value of inward and outward flows of financial assets and liabilities
Emerging markets	Dummy for whether a country is included in the J.P. Morgan index (for whether or not it can issue international bonds)
Historical/institutional variables	
Political instability	Average of (i) government stability, (ii) external conflicts, (iii) political violence and internal conflict
Post-1945 independence	Dummy for whether the country became independent after 1945
Years since independence	Date of independence minus 1945 if the country became independent after 1945
Transition countries	Dummy for whether a country is defined as a transition economy in the IMF's *World Economic Outlook*
Macroeconomic variables	
Inflation	Logarithm of 1 plus the percentage inflation rate
Reserves	Reserves as a percentage of imports

(ii) a dummy for whether or not the country is landlocked. The explanatory variables are listed in Table 8.3.

Leon and Oliva (1999) developed a multinomial qualitative response model with the dependent variable taking the value 0 to represent a fixed exchange rate regime, 1 to represent managed floating or crawling peg and 2 to represent flexible exchange rates. The explanatory variables used in this model are the following:

- Monetary shocks, measured as the 12-month average standard deviation of the residuals from an ARMA (autoregressive moving average) model of the seasonally adjusted percentage change in M1. To avoid the simultaneity problem, the lagged value is used.
- Real shocks, defined as the 12-month average standard deviation of the residuals from an ARMA model of the percentage change in manufacturing production.
- Inflation differential, measured as the difference between domestic and world inflation.
- Foreign reserves constraint, measured as the average change in international reserves during the previous 12 months.
- Openness, measured as the ratio of trade divided by manufacturing production.

The model was estimated using monthly data covering the period January 1974–July 1993. In terms of the predicted outcomes, 80 per cent of the cases were correctly predicted as a fixed exchange rate regime. The crawling peg had 88 per cent accuracy, whereas the flexible system was predicted correctly in 83 per cent of the cases only.

While the majority of empirical regime choice models are single-equation models, Savvides (1990) formulated a simultaneous-equation model providing a link between real exchange rate variability and the choice of exchange rate regime. This kind of model is motivated by the work of Stockman (1983), who examined theoretically the impact of exchange rate regime on real exchange rate variability, showing that the exchange rate regime should be neutral with respect to real exchange rate variability. His empirical tests did not support the neutrality hypothesis, confirming that variability is substantially higher under floating than fixed exchanges rates. While he tested for the impact of the exchange rate system on real exchange rate variability, a country's experience with variability may itself influence the type of regime a country adopts. Mussa (1986, p. 202) also questions the direction of causality, suggesting that differences in real exchange rate variability may have had an important influence on the choice of exchange rate regimes by particular countries.

Mussa's and Stockman's suggestion that real exchange rate variability may influence the choice of exchange rate regime has been elaborated on by Melvin (1985). Using a standard open-economy macroeconomic model, he demonstrated that the greater the variability of foreign price disturbances, the more likely that a flexible exchange rate regime will be chosen. In testing this proposition, he measured foreign price disturbances as the standard error of residuals from autoregressive regressions of the exchange rate-adjusted inflation rate of a country's major trading partner. He then noted the work of Vaubel (1978), who suggested that higher real exchange rate variability leads a country to opt for a flexible exchange rate regime.

Empirical testing of the joint determination of real exchange rate variability and the choice of the exchange rate regime makes it necessary to use a simultaneous-equation model. The model differs from standard simultaneous-equation models in that one of the endogenous variables (the exchange rate regime) is qualitative. He used a binary classification: fixed (pegged to either a single currency or a basket) and flexible (crawling peg or floating). In this model, a number of economic variables determine a latent variable (y_1^*), which represents the intention to adopt a flexible exchange rate regime. This latent variable is in turn one of the determinants of real exchange rate variability. The model is specified as

$$y_1^* = \gamma_1 y_2 + \beta_1' X_1 + u_1 \tag{8.6}$$

$$y_2 = \gamma_2 y_1^* + \beta_2' X_2 + u_2 \tag{8.7}$$

where the latent variable is unobserved. The observed variable, y_1, is equal to 1 if the flexible regime is adopted and 0 otherwise (that is, $y_1 = 1$ if $y_1^* > 0$ and $y_1 = 0$ otherwise). In this model y_2 is variability, X_1 is a vector of exogenous variables influencing the intention to adopt an exchange rate regime, X_2 is a vector of exogenous determinants of real exchange rate variability, β_1 and β_2 are vectors of coefficients and γ_1 and γ_2 are coefficients to be estimated. The explanatory variables included in X_1 and X_2 are listed in Table 8.4 (a negative sign implies that an increase in the explanatory variable leads to the adoption of flexible rates or an increase in real exchange rate variability). The remarks refer to the anticipated signs of the coefficients on the explanatory variables as postulated by Savvides.

Thus, the final model specification consists of two equations in which the dependent variables are the exchange rate regime and real exchange rate variability. The variability of the real exchange rate is measured by the standard deviation of quarterly changes in the real exchange rate. This is unlike the two measures proposed by Kenen and Rodrik (1986): the standard deviation of the real exchange rate obtained from a log-linear trend regression and the standard deviation obtained from a

Table 8.4 The explanatory variables in the Savvides (1990) model

Variable	Effect	Remarks
Variables in equation (8.6)		
Openness	−	As openness increases, the cost of adjustment to trade disequilibrium increases under fixed exchange rates
Commodity concentration	−	Countries with diversified exports experience greater stability in foreign exchange earnings and may opt for greater exchange rate flexibility
Geographical concentration	−	If exports are directed to one trading partner it may be beneficial to peg the currency to that of the major trading partner
Capital mobility	+/−	The impact of this variable is ambiguous, as there are two contrasting forces in operation. Countries where capital is highly mobile should opt for flexible rates (because the effectiveness of monetary policy decreases as the degree of international capital mobility increases). But under flexible exchange rates and high capital mobility, balance of payments equilibrium requires the current account to adjust to capital flows, imposing domestic resource allocation costs
Economic development	+	As a country develops the efficiency of its domestic product and capital markets increases, it becomes a more suitable candidate for exchange rate flexibility
Domestic disturbances	−	The greater the domestic monetary disturbances the more likely that a fixed exchange rate is adopted
Variables in equation (8.7)		
Openness	−	The more open an economy, the greater the role of traded goods prices in the overall price indices and the smaller the deviations from PPP

Table 8.4   (Continued)

Variable	Effect	Remarks
Terms of trade variability	+	The greater the variability in the terms of trade the greater will be real exchange rate variability
Variability of GDP growth	+	Greater growth variability generates increased real exchange rate variability
Domestic monetary disturbances	+	An increase in domestic monetary shocks results in real exchange rate variability. Money or domestic credit can be used. Melvin (1985) defines domestic credit shocks as the standard error of the residuals from autoregressive regressions of the growth rate of domestic credit
Domestic inflation variability	+	Greater variability in domestic cost conditions results in greater real exchange rate variability (Kortweg, 1980)
Responsiveness of trade flows	−	Real exchange rate variability depends negatively on the degree of responsiveness of trade flows to real exchange rate changes (Driskill and McCafferty, 1980)

first-order autoregressive regression. In general, the literature does not provide a clear-cut expectation as to the sign of γ_2.

As far as exchange rate regime choice is concerned, the results indicate the following:

- Confirmation of Vaubel's (1978) conjecture that flexible exchange rates are chosen when real exchange rates are more variable.
- Support for Melvin's (1985) hypothesis that the greater the foreign price shocks the more likely is a flexible system when the real exchange rate is viewed as a measure of foreign price shocks.
- Support for Melvin's second hypothesis concerning monetary disturbances.
- The coefficients on commodity concentration and economic development are, as expected, negative and positive respectively.
- International capital mobility exerts significant negative impact on exchange rate flexibility.

- The coefficients on openness and the geographical concentration are insignificant.

As far as real exchange rate variability is concerned, the results confirmed that a country with a more flexible exchange rate regime experiences lower real exchange rate variability. This result is in contrast with earlier findings, which warrants an explanation. Black (1976) and Williamson (1982) have suggested that a more flexible exchange rate arrangement, such as a crawling peg based on inflation differentials, may provide for greater real exchange rate stability. He attributed the contrasting results produced by Stockman (1983) and Mussa (1986) to the use of misspecified models that exclude real and monetary shocks.

Theoretical models of exchange rate regime choice

Some models of exchange rate regime choice are based on explicit functional equations, including the models used by Fischer (1977), Boyer (1978) and Frenkel and Aizenman (1982). In these models the choice of the exchange rate regime is affected by the assumptions supporting the model. For example, Fischer and Frenkel and Aizenman assume an optimizing criterion based on real consumption, within a model with no capital mobility and output that is independent of prices. The basic result is that flexible exchange rates are preferred when there are monetary disturbances, whereas preference goes for fixed rates when there are real shocks. In contrast, Boyer (1978) used a Mundell–Fleming-type model for a small open economy where the objective is to minimize output variability. His main conclusion is the opposite to Fischer's, concluding that it is optimal to have flexible exchange rates when there are real shocks, since these shocks have to be absorbed by generating or withdrawing external demand.

Other models include consumer optimizing behaviour. For example, Helpman (1981) developed a simple two-country model to compare the welfare levels achieved under different exchange rate regimes. He found welfare levels to be identical under both regimes. However, as Aschauer and Greenwood (1983) point out, this result is due to the assumption that output is determined exogenously. When they change this assumption and postulate that output depends on the labour force, they obtain results indicating that a country may achieve a higher welfare level under flexible exchange rates, as flexibility permits the country to choose an optimal inflation rate.

It is also possible to classify theoretical models of exchange rate regime choice into those based on what Devereux and Engel (1999) call ad hoc criteria involving the variance of inflation and output and those that investigate the optimality of exchange rate regimes from a welfare-maximizing perspective. In the first category are Turnovsky (1976, 1983), Hamada and Sakurai (1978), Flood (1979), Flood and Marion (1982), Weber (1981), Kimbrough (1983), Aizenman and Frenkel (1985) and Glick and Wihlborg (1990). In the second category are Lapan and Enders (1980), Helpman (1981), Helpman and Razin (1982), Eaton (1985), Aizenman (1994), Chinn and Miller (1998) and Neumeyer (1998).

Berger *et al.* (2001) present a standard one-period model of credibility problems in monetary policy. The model shows that the choice between fixed and flexible exchange rates depends on the trade-off between gaining credibility and losing flexibility. The Lucas supply schedule is given by

$$y = \alpha(\pi - \pi^e) + \varepsilon \tag{8.8}$$

where $\alpha > 0$ is a proxy for nominal rigidity, the extent to which unanticipated inflation has real effects, y is the logarithm of output, π is inflation and ε is a shock with zero mean and variance of σ_ε^2. Monetary policy is conducted according to the stochastic version of PPP

$$\pi = \Delta e + \pi^* + \phi \tag{8.9}$$

where Δe is the rate of change in exchange rate, π^* is the foreign inflation rate and ϕ is a mean zero shock with variance σ_ϕ^2. The shock can be interpreted as a change in the world's relative demand for domestic goods or as a part of foreign monetary policy. In general, it can be interpreted as foreign business cycle spillovers onto the domestic economy. The aim of monetary policy is to minimize deviations of output and inflation from their target levels ($y^* > 0$ and zero respectively). The loss function specified by Berger *et al.* (2001) takes the form

$$L = E[\lambda(y - y^*)^2 + \pi^2], \ \lambda > 0 \tag{8.10}$$

where E is the expectations operator. Furthermore, they specify the time-consistent rational expectations equilibrium as

$$\pi = \lambda\alpha y^* - \frac{\lambda\alpha}{1 + \lambda\alpha^2}\varepsilon \tag{8.11}$$

$$y = \frac{1}{1 + \lambda\alpha^2}\varepsilon \tag{8.12}$$

Then they proceed to specify the loss function under flexible and fixed rates, which puts them in a position to formulate a decision rule. Under flexible exchange rates, foreign inflation and the spillover shock do not affect the domestic economy, as variations in these variables are absorbed by exchange rate movements. They obtain the loss function encountered under flexible exchange rates by inserting (8.11) and (8.12) into (8.10). Hence

$$L(Flexible) = \lambda y^{*2} + (\lambda \alpha y^*)^2 + \frac{\lambda}{(1 + \lambda \alpha^2)^2} \sigma_\varepsilon^2 + \frac{\lambda^2 \alpha^2}{(1 + \lambda \alpha^2)^2} \sigma_\varepsilon^2 \quad (8.13)$$

Under fixed exchange rates, $\Delta e = 0$, which gives $\pi = \pi^* + \phi$ and $y = \alpha \phi + \varepsilon$. Hence, the loss function under fixed rates is

$$L(Fixed) = \lambda y^{*2} + \pi^{*2} + \lambda[\sigma_\varepsilon^2 + \alpha^2 \sigma_\phi^2 + 2\alpha \rho_{\varepsilon\phi} \sigma_\varepsilon \sigma_\phi] + \sigma_\phi^2 \quad (8.14)$$

where $\rho_{\varepsilon\phi}$ is the correlation coefficient between ε and ϕ. The decision rule that Berger *et al.* come up with is the following: fixed exchange rates will be preferable if L under fixed rates is less than L under flexible rates. Formally, fixed exchange rates will be chosen if

$$(\lambda \alpha y^*)^2 - \pi^{*2} > \lambda \left[\sigma_\varepsilon^2 + \alpha^2 \sigma_\phi^2 + 2\alpha \rho_{\varepsilon\phi} \sigma_\varepsilon \sigma_\phi \right]$$
$$- \frac{\lambda}{(1 + \lambda \alpha^2)^2} \sigma_\varepsilon^2 + \sigma_\phi^2 - \frac{\lambda^2 \alpha^2}{(1 + \lambda \alpha^2)^2} \sigma_\varepsilon^2 \quad (8.15)$$

The left-hand side of the inequality is the regime differences in terms of losses from average inflation. The first two terms on the right-hand side depict regime differences in terms of losses from the output variance. The last two terms are the regime differences in terms of inflation variability. Two findings are derived from this model. The first is that the case for fixed rates is strengthened if the correlation between the domestic and the spillover shocks is negative. The second is that an increase in the standard deviation of the domestic or spillover shocks unambiguously weakens the case for fixed rates if, and only if, correlation is non-negative.

Sun (2002) presents a game theory-based political–economic model that analyses exchange rate regime choice in a two-period bipartisan game. Two parties are involved in the game (a left-wing party and a right-wing party) to choose the exchange rate regime on the basis of the difference between the intertemporal distribution of the inflation cost under the two regimes. Under fixed exchange rates the inflation cost of fiscal spending is pushed to the future, whereas it is spread across time under flexible exchange rates (Tornell and Velasco, 1995). The incumbent government can influence the spending decision of the future government by determining whether the inflation cost is borne by the future government only or by both the current and future governments.

A forward-looking government chooses an exchange rate regime based on the strategic balancing of three incentives: (i) the incentive to facilitate its own future policy implementation should it win the election, (ii) the incentive to create constraints for its successor if it loses the election, and (iii) the incentive to increase the probability of reelection. This is what is likely to happen under three scenarios:

- When the incumbent government knows with certainty that it will not be in power in the next period, it has the incentive to tie the hands of its successor. A right-wing incumbent government will choose fixed exchange rates to restrain the spending of a future left-wing government, whereas a left-wing incumbent government will choose flexible rates to induce its successor to spend more.
- When the incumbent government knows with certainty that it will be in power next period, it chooses an exchange rate regime that facilitates its own future policy implementation. The best course of action would be to commit spending to what is announced at the beginning of the period, thus choosing fixed exchange rates. This applies to both parties.
- If there is electoral uncertainty, the incumbent government will try to influence the preference of the median voter (who dislikes inflation more than the left-wing party but less than the right-wing party). By choosing exchange flexible rates, a right-wing incumbent capitalizes on the inflationary reputation of the left-wing party and gains from its non-inflationary reputation. Likewise, fixed exchange rates are more conducive to increasing the chance of reelecting a left-wing government.

Flood *et al.* (1989) present a theoretical model that tracks the evolution of exchange rate regimes. The model makes it possible to view an exchange rate regime as an optimal response by policy-makers to a changing environment. They criticize typical models of exchange rate regime choice because they are based on the assumption that the underlying economic structure is time-invariant, in which case exchange rate regime choice is obtained as a once-and-for-all solution to a static optimization problem. Yet, this is not really the case in an ever-changing world.

As the underlying economic structure changes over time, the nature of the optimal exchange rate regime can be expected to vary, giving rise to some sort of evolution. This proposition seems to be supported by casual observation as countries tend to switch back and forth between exchange rate regimes. Thus, Flood *et al.* (1989) argue that 'the adoption or disbandment of various exchange rate arrangements over time may then be viewed as a predictable and optimal response to the inherently time-varying nature of the underlying state of the world'. The model they advance to track the evolution of exchange rate regime choice consists of three equations: a money market equilibrium equation, a Lucas-style output supply function and a PPP relationship. The model is subsequently used to analyse two situations: (i) a response to an unexpected event, such as a sudden large change in the desired government spending; and (ii) the possible expected return to the prior regime.

Some theoretical models of exchange rate regime choice have dealt with 'unorthodox' explanatory variables. For example, Devereux and Engel (1999) investigate the choice between fixed and flexible exchange rates in a dynamic, intertemporal general equilibrium model. They extend the work of Devereux and Engel (1998) by examining the implications of internationalized production. The conclusion they reach is that gains from floating exchange rates are greatest in the presence of internationalized production and that price setting (whether it is in terms of the currency of the producer or that of the consumer) plays an important role in the choice between fixed and flexible rates. Aizenman and Hausmann (2000) present a model that considers the interaction between exchange rate regime choice and financial structure. This is a two-period model in which the second period output is determined by the expectation-augmented Phillips curve and where there is incomplete information about the second period's real and nominal shocks. By solving the model, they conclude that two variables pertaining to the financial structure affect the regime choice: (i) reliance on working capital to finance output needs, and (ii) segmentation of the domestic capital market.

Models of macroeconomic performance

In this section, we deal with models that aim to explain the effect of exchange rate regimes on macroeconomic performance or, in general, the effect of various exchange rate regimes on other variables in the economy. This strand of research takes the form of empirical models in which macroeconomic variables are specified to depend on some explanatory variables that include the exchange rate regime. Thus, these models aim at revealing the effect of exchange rate regime on macro-economic variables after controlling for other variables. For example, Levy-Yeyati and Sturzenegger (2001) use the explanatory variables listed in Table 8.5 to test for the relationships between four macroeconomic indicators and the exchange rate regime (fixed or flexible, as indicated by a dummy variable). The four macroeconomic indicators are infla-tion, monetary growth, real interest rate and growth rate. They men-tion in particular the difficulty of modelling the credibility effect on inflation, arguing that it may be obtained by including regime dum-mies. A measure of openness is used to control for the potential disciplinary effects of international arbitrage (see Romer, 1993). A lagged dependent variable is included to capture the effect of past policies on current expectations and to control for the effect of past policies on current expectations.

Ghosh *et al.* (2002) present a comprehensive treatment of the effect of the exchange rate regime on inflation and growth. This work was motiv-ated by the mixed nature of the results and stylized facts on the relation-ship between the exchange rate regime and macroeconomic indicators. They described the results for the inflation–exchange rate regime nexus as being 'largely consistent with the predictions of the policy credibility models', whereas those pertaining to the effect on growth were 'more equivocal'.

For the purpose of empirical testing, Ghosh *et al.* (2002) use functional specifications that are slightly different from those presented in Ghosh *et al.* (1997). More or less similar specifications are used by Rogoff *et al.* (2004). To examine the relationship between inflation and the exchange rate regime, they start with a simple regression equation in which the scaled inflation rate is explained in terms of two regime dummies for fixed and intermediate regimes. The equation may be written as

$$\pi = \alpha_0 + \alpha_1 D_F + \alpha_2 D_I + \varepsilon \tag{8.16}$$

where D_F is the dummy for fixed regimes and D_I is the dummy for intermediate regimes. Since the effect of floating regimes is not explicit in the model, the coefficients α_1 and α_2 are interpreted as the inflation differentials relative to the floating regime. The scaled inflation rate is defined as

$$\pi = \frac{\Delta p}{1 + \Delta p} \tag{8.17}$$

Table 8.5 The Levy-Yeyati and Sturzenegger specifications

Dependent variable	Explanatory variables
Inflation rate	Monetary growth GDP growth Change in interest rate Openness Lagged inflation rate Exchange rate regime dummies Regional dummy (Latin America) Regional dummy (sub-Saharan countries) Regional dummy (transition countries)
Monetary growth	Lagged GDP growth Change in interest rate Openness Fiscal balance as a percentage of GDP Lagged inflation rate Exchange rate regime dummies Regional dummy (Latin America) Regional dummy (sub-Saharan countries) Regional dummy (transition countries)
Real interest rate	GDP growth Monetary growth rate Change in interest rate Net interest rate payments as a percentage of GDP Lagged inflation rate Openness Exchange rate regime dummies Regional dummy (Latin America) Regional dummy (sub-Saharan countries) Regional dummy (transition countries)
Growth rate	Investment to GDP ratio Population growth Lagged growth of government consumption Per capita GDP at the beginning of the period Initial secondary school enrolment A measure of political stability Change in terms of trade Exchange rate regime dummies Regional dummy (Latin America) Regional dummy (sub-Saharan countries) Regional dummy (transition countries)

where Δp is the unscaled inflation rate (the logarithmic change in the price level). The advantage of the scaled inflation rate is that it is robust to hyperinflationary outliers, while capturing the mass of the distribution. Obviously, the model represented by equation (8.16) is inadequate as there are missing variables. Therefore, they refine the model by adding the following explanatory variables: output growth, Δy; monetary growth, Δm; openness, O; the turnover rate of the central bank governor, G; inflationary terms of trade shocks, T; and the fiscal balance, B. Table 8.6 explains why these variables are included in the model.

The full inflation equation is written as

$$\pi = \alpha_0 + \alpha_1 D_F + \alpha_2 D_I + \alpha_3 \Delta y + \alpha_4 \Delta m + \alpha_5 O$$
$$+ \alpha_6 G + \alpha_7 \Delta T + \alpha_8 B + \varepsilon \qquad (8.18)$$

The empirical results show that all of the coefficients on the explanatory variables turned out to be significant with the expected signs, except for the terms of trade. They also reveal that inflation under fixed exchange rates is 10.5 percentage points lower than under floating rates. The inflation differential is even larger *vis-à-vis* intermediate regimes.

The growth equation contains a larger number of explanatory variables as suggested by growth theory and the numerous studies of cross-country differences in growth. Thus, the growth equation is written as

$$\pi = \beta_0 + \beta_1 D_F + \beta_2 D_I + \beta_3 I + \beta_4 O + \beta_5 \Delta T + \beta_6 S + \beta_7 X$$
$$+ \beta_8 B + \beta_9 \log C + \beta_{10} \Delta P + \beta_{11} \log P + \xi \qquad (8.19)$$

Table 8.6 Explanatory variables in the Ghosh *et al.* (2002) inflation equation

Variable	Effect	Rationale
Δy	−	Raising the demand for money, hence reducing inflation
Δm	+	The quantity theory of money
O	−	Openness raises the costs of monetary expansion, which (by the logic of the policy credibility models) should reduce inflation (Romer, 1993)
G	+	Turnover rate of the central bank governor is an inverse proxy for central bank independence (Cukierman, 1992)
ΔT	+	As in Fischer (1993)
B	+	Through direct monetization of the deficit or contribution to aggregate demand pressure

where *I* is the ratio of investment to GDP, *S* is the average number of years of schooling, *X* is the tax revenue to GDP ratio, *C* is the log of the ratio of the country's per capita GDP to that of the USA in 1970 (to capture the catch-up effect) and *P* is population. They used the model not only to examine the direct effect of the regime on growth but also the indirect effect transmitted via the effect on openness and investment. Overall, they find mixed results for the effect of exchange rate regime on growth. Specifically, they point out that while they find some evidence indicating that countries with pegged and intermediate regimes perform better on the growth front, much of the performance can be explained by country-specific effects or simultaneity bias.

Other models of exchange rate regime choice

A large number of theoretical and empirical models have been suggested to study issues pertaining to exchange rate regime choice, apart from those discussed in the previous sections (factors determining the choice and the effect of the exchange regime on growth and inflation). In this section selected studies of this kind are surveyed briefly.

Modelling the effect of currency unions

One of the issues that have been examined extensively is the effect of currency unions on trade. Much of the recent interest in this issue was sparked by Rose (2000), who found out that trading partners belonging to a currency union experienced a threefold increase in bilateral trade compared to other trading partners. This is too much of an effect if we take into account the results of the literature on the relationship between exchange rate volatility and trade. Subsequent studies by Persson (2001) and Tenreyo (2001) criticized the methodology used by Rose, producing a smaller effect of currency union on trade. Faruqee (2004) also criticized the findings of Rose on grounds other than econometric issues. He argues that the implications of the Rose study for the EMU are unclear because: (i) the analysis did not directly include countries operating under the EMU in the sample; (ii) the sample countries that did not belong to currency areas were mostly smaller, poorer countries; and (iii) the cross-sectional analysis provides a comparative benchmark across trading partners that belong to an existing currency union against those that do not.

To deal with the criticism of Rose, Glick and Rose (2002) analysed panel data to exploit the time series information associated with entering and exiting a currency union. They find that trade roughly doubles in that context, but again the sample does not cover the EMU. This is unlike the study of Micco *et al.* (2003), who examined the dynamic impact of the EMU on trade using a panel of twenty-two industrial countries and a smaller panel of fifteen members of the European Union. The panel regressions based on the gravity model suggest that the EMU has fostered further trade integration among member countries and that the positive effect has been rising over time. The European Commission (2003) provides a review of studies examining the EMU's impact on trade.

More recently, Faruqee (2004) used a gravity model to examine the trade effect of the EMU. Specifically, he examined the following issues: (i) whether or not the EMU has fostered greater trade integration among member countries, (ii) the evolution of the trade effects of the EMU over time, (iii) the distribution of the trade gains among member countries, and (iv) the policies and preconditions that have been important in positioning some European Union members to benefit more in terms of trade integration. The gravity model that he used is specified as

$$\log T_{ijt} = \alpha_{ij} + \tau_t + \beta_1 \log(Y_{it} Y_{jt}) + \beta_2 \log(y_{it} y_{jt})$$
$$+ \gamma_1 D_A + \gamma_2 D_E + \gamma_3 D_U + \varepsilon \tag{8.20}$$

where T_{ijt} is bilateral trade between country i and country j at time t, α_{ij} is the fixed effect on trade between partner countries i and j, τ_t represents common time effects for a particular year, Y is the level of GDP, y is the per capita GDP, D_A is a dummy for common membership in a free trade agreement, D_E is a dummy for membership in the European Union and D_U is a dummy for membership of the EMU. The variable of interest here is naturally D_U. This model was estimated using a panel of annual data covering the period 1992–2002 for 22 industrial countries, giving 231 country pairs. The results show that the EMU has had a positive impact on intra-area trade and that these gains have not been achieved at the expense of extra-area trade.

Modelling exchange rate stabilization against several currencies

Benassy-Quere (1999) presents a model representing a country's desire to stabilize the exchange rate of the domestic currency against three major currencies (say, the dollar, the euro and the yen). In this case, the country in question tries to minimize the loss function:

$$F = \alpha_1 [a(L)\Delta e(x/y_1) - \sigma_1]^2 + \alpha_2 [b(L)\Delta e(x/y_2) - \sigma_2]^2$$
$$+ \alpha_3 [c(L)\Delta e(x/y_3) - \sigma_3]^2 \tag{8.21}$$

where $e(x/y_i)$ is the logarithm of the exchange rate of the domestic currency, x, against currency y_i, such that $i = 1,2,3$, σ_i is the corresponding target and $a(L)$, $b(L)$ and $c(L)$ are lag polynomials, such that $a(L) = \sum a_i L_i$, $b(L) = \sum b_i L_i$ and $c(L) = \sum c_i L_i$, where L is the lag operator. If y_1 is the numeraire currency (the US dollar), then it follows that

$$\Delta e(x/y_i) = \Delta e(x/y_1) - \Delta e(y_i/y_1) \tag{8.22}$$

for $i = 1,2,3$. Hence, the optimal exchange rate policy can be represented by

$$\Delta e(x/y_1) = D + A(L)\Delta e(x/y_1) + B(L)\Delta e(y_2/y_1) + C(L)\Delta e(y_3/y_1) \tag{8.23}$$

where

$$D = \frac{\alpha_1 a(0)\sigma_1 + \alpha_2 b(0)\sigma_2 + \alpha_3 c(0)\sigma_3}{\alpha_1 a(0)^2 + \alpha_2 b(0)^2 + \alpha_3 c(0)^2} \tag{8.24}$$

$$A(L) = \frac{\alpha_1 a(0)[a(0) - a(L)]}{\alpha_1 a(0)^2 + \alpha_2 b(0)^2 + \alpha_3 c(0)^2} \tag{8.25}$$

$$B(L) = \frac{\alpha_2 b(0)b(L)}{\alpha_1 a(0)^2 + \alpha_2 b(0)^2 + \alpha_3 c(0)^2} \tag{8.26}$$

$$C(L) = \frac{\alpha_3 c(0)c(L)}{\alpha_1 a(0)^2 + \alpha_2 b(0)^2 + \alpha_3 c(0)^2} \tag{8.27}$$

Benassy-Quere further suggests that equation (8.23) can be rewritten in such a way as to make it possible to estimate the long-run coefficients. Hence, we have

$$\Delta e(x/y_1) = D + A(1)\Delta e(x/y_1)_{t-1} + \sum_{i=1}^{11} A_i^* \Delta^2 e(x/y_1)_{t-i}$$

$$+ B(1)\Delta e(y_2/y_1)_t + \sum_{i=0}^{11} B_i^* \Delta^2 e(y_2/y_1)_{t-i} + C(1)\Delta e(y_3/y_1)$$

$$+ \sum_{i=0}^{11} C_i^* \Delta^2 e(y_3/y_1)_{t-i} + \varepsilon \tag{8.28}$$

where

$$A_i^* = - \sum_{j=i+1}^{12} a_j \tag{8.29}$$

$$B_i^* = - \sum_{j=i+1}^{12} b_j \tag{8.30}$$

$$C_i^* = - \sum_{j=i+1}^{12} c_j \tag{8.31}$$

However, it has to be mentioned here that this is not the only way to estimate long-run coefficients.

Kawai (2003) examines the issue of anchors for exchange rate stabilization policies by considering the currency composition in each developing country's currency basket. The underlying hypothesis is that the estimated currency composition (a set of estimated weights) is explained by the country's share of trade with the currency area formed by the respective anchor currency. It is also postulated that non-economic factors, such as the country's geographical location and former colonial relationships, may explain the currency composition of the basket. Using daily data, Kawai (2003) estimated the following regression equation to investigate the roles of the US dollar, yen and euro:

$$\Delta e(x/y) = \alpha_0 + \alpha_1 \Delta e(USD/y) + \alpha_2 \Delta e(EUR/y) + \alpha_3 \Delta e(JPY/y) + \varepsilon \tag{8.32}$$

where e is the log of the exchange rate, x is the domestic currency and y is a numeraire, which in this case is the Swiss franc. The estimated coefficients are interpreted as the weights assigned by the authorities to the corresponding currencies in their exchange rate policies. The ECU was used prior to the emergence of the euro.

The regression results show that in the pre-crisis period (January 1990–June 1997) the estimated coefficients on the US dollar are statistically significant and close to unity, supporting the proposition that many emerging East Asian economies were on *de facto* US dollar-pegged systems until the onset of the crisis. Little evidence was found for the role of the other two currencies. After the crisis, the results show that a few countries returned to the pre-crisis pattern (China and Hong Kong), whereas others departed from that pattern (Indonesia). The results also show that Korea and Thailand shifted to a currency basket with large weights assigned to the US dollar and Japanese yen.

Kawai and Akiyama (2000) conducted a similar exercise. The results of their regression analysis indicate that the more a developing country trades with a major currency area, the larger will be the proportion of this currency in the country's exchange rate stabilization policy. They found that the weight assigned to the US dollar in a particular country's currency basket is positively correlated with the size of the dollar area with which this country trades. The results also reveal that the observed exchange rate arrangements are largely consistent with the reported exchange rate policies, with some exceptions. Furthermore, Kawai and Akiyama suggest the following:

- Many developing countries have shifted from fixed to flexible exchange rates. However, they often exhibit a preference for stable exchange rates *vis-à-vis* a single currency or a currency basket.
- The US dollar is the most favoured anchor currency for exchange rate stabilization in the developing world.
- The Japanese yen does not play a major role as an anchor currency, even in East Asia.
- Developing Europe uses the US dollar, the euro, or a basket thereof as a loose anchor.
- The Middle East includes countries that have successfully stabilized exchange rates *vis-à-vis* the dollar and the SDR.
- Latin America is a *de facto* dollar area, and even countries that do not officially peg to the US dollar do assign significant weight to the dollar.
- A developing country's choice of anchor currencies for exchange rate stabilization depends largely on the country's geographical location and its past colonial ties.

Some other economists have come up with models of basket pegs. Turnovsky (1982) used a general equilibrium model of a small open economy to derive the optimal weights in a currency basket on the assumption that the policy objective is to minimize the variance of income. The optimal weights are shown to depend on variances, covariances and partial derivatives. Likewise, Bhandari (1985) used a three-country general equilibrium model with stochastic monetary and real disturbances to analyse the basket peg. The policy objectives he considered are: (i) minimization of the variances of domestic output around its expected value as well as its full-information level, (ii) minimization of the variance of the domestic money supply, and (iii) minimization of the variance of the trade-weighted real exchange rate.

Monetary independence and exchange rate regimes

Empirical models have been suggested to test the effect of exchange rate regime choice on the sensitivity of domestic interest rates to foreign interest rates, which boils down to studying the relationship between the exchange rate regime and monetary independence. If floating exchange rates allow monetary independence, then domestic interest rates should be less sensitive to foreign interest rates under floating rates. Focusing on some countries whose regimes can be clearly described as currency boards or floating regimes, Borensztein *et al.* (2001) found some evidence that is consistent with the traditional view. On the other hand, selected country evidence reported in Frankel (1999) and Hausmann *et al.* (1999) confirms the alternative view.

Frankel *et al.* (2002) extended the literature on this issue by using a model that can be written as

$$r_{i,t} = \alpha_i + \beta r_t^* + \gamma' X_{i,t} + \varepsilon_t \tag{8.33}$$

where r is the domestic nominal interest rate of country i at time t, r_t^* is the international interest rate and $X_{i,t}$ is a set of control variables, including dummy variables that control for turbulent periods. The empirical results derived from this model reveal the following: (i) over the 1990s all exchange rate regimes exhibited high sensitivity of domestic interest rates to international rates, (ii) floating regimes allow for increased monetary independence but only in the sense of the speed of adjustment of domestic interest rates towards the long-run one-for-one relation, and (iii) only the Japanese and German interest rates do not show sensitivity to the US rates.

The model used for this purpose is similar to what has been used in some studies to test the trilemma (the inconsistency of fixed exchange rates, capital mobility and monetary independence). Tests of the trilemma are typically indirect, but a more direct approach was proposed by Rose (1996), who compared the predictions of the monetary model of exchange rates with actual exchange rate movements conditional on capital controls and the exchange rate regime. Obstfeld *et al.* (2004a) suggest a natural alternative by measuring monetary policy not by a quantity (money) but by a price, which is the short-term interest rate, because it is the actual instrument used by the central bank to implement monetary policy. Several other studies have followed this track, including Frankel *et al.* (2002), Obstfeld *et al.* (2004b) and Shambaugh (2004). The simple equation used by Obstfeld *et al.* (2004a) takes the form

$$\Delta r_{it} = \beta \Delta r_{bit} + \varepsilon_{it} \qquad (8.34)$$

where r_{it} is the nominal interest rate in country i at time t, r_{bit} is the interest rate in the base country and u_{it} is a random shock. Fixed effects (constant terms) are omitted on the grounds that deterministic trends in interest rates are implausible and that they turn out to be statistically insignificant anyway. The empirical results provide support for the prevalence of the trilemma during the interwar period.

Exchange rate regimes and the effect of terms of trade shocks

There has been little work on the relationship between exchange rate regimes and the way in which the terms of trade shocks affect growth and other measures of economic performance. In fact, papers investigating empirically the way in which terms of trade disturbances affect economic growth and growth volatility tend to ignore the role played by the exchange rate regime in the transmission process. Edwards and Levy-Yeyati (2003) conducted a literature search using EconLit and came up with the finding that 165 papers with the words 'exchange rate regimes' and 'growth' in the titles or the abstract were published between 1969 and 2002. They also found that during the same period, 98 papers with the words 'terms of trade' and 'growth' were published. But only three papers that had all terms were published during the period. One of these papers is Broda (2001), who provides one of the few empirical analyses of how terms of trade shocks affect real economic performance under alternative exchange rate regimes. He uses a VAR analysis to assess the way in which terms of trade shocks affect growth. He finds that a 10 per cent deterioration in the terms of trade has a greater negative effect under fixed than under flexible exchange rates.

Edwards and Levy-Yeyati (2003) investigate the hypothesis that terms of trade disturbances have a smaller effect on growth under a flexible exchange rate regime than otherwise. They also analyse whether negative and positive terms of trade shocks have asymmetric effects on growth, and whether the magnitude of these asymmetries depends on the exchange rate regime. For this purpose, they used a model consisting of two equations: a long-run GDP growth equation and another equation that captures the growth dynamic process. These equations are specified as

$$g_j^* = \alpha + \mathbf{x}_j \beta + \mathbf{r}_j \theta + \omega_j \qquad (8.35)$$

$$\Delta g_{t,j} = \lambda [g_j^* - g_{t-1,j}] + \varphi v_{t,j} + \gamma u_{t,j} + \xi_{t,j} \qquad (8.36)$$

where g_j^* is the long-run real per capita GDP growth in country j, $\mathbf{x}_j$ is a vector of structural, institutional and policy variables that determine long-run growth, $\mathbf{r}_j$ is a vector of regional dummies, α, β and θ are parameters and ω_j is a heteroscedastic error term. In equation (8.36), $g_{t,j}$ is the rate of growth of per capita GDP in country j in period t. The terms v and u are shocks, assumed to have a zero mean, finite variances and zero covariances (v is an external terms of trade shock, whereas u captures other shocks, including political shocks). In this model the question whether or not the exchange rate regime has a direct effect on the long-term growth rates is indicated by whether α is different for countries with different exchange rate regimes. The parameter φ tells us whether floating exchange rates allow better absorption of foreign shocks (expected to be smaller in countries with floating rates). The model was estimated for a sample of 183 countries over the period 1974–2000, producing the following results:

- Terms of trade shocks get amplified in countries with more rigid rates. This means that countries with flexible rates are better able to accommodate real external shocks.
- An asymmetric response of output to terms of trade shocks. The output response is larger for negative than for positive shocks.

9
Case Studies

Exchange rate regime choice in a postwar country: Iraq

This case study draws heavily on Moosa (2004a, 2004b). Iraq is a case of a postwar country that experienced hyperinflation resulting from excessive currency printing. Between 1991 and 1995, the nominal value of the currency in circulation jumped from 22 billion to 584 billion, giving rise to an average annual inflation rate of 250 per cent. Monetary reform in post-Saddam Iraq is an issue that has been dealt with in the academic literature (for example, Hanke, 2003a; Roubini and Sester, 2003), in the media (for example, Hanke, 2003b) and in policy documents (for example, Sanford, 2003). King (2004) used the case of Iraq to demonstrate that expectations of future collective decisions can have a major impact on the value of a currency, irrespective of the policies pursed by the current government.

One of the major tasks facing any civilian authority in a postwar situation is to get the economy up and running. Central to this effort is putting in place stable monetary conditions as a prerequisite for the success of economic reconstruction. This is particularly the case if the country in question has been enduring macroeconomic mismanagement and inflationary monetary policy, which were the conditions that Iraq endured for many years under the regime of Saddam Hussein. The question that had to crop up, therefore, was the choice of exchange rate regime, as this choice is a critical component of monetary reform in Iraq. As expected, the views on this issue diverge between the extremes of dollarization and free floating.

I argue that the optimal exchange rate regime under the prevailing conditions is a currency board, while arguing against suggestions for adopting managed floating and other regimes. The basis of the argument for a currency board and against managed floating is that the former imposes the discipline that the Central Bank of Iraq (CBI) needs after years of monetary abuse. It is also argued that while a currency board is a rather stringent system, it is an extreme measure that is needed to deal with an extreme situation. There is no better way to curb the temptation to monetize the deficit than a currency board, whereby the central bank keeps a full foreign exchange cover at a fixed exchange rate.

One argument against a currency board for Iraq is that the foreign currency reserves needed to run the exchange rate arrangement can and should be used more appropriately for the reconstruction of the country. Some counter-arguments can be suggested. The first is that this is a price worth paying to achieve monetary stability and restore confidence in the currency. The other counter-argument is that the foreign exchange reserves required for a full cover are rather small relative to the total cost of reconstruction. Assuming that the monetary base/GDP ratio is 0.1 and that GDP in 2003 is $25 billion, the initial cover required is $2.5 billion. This is a small fraction of the $100 billion or so needed to finance reconstruction. The amount required for this purpose should be readily available from the frozen Iraqi assets. Moreover, keeping full reserves at the CBI gives it more credibility at a time when potential transaction partners associate it with bankruptcy. This is not to mention that the CBI needs to hold some reserves under other exchange rate arrangements, albeit smaller amounts.

The arguments against a currency board for Iraq are the following:

- Difficulties of managing external shocks.
- The requirement of a strong fiscal policy in place.
- The possibility of serious consequences if an inappropriate level of the fixed exchange rate is selected.

While there are no problems with these arguments in a general sense, I find it unacceptable to put forward propositions that do not take into account the specifics of the situation in Iraq and its priorities. Hence, consider the following counter-arguments:

- To start with, the argument about shocks is mostly applicable to a developed country with a diversified export base, not to a country that derives 95 per cent of its foreign exchange revenue from a commodity that is priced in US dollar terms. Iraq will be (for a long time to come) selling oil only, using the dollar-denominated revenues to buy goods (and services) denominated in dollars, euros and yen. Hence, envisaging that the exchange rate can be used as a macroeconomic policy tool under the present conditions is bizarre, to say the least. The only shock that matters for Iraq would be an oil price or demand shock, but in this case the exchange rate is totally irrelevant.

- A strong fiscal policy would be an outcome of a currency board, because this arrangement prevents the monetization of the budget deficit. Fiscal policy will be disciplined by the presence of a mechanism preventing the government from financing the deficit by printing currency. In the absence of a well-developed tax system and capital markets, deficit spending is difficult.

- I agree that serious consequences would arise if the wrong level of the exchange rate were chosen. If there is any truth to the proposition that the market is the best determinant of prices (including exchange rates), then a rate that is close to the market rate should be chosen. In any case, this will be a problem under managed floating as well (what is the level of the exchange rate that is compatible with the fundamentals?).

Those opposing a currency board for Iraq along these lines argue for managed floating. However, it is possible to present the following arguments against managed floating:

- Managed floating requires intervention in the foreign exchange market, which the staff of the CBI cannot handle (lack of expertise and training). It will take time, effort and resources to make them capable of executing this function. This is reality, not macroeconomics.

- A priority for Iraq is a stable currency, both internally and externally. This objective can be best achieved by the establishment of a currency board, not through managed floating.

- Another priority is to regain confidence in the CBI of regional and international banks that stopped dealing with it towards the end of the 1980s when they realized that it was bankrupt. Keeping a full-reserve cover would help regain confidence in the CBI.

- Managed floating with little reserves will encourage speculative attacks against the currency. A currency collapse is the shock that Iraq must avoid in the immediate future. Moreover, we have learnt through the bitter experiences of several central banks that foreign exchange market intervention does not work unless all objectives of monetary policy are subordinated to the objective of defending the domestic currency.

One way to advocate the choice of a currency board for Iraq is to argue that other exchange rate arrangements are not suitable under the present conditions. Free floating is not a viable system. Indeed, no country operates free floating in the sense that there is no foreign exchange market intervention whatsoever. Managed floating that aims at keeping the exchange rate within a certain range requires: (i) identifying a range within which the exchange rate should be kept, and (ii) executing foreign exchange operations to achieve this objective. The first requirement is similar to what is encountered under a currency board when a decision is taken on the fixed rate, which means that this regime has no advantage over a currency board in this respect. Executing foreign exchange operations is a big problem because the CBI personnel lack the experience of trading and familiarity with the underlying technology. Moreover, Iraq's telecommunications infrastructure is not developed adequately to allow a smooth working of these operations. Hence, managed floating is not a viable alternative under the present conditions. Finally, a fixed but adjustable exchange rate has been proved to be a 'dinner invitation' for currency speculators.

In a discussion paper, Roubini and Sester (2003) considered the options available to Iraq with respect to the exchange rate regime choice. While the Roubini–Sester arguments make sense in general terms, they overlook the special situation of Iraq, not as an oil exporter but as a country suffering from the ramifications of years of macroeconomic mismanagement, which has resulted in a loss of credibility. The conclusion is that the severe situation of Iraq requires a severe measure like a currency board.

The first argument they put forward is that the monetary policy autonomy made possible by floating would help Iraq adjust to an oil supply shock. Fine, but the claim that floating provides policy independence is not substantiated by practical experience. One of the aspects of dissatisfaction with the present international monetary system is that floating exchange rates have not delivered the policy independence promised by macroeconomic theory. But then if we assume that floating does provide the ability to conduct an independent monetary policy, what will the Iraqis do with it? The CBI does not have the tools, the financial markets and the institutional sophistication required to run an independent monetary policy. This brings about Schuler's (2003) argument whereby he casts doubt on the benefits of monetary sovereignty.

Argument two is that floating facilitates the real adjustment needed in the face of oil price volatility. This argument is based on the unrealistic assumption that lower oil prices and revenues will bring about depreciation of the domestic currency and vice versa. There is no guarantee that this will happen, as experience shows that the exchange rates of commodity-exporting countries do not bear a constant and consistent relation to commodity prices. It is extremely hazardous to relate the exchange rate to one factor only, even if it is oil prices in the case of an oil-exporting country.

Argument three is that floating helps the government manage the mismatch between its volatile revenues from oil and fixed domestic costs. This argument again rests on the assumption that the domestic currency will depreciate when dollar-denominated oil revenues decline, which would maintain the domestic currency value of revenues, enabling the government to meet its domestic costs. Even if we make the heroic assumption that the exchange rate bears a systematic relation to oil revenues, most of the expenditure of the Iraqi government (at least in the immediate future) will be on foreign currency-denominated imports, which makes the exchange rate of the Iraqi dinar against the US dollar irrelevant. The major domestic currency cost item is the government's wage bill, which is no more than 15 per cent of total oil revenue. A large portion of the wage bill can be financed by domestic sources of government revenue, in which case the exchange rate factor becomes irrelevant.

The fourth argument is based on the observation that Mexico and Canada (commodity exporters) are quite closely integrated into the US economy, and yet they opt for floating currencies rather than dollarization. Again, this argument is valid on the surface but there is a big difference between Mexico and Canada, on one hand, and Iraq, on the other. These countries (particularly Canada) have not experienced the macroeconomic mismanagement and the loss of credibility that Iraq has experienced. Moreover, the exchange rate works as a policy tool for these countries, which compete in the large US market by exporting a variety of goods. Iraq is not in the same position because it does not have a diversified export base like those of Canada and Mexico. For Iraq, the exchange rate is not a policy tool, but rather the means to put an end to hyperinflation and the loss of credibility. The right comparison should be with countries like Bulgaria rather than Canada and Mexico. Bulgaria was saved from hyperinflation by a currency board whereas several other monetary stabilization programmes failed.

Argument five, which is also based on a comparison with other countries, goes as follows: Iraq should not follow the example of other oil states in the region such as Libya and Saudi Arabia, which have pegged currencies. One cannot sensibly accept the proposition that the macroeconomic performance of Libya and Saudi Arabia is entirely due to the exchange rate regime. Then, how about following the example of the United Arab Emirates, which is an oil-exporting country that has been performing rather well under a system of fixed exchange rates?

Now that we have come this far, argument six has to be based on the dismal experience of Argentina, which demonstrated that a rigid currency regime does not guarantee fiscal discipline. In response, one can raise the following question: why is it that the bad example of Argentina is cited, not the good example of Bulgaria? We will also find out that the demise of Argentina cannot be blamed on the exchange rate arrangement, which was arguably not a genuine currency board.

Finally, argument seven is the following: post-conflict countries that have adopted currency boards/dollarization (such as Bosnia and Kosovo) are planning to join the EU (it is easier to exit that way, not to managed floating). Although this argument is not convincing, it can be argued that a similar course of action for Iraq is to join the common currency envisaged by the Gulf Cooperation Council (GCC) countries.

In defending the establishment of a currency board one has to observe the following points:

- A currency board for Iraq should not be looked at as a regime that precludes the availability of a macroeconomic policy tool (the exchange rate), but rather as an arrangement that produces a stable currency, restores credibility to the CBI, and precludes the tendency to indulge in deficit financing. The exchange rate is not a viable macroeconomic policy tool for a country like Iraq.
- It is a matter of priorities, and the setting of priorities for Iraq requires the discipline provided by a currency board.
- A currency board is an extreme measure, which must be resorted to because of the presence of an extreme situation resulting from years of macroeconomic mismanagement.
- There is no harm in considering a shift from the currency board to something else in the future, once conditions have changed.

In terms of costs and benefits, I strongly believe that there is no viable alternative for a currency board as the exchange rate arrangement for Iraq under the present conditions. The current practice is not really conspicuous, presumably managed floating. Al-Saadi (2004) believes that the CBI tries, through daily auction, to maintain the rate stable at about 1,460 Iraqi dinars to the dollar. He does not only refer to the 'ambiguity surrounding the Central Bank of Iraq practice in regulating the foreign exchange rate regime', but also casts doubt on the proposition that the Iraqi economy is enjoying genuine stability as a result of the CBI policy.

Verifying exchange rate regimes: Kuwait

In January 2003, Kuwait decided to go for an exchange rate regime shift by abandoning the policy of pegging the Kuwaiti dinar (KWD) to a basket with unknown components that had been in place since 1975. The shift was towards pegging to the US dollar (USD) at the par value of 0.29964 (KWD/USD), with a band of ±3.5 per cent. The declared reason for this policy shift was to unify exchange rate regimes across member countries of the Gulf Cooperation Council (GCC), which comprises Kuwait, as well as Saudi Arabia, Qatar, the United Arab Emirates, Bahrain and Oman. The strategic objective behind this move is to introduce a common currency by 2010 as a part of a plan for a common market and a customs union (see International Monetary Fund, 2003).

The main objective of this exercise is to verify the exchange rate regime that was in place up to December 2002. We will also try to verify the exchange rate regime shift that took place in January 2003, which may be easier than the first task, because exchange rate regime verifiability is more difficult when the components (and weights) of the pegging basket are unknown. The Central Bank of Kuwait (CBK) did not declare the structure of the basket under the abandoned regime, presumably to curb speculation against the currency. In this case, verification can be based on a model of the form

$$E_{0,t} = \delta_0 + \sum_{i=1}^{n} \delta_i E_{i,t} \qquad (9.1)$$

where $E_{0,t}$ is the exchange rate of the dinar against the US dollar and $E_{i,t}$ is the exchange rate of currency i against the dollar. If equation (9.1) is expressed in a log-linear form then the estimated coefficients (which are elasticities) can be interpreted directly as the weights of the currencies in the basket. If, on the other hand, the equation is written in a linear form then weights can be calculated as elasticities at the mean values. Previous empirical work shows that there are four currencies in the basket, which are the currencies of Kuwait's main trading partners (Japan, JPY; the USA, USD; Germany, DEM; and the UK, GBP). However, results obtained from previous studies show that the basket is not import-weighted but rather that it is dominated by the US dollar (see Moosa, 1983a, 1983b, 1989, 2001b; Moosa and Al-Loughani, 1997, 1999, 2000, 2003).

Table 9.1 Basic statistics of exchange rates (1992–2002)

Exchange rate	Mean	Standard deviation	Coefficient of variation
KWD/USD	0.302	0.004	1.45
KWD/GBP	0.476	0.028	5.90
KWD/DEM	0.174	0.023	13.01
KWD/JPY	0.003	0.00032	10.65
GBP/USD	0.637	0.040	6.30
DEM/USD	1.770	0.259	14.65
JPY/USD	114.604	12.126	10.58

An exchange rate arrangement of this kind makes the exchange rate of the dinar against the dollar more stable than the exchange rates of the dinar and the dollar against other currencies. This proposition can be substantiated by examining the coefficients of variation of various exchange rates as reported in Table 9.1. These figures are calculated from monthly data covering the period January 1992–December 2002. The exchange rate against the dollar has a lower coefficient of variation than any of the other exchange rates. As we can see from Table 9.1, the most stable exchange rate is that of the KWD against the dollar, with a coefficient of variation that is far below that of any of the other exchange rates. The same can be gleaned from Figure 9.1, which shows that the KWD/USD rate is more stable than the exchange rates of the yen against either the dollar or the dinar.

We can also observe from Figure 9.1 that the exchange rates of the dinar and the dollar against the yen have the same pattern of volatility and that they are highly correlated. This is again a reflection of the fact that the basket has a dollar component with a heavier weight than those of the other currencies combined. In fact, because of the very structure of the basket and the dominance of the dollar, the exchange rate arrangement leads to the following behavioural patterns:

- When the dollar appreciates or depreciates against other currencies, the dinar does likewise.
- When the dinar appreciates against other currencies, it depreciates against the dollar and vice versa.

These propositions have some support from actual figures. Table 9.2 shows that the dollar and the dinar move in the same direction against other currencies. Because the dollar appreciated against the dinar during

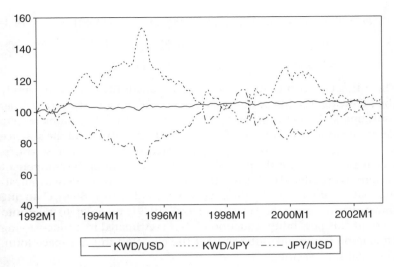

Figure 9.1 The stability of the KWD/USD exchange rate

this period, the latter appreciated but less than proportionately against the pound and the mark. We can also see that the dinar depreciated more than proportionately against the yen.

With these indications, the basket model may be specified as follows:

$$E_{0,t} = \delta_0 + \delta_1 E_{1,t} + \delta_2 E_{2,t} + \delta_3 E_{3,t} + \varepsilon_t \tag{9.2}$$

where $E_{1,t}$, $E_{2,t}$ and $E_{3,t}$ are respectively the exchange rates against the dollar of the yen, mark and pound. When this equation is estimated by OLS over the sample period we obtain the following (t statistics in parentheses):

Table 9.2 Percentage changes in the exchange rates of the dollar and dinar

Exchange rate	Percentage change	Dollar	Dinar
KWD/USD	3.13	↑	
KWD/GBP	−8.36		↑
GBP/USD	12.54	↑	
KWD/JPY	8.52		↓
JPY/USD	−4.96	↓	
KWD/DEM	−11.85		↑
DEM/USD	17.00	↑	

$$E_{0,t} = 0.26046 + 0.0000544E_{1,t} + 0.00944E_{2,t} + 0.029011E_{3,t} \qquad (9.3)$$

$$(46.93) \qquad (2.20) \qquad\qquad (6.98) \qquad\qquad (3.55)$$

$$R^2 = 0.62 \quad DW = 0.132 \quad DF = -2.01 \quad ADF(12) = -0.99$$

The estimated coefficients, which are all statistically significant, imply the following weights in the basket: dollar (86.3 per cent), yen (2.1 per cent), mark (5.5 per cent) and pound (6.1 per cent). The problem here lies in the low value of the coefficient of determination and the absence of a cointegrating relationship as indicated by the DF/ADF statistics. One reason for that is the possibility that the weights of the component currencies are altered over time. In fact, there is strong evidence indicating that the dinar was devalued against the dollar in 1986 by changing the structure of the basket (see Moosa, 1989). In order to take into account this possibility, equation (9.2) is reestimated in a time-varying parametric framework, after writing the equation in state space form. The final state vector is

$$E_{0,t} = 0.23977 + 0.000150E_{1,t} + 0.009897E_{2,t} + 0.03747E_{3,t} \qquad (9.4)$$

$$(64.43) \qquad (6.67) \qquad\qquad (4.56) \qquad\qquad (5.77)$$

$$R^2 = 0.96 \quad Q(9) = 10.13 \quad H(43) = 0.09$$

where Q is the Ljung–Box test statistic for serial correlation (distributed as χ^2 with 9 degrees of freedom) and H is a test statistic for heteroscedasticity that has an F distribution with (43, 43) degrees of freedom. Obviously, equation (9.4) is better than equation (9.3) in terms of the goodness of fit and diagnostics. It also produces a more plausible weight for the yen, given that Japan was the largest trading partner under most of the sample period (it is the European Union now). The weights assigned to the four currencies (calculated at the end of the sample period) are as follows: dollar (80.1 per cent), yen (6.2 per cent), mark (6.1 per cent) and pound (7.6 per cent). So, while the structure of the basket is confirmed, it seems that the Central Bank of Kuwait has been in the habit of changing the structure of the basket. Figure 9.2 shows how the coefficient that reflects the weight of the dollar and the weight itself changed over the sample period. The coefficient is extracted as a stochastic trend from the estimated model, whereas the weight is estimated as the current value of the KWD/USD exchange rate (this is why it looks so volatile). One reason for changing the weights is the desire to create uncertainty to deter speculation and arbitrage (for more details, see Moosa, 2003, Chapter 3).

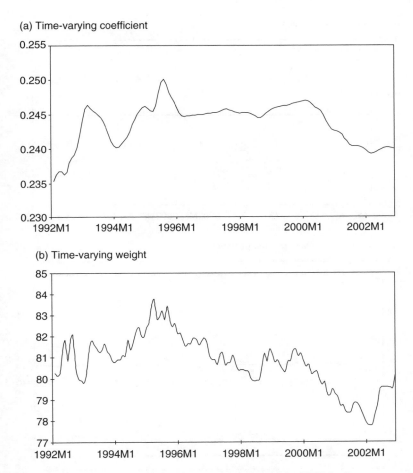

Figure 9.2 The coefficient and weight of the dollar in the KWD basket

Now, we turn to the regime shift in January 2003. The first thing to do is to find out if there is a structural break in the time path of the exchange rate in January 2003. Thus, a structural time series model is specified in which the exchange rate is determined by its time series components: trend, cycle and random components along the lines suggested by Harvey (1989). This model is then estimated over the period January 1992–December 2002 and used to forecast out of sample over the period January–September 1993. The predictive failure test statistic (distributed as $\chi^2(9)$) turned out to be insignificant at 3.49,

(a) Actual versus par value

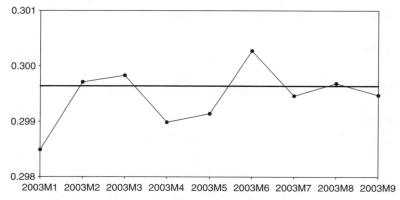

(b) Percentage deviation from the par value

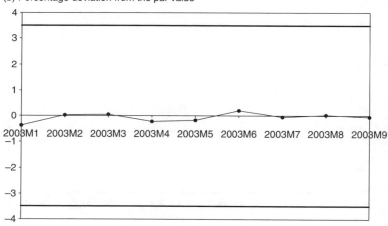

Figure 9.3 Deviation of the KWD/USD rate from the par value

whereas the CUSUM test statistic (distributed as t(130)) turned out to be insignificant at 0.41. Hence, there is no indication of a structural break, but this may not necessarily indicate that there was no exchange rate regime shift.

We can readily see from the data that the exchange rate became exceptionally stable in 2003. The coefficient of variation of the exchange rate over the first nine months of 2003 turned out to be 0.17 per cent, compared to a much higher coefficient of variation of 0.97 per cent previously. One would expect that the exchange rate between the dinar and the dollar would be more stable under a single-currency peg (to the dollar) than under a basket peg. Moreover, it seems that the CBK managed (through intervention, one has to presume) to keep the exchange rate very close to the preannounced par value of 0.29964, and this is an observation that can be detected from Figure 9.3. In Figure 9.3(a) the

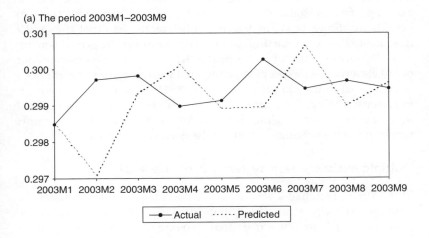

(a) The period 2003M1–2003M9

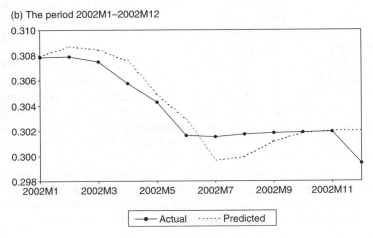

(b) The period 2002M1–2002M12

Figure 9.4 Actual and predicted KWD/USD exchange rate

actual value of the exchange rate is plotted against the par value, whereas Figure 9.3(b) plots the percentage deviation, which is well within the ±3.5 per cent band. The average absolute deviation was 0.13 per cent.

Another exercise that can be used to verify the regime change is to test the out-of-sample predictive power of the model. If there was a regime shift in January 2003, the model should be able to predict the exchange rate much better in 2002 than in 2003. Thus, the model is estimated up to December 2002 to forecast the exchange rate in 2003, and then it is reestimated over the period up to December 2001 to forecast the exchange rate in 2002. The actual and predicted values for the two periods are shown in Figure 9.4. It can be readily seen that the model does a better job of predicting the exchange rate over the period January 2001–December 2002. Over this period there are direction errors in four out of eleven cases (36 per cent), compared with seven out of eight cases (88 per cent) in the sample covering 2003. Thus, while the evidence is not overwhelming, there are strong indications that the CBK indulged in an exchange rate regime shift in January 2003. More data points covering the post-change period will be needed for this exercise.

Multiple exchange rate systems: Peru, 1984–87

In the 1980s, Peru had a very interesting and rather complex system of multiple exchange rates. The system involved five different exchange rates: an official rate (O), a free (financial) rate (F), a premium rate (P), a special rate (S), and a super special rate (SS). Table 9.3 lists the exchange rates applicable to various current account and capital account transactions during the period 1984–87.

Figure 9.5 displays the developments of the five rates (per one US dollar) and the associated premia (in per cent) over the period 1984–87. Figure 9.5(a) shows that the official rate went up from 5.20 in 1984 to 25.24 in 1987, whereas the free rate and the premium rate went up from 5.38 to 19.28 and from 5.92 to 21.21, respectively. The special and super special rates were introduced in 1987. As we can see from Figure 9.5(b), the premia of the free and pemium rates over the official rate jumped in 1985 but they were stable in 1986 and 1987. In 1987 the premia associated with the special and super special rates were 60.2 and 84.2 per cent respectively. The average rate at which the central bank bought the domestic currency from importers was below the rate at which it sold the domestic currency to exporters, which means that the system had adverse fiscal consequences for the central bank.

(a) Exchange rates (per one US dollar)

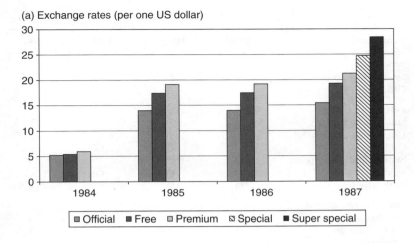

(b) Premium over the official rate

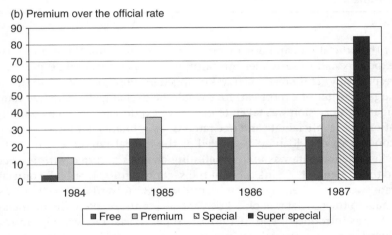

Figure 9.5 The multiple exchange rates of Peru (1984–87)

Now, let us try to read Table 9.3 (p. 240). In 1984, all current account transactions and capital account transactions listed in the table were settled at the official rate. In 1985, imports were settled at the official rate, but some changes were introduced to the settlement of small and large mine exports as well as the non-traditional exports. Mine exporters had to surrender 95 per cent of their foreign exchange earnings

Table 9.3   Peru's multiple exchange rates (1984–87)

Transaction	1984	1985	1986	1987
Imports				
Essential imports	O	O	O	O
Other imports	O	O	F	F
Exports				
Small mine exports	O	95/5	45/55	35/65
Large mine exports	O	95/5	63/35	55/45
Oil exports	O	O	O	55/45
Non-traditional exports	O	80/20	P	P
Services	O	O	O	O
Authorized transfers	O	O	O	O, F
Financial transactions				
New loans	O	O	O	F
Bank accounts	O	O + 3%	O, F	O, F, SS
Repatriation	–	–	–	S

at the official rate and 5 per cent only at the free rate. Non-traditional exporters had to surrender the earning at 80 per cent and 20 per cent respectively. This breakdown was changed in subsequent years so that a larger portion of export earnings would be exchanged at the free rate. In 1987, a decision was taken to exchange export earnings at a combination of the official rate and free rate. As far as financial transactions are concerned, new loans were settled at the official rate except in 1987 when the free rate was used. Interesting changes occurred with respect to the settlement of bank account transactions. In 1984, only the official rate was used, then there was a shift in 1985 towards a rate that was equal to the official rate plus 3 percentage points. In 1986, the financial rate was introduced, and in 1987 the super special rate was also introduced. Finally, a special rate was introduced in 1987, to settle transactions involving repatriation. Dornbusch and Kuenzler (1993) argue that this arrangement, together with the accompanying tariff and licensing policies, had an adverse effect on the real price of imports and exports in terms of domestic goods.

Exchange rate regimes and inflation: 1970–72 to 1988–89

As we have seen, there is no clear-cut evidence on the relationship or the direction of causation between the exchange rate regime and inflation.

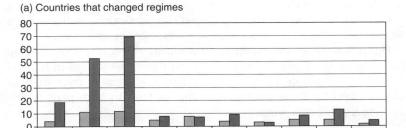

(a) Countries that changed regimes

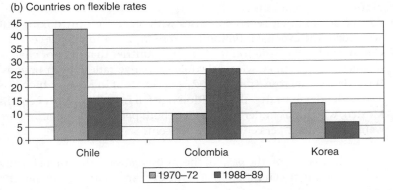

(b) Countries on flexible rates

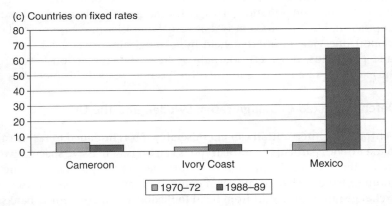

(c) Countries on fixed rates

Figure 9.6 Exchange rate regimes and inflation

The theory is not that helpful either, as economists have cast a lot of doubt on the validity of the hypotheses linking flexible exchange rates to inflation. This case study seems to verify these propositions.

Figure 9.6 shows the inflation rates during the period 1970–72 and 1988–89 for three groups of countries: (a) those that shifted from fixed to flexible exchange rates, (b) those that had flexible rates in both periods, and (c) those with fixed exchange rates in both periods. We can observe the following:

- In three cases (Costa Rica, Nigeria and Turkey), the regime shift caused (was associated with) a sharp rise in inflation. It is not clear whether this observation should be interpreted as implying that the regime shift led to more inflation or that higher inflation compelled those countries to shift from fixed to flexible rates (it could be that neither of these interpretations is valid).
- For six of the other seven countries with a regime shift (taking out Sri Lanka), the average inflation rate rose from 4.4 to 6.7 per cent.
- Compare now the inflation rates in the countries that did not change regimes. In Colombia, with a flexible exchange rate in both periods, the inflation rate rose from 9.8 to 27 per cent. But in Korea, which was also under flexible rates, the inflation rate fell from 14 to 6 per cent. In Mexico, which was under fixed rates in both periods, the inflation rate went up from 5.2 per cent to 67.1 per cent.

Hence, it appears (on the basis of these observations) that there is truly no connection between inflation and the exchange rate regime. But the connection could be obscured by the failure to control for the effect of other variables on inflation. This is the danger of relying on casual empiricism, but the problem is that casual empiricism is often used to support one view or another held by ideologically driven economists (and politicians, observers, journalists, etc.). The connection between the exchange rate regime and inflation has not escaped this practice.

Defending fixed exchange rates: Sweden and the UK

Central bank intervention can fail miserably if it is intended to reverse a market trend, particularly if the trend is caused by a massive speculative attack. If central bank intervention is intended for the purpose of maintaining a fixed exchange rate, then failure of intervention may mean an exchange rate regime shift from fixed to flexible rates. The central banks of Sweden (the Sveriges Riskbank) and the UK (the Bank of England) have some unhappy memories of the early 1990s. They faced similar problems, reacted differently, but ended up doing the same thing and losing a lot of money in the process.

Let us examine the Swedish experience first. Following its decision to join the European Union, this Scandinavian country pegged its currency (the krona) to the ECU in May 1991 (a description of the ECU can be found in Chapter 6). During the EMS crisis of September 1992, the Swedish currency came under selling pressure fuelled by speculation. The Swedish central bank reacted not by intervening in the foreign exchange market, but by using the interest rate as a policy tool. Thus, the overnight lending rate of the bank was raised to 500 per cent and maintained at that level for four days starting on 16 September 1992. Within two weeks, the central bank was able to lower its interest rate to a more realistic level, thus claiming victory against speculators. But that was not the end of the story, because raising the interest rate to such an ultra-high level weakened the economy at large and the banking sector in particular. This is a classic case of subordinating all objectives of monetary policy to the objective of defending the exchange rate (Obstfeld and Rogoff, 1995).

Speculators observed the fragile state of the economy and the banking sector, and by mid-November 1992 they decided to launch another attack on the currency (presumably by selling it short). Because the economic and financial conditions were fragile, the Swedish central bank was not on this occasion in a position to raise interest rates, not even to 20 per cent, and so foreign exchange intervention was the only way to defend the currency. By 19 November, the Swedish central bank could no longer support the currency, and so it had to face the inevitable: abandoning the fixed exchange rate system and floating the krona. Subsequently, the krona depreciated under selling pressure, which had some positive effects on the Swedish economy. But in the process, the Riksbank suffered substantial capital losses on its reserve position.

The case of Britain was more typical, resembling the subsequent case of the Thai central bank during the Asian crisis: massive central bank intervention that ultimately failed, producing capital loss for the central bank and capital gains for speculators. By 16 September 1992, the British currency was under severe pressure but, unlike its Swedish counterpart, the Bank of England was not in a position to raise interest rates, first because the British economy was in a bad shape at that time, and also because it was not politically acceptable to raise interest rates to a high level, given the sensitivity of mortgage rates. The massive intervention efforts proved to be totally ineffective, and the Bank of England ended up losing billions of pounds' worth of currency reserves. Eichengreen (1999a) uses this case to demonstrate his thoughts on the exit strategy.

Adopting and abandoning a currency board: Argentina

Argentina had a long history of monetary instability, high inflation and slow growth. During the 1980s, a series of stabilization programmes failed, as chronically large money-financed deficits led to capital flight and informal dollarization. By mid-1989, the economy was in hyper-inflation (Figure 9.7), public confidence in the domestic currency had evaporated, and the dollar became the unit of account and played a major role as the medium of exchange. When Domingo Cavallo was appointed as the Minister of the Economy in January 1991, he wasted no time in pushing the idea of a currency board as a means of avoiding the monetization of the deficit. In March 1991, the Convertibility Law was passed by Congress, fixing the parity at 10,000 australes to the dollar (which became one Argentine peso per dollar in 1992).

The new currency board was to be managed by an independent central bank. The arrangement differed from a classic currency board in a number of respects to allow for an activist monetary policy. Corden (2002) argues that the Convertibility Plan did not really establish an 'orthodox' currency board but something close. To start with, the exchange rate could be altered by legislation by Congress. Second, the

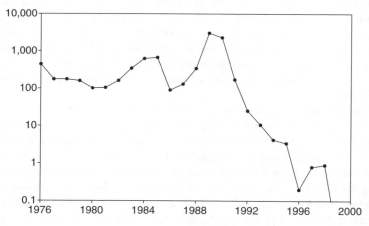

Figure 9.7   The inflation rate in Argentina (logarithmic scale)

monetary base was not required to change one-for-one with foreign exchange reserves. Third, declines in foreign exchange reserves could be sterilized to a very limited extent, which is what Corden describes as 'pragmatic modification of the usual scheme'.

As a result of adopting the currency board, inflation fell from over 1,000 per cent in 1989–90 to 25 per cent in 1992, and it effectively disappeared by 1996. Growth reached more than 8 per cent in 1991–92, having been negative for most of the 1980s. Things, however, started to change in 1995 when Argentina got a shock from the Mexican crisis following the collapse of the Mexican peg in December 1994. The second major crisis followed the collapse of the Brazilian peg in early 1999. Growth turned negative in 1999, as the Brazilian devaluation made the Argentine economy less competitive. A combination of external shocks and some structural weaknesses resulted in very high unemployment. While (price) inflation fell, wage inflation did not, which (coupled with the dollar appreciation and the Brazilain devaluation) led to a loss of competitiveness.

Towards mid-2000, and in the midst of recession, the Minister of the Economy, Domingo Cavallo, was desperately trying to deal with Argentina's debt problem as the country's risk premium went up to 20 percentage points. By 2001, public debt was some 50 per cent of GDP. There was also the problem of disagreement with the provinces about the transfer of revenue. As conditions deteriorated, Cavallo resorted to restructuring the public debt and negotiating with the provinces. In December 2001, the government implemented a deposit freeze as a measure to quell a growing run on the banking system. Naturally, problems followed as the public lost their savings.

In early 2002, Eduardo Duhalde was appointed as president by Congress, and his government wasted no time in denouncing the old economic policy (including the Convertibility Plan) as inefficient, recessionary and corrupt. The peso was devalued, public debt was defaulted on and dollar-denominated private debt was converted into pesos at different arbitrary rates. What made things worse was that the Argentine economy was (unofficially) a dollarized economy. Bank and corporate balance sheets were wrecked, with devastating effects on the economy. There was a massive collapse of the demand for money (pesos). The government undertook various measures but it was not possible to break the cycle of rising interest rates and falling growth. The end of the currency board came on 6 January 2002 when the Law of Public Emergency granted the president special powers to devalue the peso. The Argentine currency board ceased to exist.

What are the lessons that have been learnt from the Argentine experience? During most of the 1990s, Argentina was admired by the international financial community and the proponents of super-fixed exchange rates in particular. Mussa (2002) pointed out how, and despite the initial IMF scepticism, the Argentine experience became increasingly popular in the Washington policy circles. Ricardo Hausmann of the International Development Bank was so impressed by the Argentine experience that he argued for the adoption of a currency board by Brazil and Mexico to follow the Argentine example (*La Nacion*, 6 April 2001).

Edwards (2002) points out that most supporters of hard pegs have not changed their minds and continue to believe that these exchange rate regimes are still the solution for many problems in emerging countries. They followed, according to Edwards, a strategy of 'bastardization' of the Argentine experience, suggesting that dollarization would be the way out. Even the *Wall Street Journal* that had always praised the Argentine experience started arguing that Argentina did not really have a 'true' currency board, let alone sound monetary policy.

What was the problem? Argentina's problem was one of unsustainable public debt dynamics, partly reflecting the slowdown of growth after 1998 (Ghosh *et al.*, 2002). One explanation is the end of structural reform during President Menem's second term. But the root of unsustainable debt was fiscal profligacy, which had several dimensions, including the uneasy fiscal relations between the provinces and the central government that were never resolved. Ghosh *et al.* (2002) conclude that the currency board probably played only a minor role in the failure of Argentina's decade-long stabilization episode. Again, this case study highlights the hazard of attributing major successes and failures entirely or predominantly to the underlying exchange rate regime.

Exchange rate regime choice after the Asian crisis

The five countries engulfed by the Asian crisis of 1997–98 were Thailand, Indonesia, Malaysia, Korea and the Philippines. The crisis started in Thailand, where there had been over-investment in real estate and an asset price bubble that had already burst in 1994. The situation deteriorated sharply in 1996 when the terms of trade worsened severely. The Japanese banking crisis led to a slowing down of capital inflows and the depreciation of the yen against the dollar to which the Thai currency is pegged.

Before the onset of the crisis in 1997, the countries that experienced the crisis had impressive records of economic performance. It is no wonder then that no one predicted the crisis (the IMF was on the verge of 'promoting' these countries from the status of being 'developing' just before the emergence of the crisis). Asian countries were complacent for a long time because of their success. They did not have the problems that faced Latin American countries in the 1980s (large fiscal deficits, heavy public debt burden and rapid monetary expansion). This complacency prevented the countries from dealing with the problem until it was too late.

The underlying causes of the Asian crisis have been clearly identified. First, substantial foreign short-term funds became available at relatively low interest rates, as foreign investors shifted massive amounts of capital into Asia. The problem was inefficiency of the allocation of borrowed foreign funds because of weak banking systems, poor corporate governance and limited absorptive capacity. Second, the fixed exchange rate regime gave the borrowers a false sense of security, encouraging them to take on dollar-denominated debt. Third, exports were weak by the mid-1990s because of the appreciation of the US dollar and China's devaluation of its currency in 1994. Thus, the crisis had to happen, producing massive capital outflows, depreciating currencies and collapsing stock markets.

Financial fragility was, however, the main culprit. This factor involved five aspects:

- Many financial institutions and corporations had borrowed foreign currency funds without adequate hedging, making them vulnerable to changes in exchange rates.
- The borrowed funds were largely short-term while assets were long-term, creating a maturity mismatch and the possibility of a liquidity attack similar to what happens in the case of a bank run.
- Stock and real estate prices had risen substantially, posing the risk of subsequent asset price deflation.
- Credit was often poorly allocated, contributing to the problem faced by banks and other financial institutions.
- Financial fragility reflected ineffective financial supervision and regulation in the context of financial sector liberalization. Moreover, capital account liberalization was poorly executed, encouraging short-term borrowing, while limited exchange rate flexibility led borrowers to underestimate foreign exchange risk. Monetary policies allowed domestic credit to expand at a rapid pace.

Let us now concentrate on the exchange rate factor. The East Asian currencies with a large weight on the US dollar in their baskets in the pre-crisis period became overvalued in real effective terms because of both higher domestic inflation than in the USA and the US dollar's appreciation against major currencies since mid-1995. The emergence of real effective overvaluation of the currencies was an important factor behind the mounting speculative pressure that developed in the foreign exchange market in 1997. This was compounded with the weakness of domestic financial institutions. Hence, the *de facto* US dollar peg system was one of the underlying triggers of the currency crisis. It provided exchange rate stability, which benefited East Asian economies for a long time by creating stable environment for trade and FDI-driven economic development and growth. According to McKinnon (2000), exchange rate stability was an important factor behind the remarkable economic performance during the East Asian miracle of the mid-1960s through to the mid-1990s. By choosing the US dollar as an anchor, East Asian countries benefited because (i) the US dollar was used extensively as an invoicing currency for international trade, and (ii) the appreciation of the yen against the dollar in the 1980s helped these countries receive FDI (foreign direct investment) from Japan. However, when the yen started to depreciate against the dollar in mid-1995, Japanese FDI inflows began to lose momentum.

The problem is that *de facto* fixed exchange rates provided a misguided perception that foreign currency-denominated inflows posed little risk for both domestic borrowers and foreign lenders. Even if countries may benefit from stable exchange rates at normal times, maintaining an overvalued currency at a time of speculative attack would be difficult. Hence, there were two mistakes: (i) the failure to adopt macroeconomic policies consistent with and supportive of fixed exchange rates, and (ii) the failure to adjust the exchange rate at an early stage before serious speculative pressure mounted in the foreign exchange market.

The Asian crisis of 1997–98 forced many economies in the region to shift away from *de facto* US dollar-pegged regimes to flexible exchange rates. The US dollar had played a dominant role as an international anchor currency in the region until the outbreak of the crisis in the summer of 1997. During the crisis, the anchor-currency role of the US dollar was substantially reduced, at least temporarily, due to a general shift to more flexible rates. But as the currency crisis subsided in the second half of 1998, Asian economies generally restored exchange rate stability (with the exception of Indonesia), though in a less pronounced way than in the pre-crisis period. The restoration of exchange rate stability has been accompanied by a greater role of the US dollar in some countries and a greater role of the Japanese yen in others.

The question that arises once more pertains to the post-crisis optimal exchange rate regime. Kawai (2003) recommends a currency basket system based on the US dollar, the Japanese yen and the euro in a way that reflects the importance of the USA, Japan and the European Union as the region's major trading partners. The objective in this case is to achieve real effective exchange rate stabilization by loosely tying their exchange rates to a currency basket, supported by consistent and sustainable macroeconomic policy. The USA is no longer the main partner. For example, Japan is the biggest provider of FDI, whereas the EU is the largest bank lender. Hence, exchange rate stabilization against the US dollar only is no longer desirable, which makes exchange rate stabilization versus a well-balanced basket comprising the three major currencies a more reasonable option. Actual weights would depend on the relative importance of the USA, Japan and the European Union as trading partners and FDI sources, future expectations of movements of the yen/dollar exchange rate and the perceived success of the euro. To ensure intra-regional exchange rate stability individual countries must choose similar baskets. This policy is also consistent with inflation targeting if the weights assigned to currencies are the same rates assigned to foreign inflation rates, particularly over the long run when PPP tends to hold.

References

Aghevli, B. and Montiel, P. (1991) *Exchange Rate Policy in Developing Countries*, IMF Occasional Papers, No. 78.

Aghion, P., Baqcchetta, P. and Banerjee, A. (1999) *Capital Markets and the Instability of Open Economies*, CEPR Discussion Papers, No. 2083.

Aghion, P., Baqcchetta, P. and Banerjee, A. (2000) 'Currency Crises and Monetary Policy in an Economy with Credit Constraints', mimeo, UCL.

Aizenman, J. (1994) 'Monetary and Real Shocks, Productive Capacity and Exchange Rate Regimes', *Economica*, 61, 407–34.

Aizenman, J. and Frenkel, J.A. (1985) 'Optimal Wage Indexation, Foreign Exchange Intervention and Monetary Policy', *American Economic Review*, 75, 402–23.

Aizenman, J. and Hausmann, R. (2000) *Exchange Rate Regimes and Financial Market Imperfections*, NBER Working Papers, No. 7738.

Alesina, A. and Barro, R. (2002) 'Currency Unions', *Quarterly Journal of Economics*, 117, 409–36.

Alesina, A. and Wagner, A. (2003) *Choosing (and Reneging on) Exchange Rate Regimes*, NBER Working Papers, No. 9809.

Alexander, S.S. (1952) 'Effects of Devaluation on a Trade Balance', IMF Staff Papers, 2, 263–78.

Al-Saadi, S.Z. (2004) 'Oil Revenues and the Foreign Exchange Regime in Iraq', *Middle East Economic Survey*, 47, September.

Arize, A.C. (1995) 'The Effects of Exchange Rate Volatility on U.S. Exports: An Empirical Investigation', *Southern Economic Journal*, 62, 34–43.

Artus, J.R. and Young, J.H. (1979) 'Fixed and Flexible Exchange Rates: A Renewal of the Debate', IMF Staff Papers, 26, 654–98.

Aschauer, D. and Greenwood, J. (1983) 'A Further Exploration in the Theory of Exchange Rate Regimes', *Journal of Political Economy*, 91, 868–75.

Asian Policy Forum (2000) *Policy Recommendations for Preventing Another Capital Account Crisis*, Tokyo: Asian Development Bank Institute.

Bacchetta, P. (2000) 'Monetary Policy with Foreign Currency Debt', mimeo, University of Lausanne.

Baldwin, R. and Krugman, P. (1989) 'Persistent Trade Effects of Large Exchange Rate Shocks', *Quarterly Journal of Economics*, 104, 635–65.

Balino, T. and Enoch, C. (1997) *Currency Board Arrangements: Issues and Experiences*, IMF Occasional Papers, No. 151.

Ball, L. (1999) 'Policy Rules for Open Economies', in Taylor, J.B. (ed.), *Monetary Policy Rules*, Chicago: University of Chicago Press.

Barro, R. and Gordon, D. (1983) 'Rules, Discretion and Reputation in a Model of Monetary Policy', *Journal of Monetary Economics*, 12, 101–21.

Bartolini, L. (1996) 'Are Exchange Rates Excessively Volatile? And What Does Excessively Volatile Mean, Anyway?', IMF Staff Papers, 43, 72–96.

Baxter, M. and Stockman, A. (1989) 'Business Cycle and Exchange Rate Regime: Some International Evidence', *Journal of Monetary Economics*, 23, 377–400.

Benassy-Quere, A. (1999) 'Exchange Rate Regimes and Policies: An Empirical Analysis', in Collingnon, S., Pisani-Ferry, J. and Park, Y.C. (eds), *Exchange Rate Policies in Emerging Asian Countries*, London: Routledge.

Berg, A. and Borensztein, E. (2000) 'Full Dollarization: The Pros and Cons', *Economic Issues*, No. 24.

Berg, A. and Borensztein, E. (2003) 'The Pros and Cons of Full Dollarization', in Salvatore, D., Dean, J.D. and Willett, T.D. (eds), *The Dollarization Debate*, Oxford: Oxford University Press.

Berger, H., Jensen, H. and Schjelderup, G. (2001) 'To Peg or not to Peg? A Simple Model of Exchange Rate Regime Choice in Small Economies', *Economics Letters*, 73, 161–7.

Berger, H., Sturn, I. and de Hann, J. (2000) *An Empirical Investigation into Exchange Rate Regime Choice and Exchange Rate Volatility*, CESIFO Working Papers, No. 263.

Bhandari, J.S. (1982) 'Staggered Wage Setting and Exchange Rate Policy in an Economy with Capital Assets', *Journal of International Money and Finance*, 1, 275–92.

Bhandari, J.S. (1985) 'Experiments with Optimal Currency Composite', *Southern Economic Journal*, 51, 711–30.

Bhandari, J.S. and Vegh, C.A. (1990) 'Dual Exchange Markets under Incomplete Separation: An Optimization Model', *IMF Staff Papers*, 37, 146–67.

Bird, G. (1979) 'The Choice of Exchange Rate Regime in Developing Countries', *Philippine Economic Journal*, 18, 148–62.

Black, S.W. (1976) 'Exchange Policies for Less Developed Countries in a World of Floating Rates', *Princeton Essays in International Finance*, No. 119.

Bofinger, P. and Wollmershauser, T. (2001) *Managed Floating: Understanding the New International Monetary Order*, Warsburg Economic Papers, No. 30, May.

Bordo, M.D. (1993) 'The Bretton Woods System: An Historical Overview', in Bordo, M.D. and Eichengreen, B. (eds), *Retrospective on the Bretton Woods System*, Chicago: University of Chicago Press.

Bordo, M.D. (2003) *Exchange Rate Regime Choice in Historical Perspective*, NBER Working Papers, No. 9654.

Bordo, M.D. and Kydland, F.E. (1996) 'The Gold Standard as a Commitment Mechanism', in Bayoumi, T., Eichengreen, B. and Taylor, M.P. (eds), *Economic Perspectives on the Classical Gold Standard*, New York: Cambridge University Press.

Bordo, M.D. and Schwartz, A.J. (1997) 'Why Clashes between Internal and External Stability Goals End in Currency Crises: 1797–1994', in Tavalas, G.S. (ed.), *The Collapse of Exchange Rate Regimes: Causes, Consequences and Policy Responses*, Dordrecht: Kluwer.

Bordo, M.D. and Schwartz, A.J. (1999) 'Monetary Policy Regimes and Economic Performance: The Historical Record', in Taylor, J. and Woodford, M. (eds), *Handbook of Macroeconomics*, New York: Elsevier.

Borensztein, E., Zettelmeyer, J. and Philippon, T. (2001) *Monetary Independence in Emerging Markets: Does the Exchange Rate Make a Difference*, IMF Working Papers, No. WP/01/1.

Bosco, L. (1987) 'Determinants of Exchange Rate Regimes in LDCs: Some Empirical Evidence', *Economic Notes*, 1, 110–43.

Boyer, R. (1978) 'Optimal Foreign Exchange Market Intervention', *Journal of Political Economy*, 86, 1045–55.

Branson, W.H. and Katseli-Papaefstratiou, L.T. (1981) 'Exchange Rate Policy in Developing Countries', in Grossman, S. and Lundberg, E. (eds), *The World Economic Order: Past and Present*, London: Macmillan.

Broda, C. (2001) 'Coping with Terms-of-Trade Shocks: Pegs versus Floats', *American Economic Review*, 91, 376–80.

Bruno, M. (1991) 'High Inflation and the Nominal Anchors of an Open Economy', *Princeton Essays in International Finance*, No. 183.

Bubula, A. and Otker-Robe, I. (2002) *The Evolution of Exchange Rate Regimes Since 1990: Evidence from De Facto Policies*, IMF Working Papers, No. WP/02/155.

Bubula, A. and Otker-Robe, I. (2003) *Are Pegged Exchange Rate Regimes More Crisis Prone?*, IMF Working Papers, No. WP/03/223.

Caballero, R.J. and Krishnamurthy, A. (2001) *Vertical Analysis of Crises and Intervention: Fear of Floating and Ex-Ante Problems*, NBER Working Papers, No. 8428.

Caballero, R.J. and Krishnamurthy, A. (2002) 'Excessive Dollar Debt: Financial Development and Underinsurance', unpublished paper, MIT.

Calvo, G.A. (1999) 'Fixed versus Flexible Exchange Rates: Preliminaries of a Turn-of-Millennium Rematch', unpublished paper, University of Maryland.

Calvo, G.A. (2001) 'Capital Markets and the Exchange Rate with Special Reference to the Dollarization Debate in Latin America', *Journal of Money, Credit and Banking*, 33, 312–34.

Calvo, G.A. and Mendoza, E.G. (2000) 'Capital Market Crises and Economic Collapse in Emerging Markets: An Informational-Frictions Approach', *American Economic Review* (Papers and Proceedings), 90, 59–64.

Calvo, G.A. and Mishkin, F.S. (2003) *The Mirage of Exchange Rate Regimes for Emerging Market Countries*, NBER Working Papers, No. 9808.

Calvo, G.A. and Reinhart, C.M. (2002) 'Fear of Floating', *Quarterly Journal of Economics*, 117, 379–408.

Calvo, G.A., Reinhart, C.M. and Vegh, C.A. (1995) 'Targeting the Real Exchange Rate: Theory and Evidence', *Journal of Development Economics*, 47, 97–133.

Canavan, C. and Tommasi, M. (1997) 'On the Credibility of Alternative Exchange Rate Regimes', *Journal of Development Economics*, 54, 101–22.

Caramazza, F. and Aziz, J. (1998) 'Fixed or Flexible? Getting the Exchange Rate Right in the 1990s', *Economic Issues*, No. 13.

Carew, E. and Slatyer, W. (1989) *FOREX: The Techniques of Foreign Exchange*, Sydney: Allen & Unwin.

Cassel, G. (1936) *The Downfall of the Gold Standard*, London: Frank Cass & Co.

Cespedes, L.F., Chang, R. and Velasco, R. (2000) *Balance Sheets and Exchange Rate Policy*, NBER Working Papers, No. 7840.

Chang, R. and Velasco, A. (2000) 'Exchange Rate Policy for Developing Countries', *American Economic Review*, (Papers and Proceedings), 90, 71–5.

Chinn, D.M. and Miller, J. (1998) 'Fixed vs. Floating Rates: A Dynamic General Equilibrium Analysis', *European Economic Review*, 42, 1221–94.

Choudhry, T. (2001) 'Exchange Rate Volatility and the United States Exports: Evidence from Canada and Japan', mimeo, University of Southampton.

Chowdhury, A.R. (1993) 'Does Exchange Rate Volatility Depress Trade Flows? Evidence from Error-Correction Models', *Review of Economics and Statistics*, 75, 700–6.

Collier, P. and Joshi, V. (1989) 'Exchange Rate Policy in Developing Countries', *Oxford Review of Economic Policy*, 5, 94–113.

Collins, S.M. (1996) 'On Becoming More Flexible: Exchange Rate Regimes in Latin America and the Caribbean', *Journal of Development Economics*, 51, 117–38.

Connolly, M. (1982) 'Choice of an Optimum Peg for a Small Open Country', *Journal of International Money and Finance*, 1, 153–64.

Corbo, V. (2003) 'Is it Time for a Common Currency for the Americas?', in Salvatore, D., Dean, J.D. and Willett, T.D. (eds), *The Dollarization Debate*, Oxford: Oxford University Press.

Corden, W.M. (2002) *Too Sensational: On the Choice of Exchange Rate Regimes*, Cambridge, Mass.: MIT Press.

Crockett, A.B. and Nsouli, S.M. (1977) 'Exchange Rate Policies for Developing Countries', *Journal of Development Studies*, 13, 125–43.

Cuddington, J.T. and Otto, S.K. (1990) *Choice of Exchange Rate Regime: A Multinomial Logit Model*, George Town University, Working Paper No. 90-18.

Cuddington, J.T. and Otto, S.K. (1991) *Analysis of the Choice of Exchange Rate Regimes in the 1980s*, George Town University, Working Paper No. 91-02.

Cukierman, A. (1992) *Central Bank Strategy, Credibility and Independence*, Cambridge, Mass.: MIT Press.

Cukierman, A., Webb, S.B. and Neyapti, B. (1992) 'Measuring the Independence of Central Banks and its Effects on Policy Outcomes', *World Bank Economic Review*, 6, 353–98.

Cushman, D. (1986) 'Has Exchange Risk Depressed International Trade? The Impact of Third-Country Exchange Risk', *Journal of International Money and Finance*, 5, 361–79.

Cushman, D. (1988) 'U.S. Bilateral Trade Flows and Exchange Risk During the Floating Period', *Journal of International Economics*, 24, 317–30.

Dedola, L. and Leduc, S. (2001) *Why is the Business Cycle Behavior of Fundamentals Alike Across Exchange Rate Regimes?*, Oesterreichische Nationalbank Working Papers, No. 53.

Dehejia, V. (2003) *The Choice of Monetary/Exchange Rate Regime: Concepts and Arguments*, Carleton Economic Papers, No. CEP03–12.

Dehejia, V. and Rowe, N. (2001) 'Macroeconomic Stabilization: Fixed Exchange Rates vs Inflation Targeting', mimeo, Department of Economics, Carleton University, November.

Devereux, M.B. and Engel, C. (1998) *Fixed vs. Floating Exchange Rates: How Price Setting Affects the Optimal Choice of Exchange-Rate Regime*, Working Paper, University of Washington.

Devereux, M.B. and Engel, C. (1999) *The Optimal Choice of Exchange-Rate Regime: Price Setting Rules and Internationalized Production*, NBER Working Papers, No. 6992.

de Zamaroczy, M. and Sa, S. (2003) *Economic Policy in a Highly Dollarized World*, IMF Occasional Papers, No. 219.

Dominguez, K.M. and Frankel, J.A. (1993) *Does Foreign Exchange Intervention Work?*, Washington, DC: Institute for International Economics.

Dornbusch, R. (1986) 'Special Exchange Rates for Capital Account Transactions', *World Bank Economic Review*, 1, 3–33.

Dornbusch, R. (2001) 'Fewer Monies, Better Monies: Discussion on Exchange Rates and the Choice of Monetary Policy Regimes', *American Economic Review*, 91, 238–42.

Dornbusch, R. and Kuenzler, L.T. (1993) 'Exchange Rate Policy: Options and Issues', in Dornbusch, R. (ed), *Policymaking in the Open Economy: Concepts and Case Studies in Economic Performance*, New York: Oxford University Press.

Doyle, E. (2001) 'Exchange Rate Volatility and Irish–U.K. Trade, 1979–1992', *Applied Economics*, 33, 249–65.

Dreyer, J.S. (1978) 'Determinants of Exchange Rate Regimes for Currencies of Developing Countries: Some Preliminary Results', *World Development*, 6, 437–45.

Driskill, R.A. and McCafferty, S.A. (1980) 'Exchange Rate Variability, Real and Monetary Shocks, and the Degree of Capital Mobility Under Rational Expectations', *Quarterly Journal of Economics*, 95, 577–86.

Duttagupta, R. and Otker-Robe, I. (2003) *Exits from Pegged Regimes: An Empirical Analysis*, IMF Working Papers, No. WP/03/147.

Eaton, J. (1985) 'Optimal and Time Consistent Exchange Rate Management in an Overlapping Generations Economy', *Journal of International Money and Finance*, 4, 83–100.

The Economist (1999) 'Global Finance: Time for a Redesign', 30 January, 1–18.

Edwards, S. (1996) *The Determinants of the Choice Between Fixed and Flexible Exchange Rate Regimes*, NBER Working Papers, No. 5756.

Edwards, S. (1999) 'The Choice of Exchange Rate Regime in Developing and Middle Income Countries', in Takatoshi, I. and Kruger, A.O. (eds), *Changes in Exchange Rates in Rapidly Developing Countries: Theory, Practice and Policy Issues*, NBER–East Asia Seminar on Economics, Vol. 7, Chicago: University of Chicago Press.

Edwards, S. (2001) *Exchange Rate Regimes, Capital Flows and Crisis Prevention*, NBER Working Papers, No. 8529.

Edwards, S. (2002) *The Great Exchange Rate Debate After Argentina*, NBER Working Papers, No. 9257.

Edwards, S. (2003) 'Dollarization: Myths and Realities', in Salvatore, D., Dean, J.D. and Willett, T.D. (eds), *The Dollarization Debate*, Oxford: Oxford University Press.

Edwards, S. (2004) 'Thirty Years of Current Account Imbalances, Current Account Reversals and Sudden Stops', IMF Staff Papers, 51, 1–49.

Edwards, S. and Levy-Yeyati, E. (2003) *Flexible Exchange Rates as Shock Absorbers*, NBER Working Papers, No. 9867.

Edwards, S. and Magendoza, I.I. (2002) *Dollarization, Inflation and Growth*, NBER Working Papers, No. 8671.

Eichengreen, B. (1992) *Golden Fetters: The Gold Standard and the Great Depression*, New York: Oxford University Press.

Eichengreen, B. (1994) *International Monetary Arrangements for the 21st Century*, Washington, DC: Brookings Institution.

Eichengreen, B. (1996) *Globalizing Capital: A History of the International Monetary System*, Princeton, NJ: Princeton University Press.

Eichengreen, B. (1999a) 'Kicking the Habit: Moving from Pegged Rates to Greater Exchange Rate Flexibility', *Economic Journal*, 109, C1–C14.

Eichengreen, B. (1999b) *Toward a New Financial Architecture: A Practical Post-Asian Agenda*, Washington, DC: Brookings Institution.

Eichengreen, B. (2003) 'What Problems can Dollarization Solve?', in Salvatore, D., Dean, J.D. and Willett, T.D. (eds), *The Dollarization Debate*, Oxford: Oxford University Press.

Eichengreen, B. and Haussmann, R. (1999) *Exchange Rates and Financial Fragility*, NBER Working Papers, No. 7418.

Einzig, P. (1970) *The Case Against Floating Exchanges*, London: Macmillan.

Ellsworth, P.T. and Leith, J.C. (1975) *The International Economy*, New York: Macmillan.

Enoch, C. and Gulde, A. (1997) *Making a Currency Board Operational*, IMF Papers on Policy Analysis and Assessment, No. 97/10.

Estevadeordal, A., Frantz, B. and Taylor, A.M. (2003) 'The Rise and Fall of World Trade, 1870–1939', *Quarterly Journal of Economics*, 118, 359–407.

Ethier, W. (1973) 'International Trade and the Forward Foreign Exchange Market', *American Economic Review*, 63, 494–503.

European Commission (2003) *Quarterly Report on the Euro Area*, No. 3, September.

Faruqee, H. (2004) *Measuring the Trade Effects of EMU*, IMF Working Papers, No. WP/04/154.

Fatas, A. and Rose, A.K. (2001) 'Do Monetary Handcuffs Restrain Leviathan? Fiscal Policy in Extreme Exchange Rate Regimes', IMF Staff Papers, 47, 40–61.

Fischer, S. (1977) 'Stability and Exchange Rate Systems in a Monetarist Model of the Balance of Payments', in Aliber, R.Z. (ed.), *The Political Economy of Monetary Reform*, London: Macmillan.

Fischer, S. (1993) 'Role of Macroeconomic Factors in Growth', *Journal of Monetary Economics*, 32, 485–512.

Fischer, S. (2001) 'Is the Bipolar View Correct?', *Journal of Economic Perspectives*, 15, 3–24.

Flanders, M.J. and Helpman, E. (1978) 'On Exchange Rate Policies for Small Countries', *Economic Journal*, 46, 44–58.

Fleming, M. (1962) 'Domestic Financial Policies under Fixed and under Floating Exchange Rates', IMF Staff Papers, 9, 369–80.

Flood, R.P. (1979) 'Capital Mobility and the Choice of Exchange Rate Regime', *International Economic Review*, 2, 405–16.

Flood, R.P., Bhandari, J.S. and Horne, J.P. (1989) 'Evolution of Exchange Rate Regimes', IMF Staff Papers, 36, 810–35.

Flood, R.P. and Marion, N.P. (1982) 'The Transmission of Disturbances under Alternative Exchange-Rate Regimes with Optimal Indexing', *Quarterly Journal of Economics*, 96, 43–66.

Flood, R.P. and Marion, N.P. (1991) *Exchange Rate Regime Choice*, IMF Working Papers, No. 91/90.

Flood, R.P. and Rose, A.K. (1995) 'Fixing the Exchange Rate: A Virtual Quest for Fundamentals', *Journal of Monetary Economics*, 36, 3–37.

Flood, R.P. and Rose, A.K. (1999) 'Understanding Exchange Rate Volatility without the Contrivance of Macroeconomics', *Economic Journal*, 109, F660–F672.

Frankel, J.A. (1995) 'Monetary Regime Choice for a Semi-Open Country', in Edwards, S. (ed.), *Capital Controls, Exchange Rates and Monetary Policy in the World Economy*, Cambridge: Cambridge University Press.

Frankel, J.A. (1999) *No Single Currency Regime is Right for All Countries or At All Times*, NBER Working Papers, No. 7338.

Frankel, J.A. (2003) *Experience of and Lessons from Exchange Rate Regimes in Emerging Economies*, NBER Working Papers, No. 10032.

Frankel, J.A., Fajnzylber, E., Schmukler, S.L. and Serven, L. (2001) 'Verifying Exchange Rate Regimes', *Journal of Development Economics*, 66, 351–86.

Frankel, J.A. and Rose, A.K. (2002) 'An Estimate of the Effect of Common Currencies on Trade and Income', *Quarterly Journal of Economics*, 117, 437–66.

Frankel, J.A., Schmukler, S.L. and Serven, L. (2002) *Global Transmission of Interest Rates: Monetary Independence and Currency Regimes*, NBER Working Papers, No. 8828.

Frankel, J.A. and Wei, S.J. (1992) 'Trade Blocs and Currency Blocs', Paper presented at the CEPR Conference on the Monetary Future of Europe, La Coruna, Spain.

Frankel, J.A. and Wei, S.J. (1993) 'Is There a Currency Bloc in the Pacific?', in Blundell-Wignall, A. and Grenville, S. (eds), *Exchange Rates, International Trade and Monetary Policy*, Sydney: Reserve Bank of Australia, 275–307.

Frankel, J.A. and Wei, S.J. (1994) 'Yen Bloc or Dollar Bloc?: Exchange Rate Policies of the East Asian Economies', in Ito, T. and Krueger, A. (eds), *Macroeconomic Linkage: Savings, Exchange Rates, and Capital Flows*, Chicago: University of Chicago Press.

Frankel, J.A. and Wei, S.J. (1995) 'Emerging Currency Bloc?', in Genberg, H. (ed.), *The International Monetary System*, Spring, 111–70.

Frenkel, J.A. and Aizenman, J. (1982) 'Aspects of the Optimal Management of Exchange Rates', *Journal of International Economics*, 13, 231–56.

Frenkel, J.A. and Goldstein, M. (1986) 'A Guide to Target Zones', IMF Staff Papers, 33, 633–73.

Frenkel, J.A. and Razin, A. (1986) *The Limited Viability of Dual Exchange-Rate Regimes*, NBER Working Papers, No. 1902.

Friedman, M. (1953) 'The Case for Flexible Exchange Rates', in *Essays in Positive Economics*, Chicago: University of Chicago Press.

Garber, P.M. and Svensson, L. (1995) 'The Operation and Collapse of Fixed Exchange Rate Regimes', in Grossman, G.M. and Rogoff, K. (eds), *Handbook of International Economics*, Vol. 3, Amsterdam: North Holland, 1865–1911.

Gavin, M. and Perotti, R. (1998) 'Fiscal Policy in Latin America', *NBER Macroeconomics Annual*, Cambridge, Mass.: National Bureau of Economic Research.

Ghosh, A.R., Gulde, A.M and Wolf, H.C. (2000) 'Currency Boards: More Than a Quick Fix', *Economic Policy*, 31, 270–335.

Ghosh, A.R., Gulde, A.M. and Wolf, H.C. (2002) *Exchange Rate Regimes: Choices and Consequences*, Cambridge, Mass.: MIT Press.

Ghosh, A.R., Gulde, A.M., Ostry, J.D. and Wolf, H.C. (1997) *Does the Nominal Exchange Rate Regime Matter?*, NBER Working Papers, No. 5874.

Giavazzi, F., Micossi, S. and Miller, M. (eds) (1988) *The European Monetary System*, Cambridge: Cambridge University Press.

Glick, R. and Rose, A.K. (2002) 'Does a Currency Union Affect Trade? The Time Series Evidence', *European Economic Review*, 46, 1125–51.

Glick, R. and Wihlborg, C. (1990) 'Real Exchange Rate Effects of Monetary Shocks under Fixed and Flexible Exchange Rates', *Journal of International Economics*, 28, 267–90.

Goldstein, M. (2002) 'Managed Floating Plus', *Policy Analyses in International Economics*, No. 66, Washington, DC: Institute for International Economics.

Grilli, V. and Kaminsky, G. (1991) 'Nominal Exchange Rate Regimes and the Real Exchange Rate: Evidence from the United States and Great Britain, 1885–1986', *Journal of Monetary Economics*, 27, 191–212.

Grubel, H.G. (1977) *International Economics*, Homewood, Ill.: Irwin.

Guidotti, P. (1988) 'Insulation Properties under Dual Exchange Rates', *Canadian Journal of Economics*, 21, 799–813.

Guitian, M. (1994) 'The Choice of an Exchange Rate Regime', in Barth, R.C. and Wong, C.H. (eds), *Approaches to Exchange Rate Policy*, Washington, DC: International Monetary Fund.

Gulde, A.M., Hoelscher, D., Ize, A., Marston, D. and De Nicolo, G. (2004) *Financial Stability in Dollarized Economies*, IMF Occasional Papers, No. 230.

Hamada, K. and Sakurai, M. (1978) 'International Transmission of Stagflation under Fixed and Flexible Exchange Rates', *Journal of Political Economy*, 86, 877–95.

Hamman, A.J. (2001) 'Exchange Rate Based Stabilization: A Critical Look at the Stylized Facts', IMF Staff Papers, 48, 111–38.

Hanke, S. (2003a) 'An Iraq Currency Game Plan', *International Economy*, Summer.

Hanke, S. (2003b) 'Dinar Plan', *Wall Street Journal*, 22 July.

Harvey, A.C. (1989) *Forecasting: Structural Time Series Models and the Kalman Filter*, Cambridge: Cambridge University Press.

Hausmann, R. (1999) 'Should There Be 5 currencies or 105?' *Foreign Policy*, 116, 65–79.

Hausmann, R., Gavin, M., Pages-Serra, C. and Stein, E. (1999) 'Financial Turmoil and the Choice of Exchange Rate Regime', mimeo, Inter-American Development Bank.

Hausmann, R., Panizza, U. and Stein, E. (2001) 'Why Do Countries Float the Way They Float?', *Journal of Development Economics*, 66, 387–414.

Heller, R.H. (1978) 'Determinants of Exchange Rate Practices', *Journal of Money, Credit and Banking*, 10, 308–21.

Helpman, E. (1981) 'An Exploration in the Theory of Exchange Rate Regimes', *Journal of Political Economy*, 89, 865–90.

Helpman, E. and Razin, A. (1982) 'A Comparison of Exchange Rate Regimes in the Presence of Imperfect Capital Markets', *International Economic Review*, 23, 365–88.

Hernandez, L. and Montiel, P. (2001) *Post-Crisis Exchange Rate Policy in Five Asian Countries: Filling the 'Hollow Middle'?*, IMF Working Papers, No. WP/01/170.

Ho, C. (2003) 'Contemplating the Credibility of Currency Boards', in Ho, L.S. and Yuen, C.W. (eds), *Exchange Rate Regimes and Macroeconomic Stability*, Boston, Mass.: Kluwer.

Holden, P., Holden, M. and Suss, E.C. (1979) 'The Determinants of Exchange Rate Flexibility: An Empirical Investigation', *Review of Economics and Statistics*, 61, 327–33.

Honkapoja, S. and Pikkarainen, P. (1994) 'Country Characteristics and the Choice of the Exchange Rate Regime: Are Mini Skirts Followed by Maxis?', in Akerholm, J. and Giovannini, A. (eds), *Exchange Rate Policies in the Nordic Countries*, London: Centre for Economic Policy Research.

Hooper, P. and Kohlhagen, S.W. (1978) 'The Effect of Exchange Rate Uncertainty on the Prices of and Volume of International Trade', *Journal of International Economics*, 8, 483–511.

International Monetary Fund (1984) *The Exchange Rate System: Lessons of the Past and Options for the Future*, IMF Occasional Papers, No. 30.

International Monetary Fund (1998) *Exit Strategies: Policy Options for Countries Seeking Greater Exchange Rate Flexibility*, IMF Occasional Papers, No. 168.

International Monetary Fund (2003) *Monetary Union Among Member Countries of the Gulf Co-operation Council*, IMF Occasional Papers, No. 223.

Irwin, G. (2004) 'Currency Boards and Currency Crises', *Oxford Economic Papers*, 56, 64–87.

Jeanne, O. and Rose, A.K. (1999) *Noise Trading and Exchange Rate Regimes*, NBER Working Papers, No. 7104.

Johnson, H.G. (1972) 'The Case for Flexible Exchange Rates', in *Further Essays in Monetary Economics*, London: Allen & Unwin.

Juhn, G. and Mauro, P. (2002) *Long-Run Determinants of Exchange Rate Regimes: A Simple Sensitivity Analysis*, IMF Working Papers, No. WP/02/104.

Kawai, M. (2003) 'Recommending a Currency Basket System for Emerging East Asia', in Ho, L.S. and Yuen, C.W. (eds), *Exchange Rate Regimes and Macroeconomic Stability*, Dordrecht: Kluwer.

Kawai, M. and Akiyama, S. (1998) 'Roles of the World's Major Currencies in Exchange Rate Arrangements', *Journal of the Japanese and International Economies*, 12, 334–87.

Kawai, M. and Akiyama, S. (2000) *Implications of Currency Crisis for Exchange Rate Arrangements in Emerging East Asia*, Policy Research Working Paper No. 2502, World Bank.

Kenek, F. and Lastrapes, W.D. (1989) 'Real Exchange Rate Volatility and U.S. Bilateral Trade: A VAR Approach', *Review of Economics and Statistics*, 71, 708–12.

Kenen, P.B. (1969) 'The Theory of Optimum Currency Areas: An Eclectic View', in Mundell, R.A. and Swoboda, A. (eds), *Monetary Problems of the International Economy*, Chicago: University of Chicago Press.

Kenen, P.B. and Rodrik, D. (1986) 'Measuring and Analyzing the Effects of Short-Term Volatility in Real Exchange Rates', *Review of Economics and Statistics*, 68, 311–15.

Kimbrough, K. (1983) 'The Information Content of the Exchange Rate and the Stability of Real Output under Alternative Exchange-Rate Regimes', *Journal of International Money and Finance*, 2, 27–38.

King, M. (2004) *The Institutions of Monetary Policy*, NBER Working Papers, No. 10400.

Klein, M.W. and Marion, N.P. (1997) 'Explaining the Duration of Exchange Rate Pegs', *Journal of Development Economics*, 54, 387–404.

Klein, M.W. and Shambaugh, J.C. (2004) *Fixed Exchange Rates and Trade*, NBER Working Papers, No. 10696.

Klyuev, V. (2001) *A Model of Exchange Rate Regime Choice in the Transitional Economies of Central and Eastern Europe*, IMF Working Papers, No. WP/01/40.

Kortweg, P. (1980) 'Exchange-Rate Policy, Monetary Policy, and Real Exchange Rate Variability', *Princeton Essays in International Finance*, No. 140.

Krugman, P. (1991) 'Target Zones and Exchange Rate Dynamics', *Quarterly Journal of Economics*, 106, 669–82.

Lahiri, A. and Vegh, C.A. (2001) *Living with the Fear of Floating: An Optimal Policy Perspective*, NBER Working Papers, No. 8391.

Lapan, H.E. and Enders, W. (1980) 'Random Disturbances and the Choice of Exchange Rate Regimes in an International Model', *Journal of International Economics*, 10, 263–83.

Lee, J. (1999) 'The Effect of Exchange Rate Volatility on Trade in Durables', *Review of International Economics*, 7, 189–201.

Leon, J. and Oliva, C. (1999) 'Determinants of the Exchange Rate Regime: A Time Series Analysis for Chile', *International Economic Journal*, 13, 89–102.

Levy-Yeyati, E. and Sturzenegger, F. (2000a) *Classifying Exchange Rate Regimes: Deeds vs Words*, CIF Working Papers, Universidad Torcuato Di Tella, No. 02/2000.

Levy-Yeyati, E. and Sturzenegger, F. (2000b) *To Float or to Trail: Evidence on the Impact of Exchange Rate Regimes*, CIF Working Papers, Universidad Torcuato Di Tella, No. 01/2001.

Levy-Yeyati, E. and Sturzenegger, F. (2001) 'Exchange Rate Regimes and Economic Performance', IMF Staff Papers, 47, 62–98.

Lipschitz, L. (1978) 'Exchange Rate Policies for Developing Countries: Some Simple Arguments for Intervention', IMF Staff Papers, 25, 650–75.

Little, I.M.D, Cooper, R.N., Corden, W.M. and Rajapatirana, S. (1993) *Boom, Crisis and Adjustment: The Macroeconomic Experience of Developing Countries*, New York: Oxford University Press.

Lopez-Cordova, J.E. and Meissner, C.M. (2003) 'Exchange Rate Regimes and International Trade: Evidence from the Classical Gold Standard Era', *American Economic Review*, 93, 344–53.

Marston, R.C. (1982) 'Wages, Relative Prices and the Choice Between Fixed and Flexible Exchange Rates', *Canadian Journal of Economics*, 15, 87–103.

Masson, P. (2001) 'Exchange Rate Regime Transitions', *Journal of Development Economics*, 64, 571–86.

McKenzie, M.D. (1999) 'The Impact of Exchange Rate Volatility on International Trade Flows', *Journal of Economic Surveys*, 13, 71–106.

McKinnon, R.I. (1963) 'Optimum Currency Areas', *American Economic Review*, 53, 717–25.

McKinnon, R.I. (1979) *Money in International Exchange: The Convertible Currency System*, New York: Oxford University Press.

McKinnon, R.I. (2000) 'The East Asian Dollar Standard: Life after Death?' *Economic Notes*, 29, 31–82.

Meade, J. (1951) *The Theory of International Economic Policy*, New York: Oxford University Press.

Melvin, M. (1985) 'The Choice of an Exchange Rate System and Macroeconomic Stability', *Journal of Money, Credit and Banking*, 17, 467–78.

Mendoza, E. (2000) *On the Instability of Variance Decomposition of the Real Exchange Rate Across Exchange-Rate-Regimes: Evidence from Mexico and the United States*, NBER Working Papers, No. 7768.

Micco, A., Stein, E. and Ordonez, G. (2003) 'The Currency Union Effect on Trade: Early Evidence from EMU', *Economic Policy*, 37, 313–56.

Moosa, I.A. (1983a) 'Appreciating the KD's Fortunes', *Arab Banking and Finance*, June, 46–7.

Moosa, I.A. (1983b) 'Dinar Dissent', *Institutional Investor*, June, 53.

Moosa, I.A. (1989) 'Has the KD Been Devalued Against the Dollar?', *Arab Banker*, November/December, 26–8.

Moosa, I.A. (1997) 'On the Costs of Inflation and Unemployment', *Journal of Post Keynesian Economics*, 19, 651–66.

Moosa, I.A. (2001a) 'The Classical Gold Standard: A Miracle or a Myth', *Journal of International Economic Studies*, 15, 131–42.

Moosa, I.A. (2001b) 'Modelling and Forecasting the KD Exchange Rates', *Middle East Business and Economics Review*, 13, 39–49.

Moosa, I.A. (2002) 'Exchange Rates and Fundamentals: A Microeconomic Approach', *Economia Internazionale*, 55, 551–71.

Moosa, I.A. (2003) *International Financial Operations: Arbitrage, Hedging, Speculation, Investment and Financing*, London: Palgrave Macmillan.

Moosa, I.A. (2004a) 'Exchange Rate Regime Choice Under Hyperinflationary Conditions in a Post-War Situation: The Case of Iraq', *Economia Internazionale*, 57, 4.

Moosa, I.A. (2004b) 'The Monetary Aspects of the Reconstruction of Iraq', in Al-Kawaz, A. (ed.), *The Status Quo and the Future of the Iraqi Economy*, Kuwait: Arab Planning Institute.

Moosa, I.A. (2004c) *International Finance: An Analytical Approach*, 2nd edn, Sydney: McGraw-Hill.

Moosa, I.A. and Al-Loughani, N.E. (1997) 'An Empirical Investigation into the Causes of Deviations from Covered Interest Parity when the Domestic Currency is Pegged to a Basket', *Journal of Financial Studies*, 5, 1–16.

Moosa, I.A. and Al-Loughani, N.E. (1999) 'Testing Purchasing Power Parity when the Base Currency is Pegged to a Basket', *Accounting Research Journal*, 12, 200–11.

Moosa, I.A. and Al-Loughani, N.E. (2000) 'An Exchange Rate Forecasting Model when the Underlying Currency is Pegged to a Basket', *Economia Internazionale*, 53, 537–50.

Moosa, I.A. and Al-Loughani, N.E. (2003) 'The Role of Fundamentalists and Technicians in the Foreign Exchange Market when the Base Currency is Pegged to a Basket', *Applied Financial Economics*, 13, 78–84.

Moosa, I.A. and Bhatti, R.H. (1996) 'The European Monetary System and Real Interest Parity: Is There any Connection?', *Swiss Journal of Economics and Statistics*, 132, 223–35.

Mundell, R.A. (1961) 'A Theory of Optimum Currency Areas', *American Economic Review*, 51, 657–65.

Mundell, R.A. (1963) 'Capital Mobility and Stabilization Policy under Fixed and Flexible Exchange Rates', *Canadian Journal of Economics*, 29, 475–85.

Mundell, R.A. (1968) *International Economics*, New York: Macmillan.

Mundell, R.A. (1995) 'Exchange Rate Systems and Economic Growth', *Revista di Politica Economia*, 58, 3–36.

Mundell, R.A. (2003) 'Does Asia Need a Common Currency?', in Ho, L.S. and Yuen, C.W. (eds), *Exchange Rate Regimes and Macroeconomic Stability*, Dordrecht: Kluwer.

Murray, J.D. (2003) 'Why Canada Needs a Flexible Exchange Rate', in Salvatore, D., Dean, J.D. and Willett, T.D. (eds), *The Dollarization Debate*, Oxford: Oxford University Press.

Mussa, M. (1986) 'Nominal Exchange Rate Regimes and the Behavior of Real Exchange Rates: Evidence and Implications, in Brunner', K. and Meltzer, A.H. (eds), *Real Business Cycles, Real Exchange Rates and Actual Policies*, Amsterdam: North Holland.

Mussa, M. (2002) *Argentina: From Triumph to Tragedy*, Washington, DC: IIE.

Mussa, M., Masson, P., Swoboda, A., Jadresic, E., Mauro, P. and Berg, A. (2000) *Exchange Rate Regimes in an Increasingly Integrated World Economy*, IMF Occasional Papers, No. 193.

Neumeyer, P.A. (1998) 'Currencies and the Allocation of Risk: The Welfare Effects of a Monetary Union', *American Economic Review*, 88, 246–59.

Nitithanprapas, I. and Willett, T.D. (2002) 'Classifying Exchange Rate Regimes', Paper presented at the Annual Meeting of the Western Economic Association, Seattle, July.

Nurkse, R. (1944) *International Currency Experience: Lessons from the Interwar Period*, Geneva: League of Nations.

Obstfeld, M. and Rogoff, K. (1995) 'The Mirage of Fixed Exchange Rates', *Journal of Economic Perspectives*, 9, 73–96.

Obstfeld, M., Shambaugh, J.C. and Taylor, A.M. (2004a) 'Monetary Sovereignty, Exchange Rates, and Capital Controls: The Trilemma in the Interwar Period', IMF Staff Papers, 51, 75–108.

Obstfeld, M., Shambaugh, J.C. and Taylor, A.M. (2004b) *Global Capital Markets: Integration, Crisis, and Growth*, Cambridge: Cambridge University Press.

Obstfeld, M. and Taylor, A.M. (1998) 'The Great Depression as a Watershed: International Capital Mobility over the Long Run', in Bordo, M.D., Goldin, C.D. and While, E.N. (eds), *The Defining Moment: The Great Depression and the American Economy in the Twentieth Century*, Chicago: Chicago University Press.

Obstfeld, M. and Taylor, A.M. (2004) *Global Capital Markets: Integration, Crisis and Growth*, Cambridge: Cambridge University Press.

Oppers, S.E. (2000) *Dual Currency Boards: A Proposal for Currency Stability*, IMF Working Papers, No. WP/00/199.

Papaioannou, M.G. (2003) *Determinants of the Choice of Exchange Rate Regimes in Six Central American Countries: An Empirical Analysis*, IMF Working Papers, No. WP/03/59.

Persson, T. (2001) 'Currency Unions and Trade: How Large is the Treatment Effect?', *Economic Policy*, 33, 435–48.

Poirson, H. (2001) *How Do Countries Choose Their Exchange Rate Regimes?*, IMF Working Papers, No. WP/01/46.

Pozo, S. (1992) 'Conditional Exchange Rate Volatility and the Volume of International Trade: Evidence from the Early 1900s', *Review of Economics and Statistics*, 74, 325–9.

Qian, Y. and P. Varangis (1994) 'Does Exchange Rate Volatility Hinder Export Growth?' *Empirical Economics*, 19, 371–96.

Quirk, P.J. and Cortes-Douglas, H. (1993) 'The Experience with Floating Rates', *Finance and Development*, June, 28–31.

Quirk, P.J. and Short, B.K. (1993) *Introduction of a New National Currency: Policy, Institutional, and Technical Issues*, IMF Working Papers, No. WP/93/49.

Razin, A. and Rubenstein, Y. (2004) *Growth Effects of the Exchange Rate Regime and the Capital Account Openness in a Crisis-Prone World Market: A Nuanced View*, NBER Working Papers, No. 10555.

Redwood, J. (1997) *Our Currency, Our Country*, London: Penguin.

Reinhart, C.M. (2000) 'The Mirage of Floating Exchange Rates', *American Economic Review*, 90, 65–70.

Reinhart, C.M. and Reinhart, V.R. (2003) *Twin Fallacies about Exchange Rate Policy in Emerging Markets*, NBER Working Papers, No. 9670.

Reinhart, C.M. and Rogoff, K.S. (2004) 'The Modern History of Exchange Rate Arrangements: A Reinterpretation', *Quarterly Journal of Economics*, 119, 1–48.

Rizzo, J.M. (1998) 'The Economic Determinants of the Choice of an Exchange Rate Regime: A Probit Analysis', *Economics Letters*, 59, 283–7.

Rogoff, K.S., Husain, A.M., Mody, A., Brooks, R. and Oomes, N. (2004) *Evolution and Performance of Exchange Rate Regimes*, IMF Occasional Papers, No. 229.

Rolnick, A.J. and Weber, W.E. (1997) 'Money, Inflation and Output under Fiat and Commodity Standards', *Quarterly Review of the Federal Reserve Bank of Minneapolis*, 22, 11–17.

Romer, D. (1993) 'Openness and Inflation: Theory and Evidence', *Quarterly Journal of Economics*, 108, 869–903.

Rose, A.K. (1996) 'Explaining Exchange Rate Volatility: An Empirical Analysis of "the Holy Trinity" of Monetary Independence, Fixed Exchange Rates, and Capital Mobility', *Journal of International Money and Finance*, 15, 6, 925–45.

Rose, A.K. (2000) 'One Money, One Market: Estimating the Effect of Common Currencies on Trade', *Economic Policy*, 15, 7–46.

Rose, A.K. and van Wincoop, E. (2001) 'National Money as a Barrier to International Trade: The Real Case for Currency Union', *American Economic Review (Papers and Proceedings)*, 91, 386–90.

Roubini, N. (2001) 'Factors to be Considered in Assessing a Country's Readiness for Dollarization', mimeo, Stern School of Business, New York University.

Roubini, N. and Sester, B. (2003) *Should Iraq Dollarize, Adopt a Currency Board or Let the Currency Float?*, Working Paper, New York University, Stern School of Business.

Sachs, J. (1980) 'Wages, Flexible Exchange Rates and Macroeconomic Policy', *Quarterly Journal of Economics*, 94, 731–47.

Salvatore, D., Dean, J.D. and Willett, T.D. (eds) (2003) *The Dollarization Debate*, Oxford: Oxford University Press.

Sanford, J.E. (2003) *Iraq's Economy: Past, Present, Future*, Report for Congress, Washington, DC.

Sarno, L. and Taylor, M.P. (2002) *The Economics of Exchange Rates*, Cambridge: Cambridge University Press.

Savvides, A. (1990) 'Real Exchange Rate Variability and the Choice of Exchange Rate Regime by Developing Countries', *Journal of International Money and Finance*, 9, 440–54.

Schuler, K. (2003) 'What Use is Monetary Sovereignty?', in Salvatore, D., Dean, J.D. and Willett, T.D. (eds), *The Dollarization Debate*, Oxford: Oxford University Press.

Shambaugh, J. (2004) 'The Effect of Fixed Exchange Rates on Monetary Policy', *Quarterly Journal of Economics*, 119, 301–52.

Smith, A. (1776) *An Inquiry into the Nature and Causes of the Wealth of Nations*, London, Methuen.

Stiglitz, J. (2003) 'Financial Market Stability, Monetary Policy and the IMF', in Ho, L.S. and Yuen, C.W. (eds), *Exchange Rate Regimes and Macroeconomic Stability*, Dordrecht: Kluwer.

Stockman, A.C. (1983) 'Real Exchange Rates under Alternative Nominal Exchange-Rate Systems', *Journal of International Money and Finance*, 2, 147–66.

Summers, L. (1999a) 'Testimony before the Senate Foreign Relations Subcommittee on International Economic Policy and Export/Trade Promotion', 27 January.

Summers, L. (1999b) 'Building an International Financial Architecture for the 21st Century', *Cato Journal*, 18, 321–30.

Sun, Y. (2002) *A Political–Economic Model of the Choice of Exchange Rate Regime*, IMF Working Papers, No. WP/02/212.

Sun, Y. (2003) *Do Fixed Exchange Rates Induce More Fiscal Discipline?*, IMF Working Papers, No. WP/03/78.

Svensson, L. (1994) 'Why Exchange Rate Bands? Monetary Independence in Spite of Fixed Exchange Rates', *Journal of Monetary Economics*, 33, 157–99.

Svensson, L. (1997) 'Inflation Forecast Targeting: Implementing and Monitoring Inflation Targets', *European Economic Review*, 41, 1111–46.

Taussig, F.W. (1927) *International Trade*, New York: Macmillan.

Taylor, M.P. and Artis, M.J. (1988) *What Has the European Monetary System Achieved?*, Bank of England Discussion Papers, No. 31.

Tenreyro, S. (2001) 'On the Causes and Consequences of Currency Unions', unpublished paper, Harvard University.

Tenreyro, S. and Barro, R.J. (2003) *Economic Effects of Currency Unions*, NBER Working Papers, No. 9435.

Tornell, A. and Velasco, A. (1995) 'Fiscal Discipline and the Choice of Exchange Rate Regime', *European Economic Review*, 39, 759–70.

Tornell, A. and Velasco, A. (1998) 'Fiscal Discipline and the Choice of a Nominal Anchor in Stabilization', *Journal of International Economics*, 46, 1–30.

Tower, E. and Willett, T.D. (1976) 'The Theory of Optimum Currency Areas and Exchange Rate Flexibility', *Special Papers in International Economics*, No. 11, Princeton University.

Triffin, R. (1960) *Gold and Dollar Crisis: The Future of Convertibility*, New Haven, Conn.: Yale University Press.

Turnovsky, S. (1976) 'The Relative Stability of Alternative Exchange Rate Systems in the Presence of Random Disturbances', *Journal of Money, Credit and Banking*, 8, 29–50.

Turnovsky, S. (1982) 'A Determination of the Optimal Currency Basket', *Journal of International Economics*, 12, 333–54.

Turnovsky, S. (1983) 'Wage Indexation and Exchange Market Intervention in a Small Open Economy', *Canadian Journal of Economics*, 16, 574–92.

Vaubel, R. (1978) 'Real Exchange-Rate Changes in the European Community', *Journal of International Economics*, 8, 319–39.

Viaene, J.M. and de Vries, G.G. (1992) 'International Trade and Exchange Rate Volatility', *European Economic Review*, 36, 1311–21.

Weber, W. (1981) 'Output Variability under Monetary Policy and Exchange-Rate Rules', *Journal of Political Economy*, 89, 733–75.

Weymark, D. (1997) 'Measuring the Degree of Exchange Market Intervention in a Small Open Economy', *Journal of International Money and Finance*, 16, 55–7.

Wickham, P. (1985) 'The Choice of Exchange Rate Regime in Developing Countries: A Survey of the Literature', IMF Staff Papers, 32, 248–88.

Williamson, J. (1982) 'A Survey of the Literature on the Optimal Peg', *Journal of Development Economics*, 11, 39–61.

Williamson, J. (1983) 'The Exchange Rate System', *Policy Analyses*, No. 5, Institute for International Economics, Cambridge, Mass.: MIT Press.

Williamson, J. (1991) 'Advice on the Choice of an Exchange Rate Policy', in Classen, E.M. (ed.), *Exchange Rate Policies in Developing and Post Socialist Countries*, San Francisco: International Center for Economic Growth and ICS Press.

Williamson, J. (1999) 'Are Intermediate Regimes Vanishing?', speech given at the International Conference on Exchange Rate Regimes in Emerging Market Economies, Tokyo, 17–18 December.

Williamson, J. (2000a) 'Crawling Bands or Monitoring Bands: How to Manage Exchange Rates in a World of Capital Mobility', *International Finance*, 1.1, October, 59–79.

Williamson, J. (2000b) 'Exchange Rate Regimes for Emerging Markets: Reviving the Intermediate Option', *Policy Analyses in International Economics*, No. 60, Institute for International Economics, Washington, DC.

Williamson, J. (2002) 'The Evolution of Thought on International Exchange Rate Regimes', *Annals of the American Academy of Political and Social Science*, 579, 73–86.

Yeager, L. (1976) *International Monetary Relations*, New York: Harper & Row.

Index